D1384797

LITERATURE AND IDEOLOGY IN HAITI, 1915-1961

LITERATURE AND IDEOLOGY IN HAITI, 1915–1961

J. Michael Dash

Lecturer in French
University of the West Indies

BARNES & NOBLE BOOKS
TOTOWA, NEW JERSEY

First Published in the U.S.A. 1981 by
BARNES & NOBLE BOOKS
81, Adams Drive, Totowa,
New Jersey, 07512
ISBN 0–389–20092–1

Printed in Hong Kong

To Cheryl, Haiti's writers
and my mother

Contents

Preface

At the end of the small hours, the strand of dreams and the
senseless awakening on this frail stratum of earth already
humiliated.

Aimé Césaire, *Return to my native land*

It is perhaps significant that the figure of the solitary wanderer or
the exile so frequently appears in Haitian literature. The embittered
heroes of protest fiction during the American Occupation; the
theme of exile in all of Roumain's work; the paranoid outcast of *Griot*
poetry; Alexis's elemental, Adamic myth of Caribbean man and the
brutalised zombi of Franck Etienne's recent novels are products of
this phenomenon. It all seems to result from the nightmare of
political instability in Haitian history which has made the writer
into a refugee. Out of the anguish of the political situation a
literature is created which deals in an articulate and sensitive way
with the humiliations of Caribbean history, the ironies of the post-
Independence situation, the complex question of cultural identity
and the problem of belonging. The literature that treats these
themes is the consequence of the self-consciousness and spirit of
defiance that emerged from the trauma of the Occupation and
which proposed nothing less than the liberation of the individual
imagination from perceptual and aesthetic limitations. The result of
this daring forms the main focus of this book.

The present work grew out of research originally done for the
University of the West Indies. The thesis which looked at nationalism in post-Occupation poetry, has been broadened to include
novelists and concentrates more selectively on those influential and
sometime notorious literary and ideological figures who changed
the course of the political and literary culture of modern Haiti. The
individual chapters are linked by the chronology of the events
which followed 1915. The background, whenever useful, is sketched
in and the work concludes with the murder of Jacques-Stéphen

Alexis in 1961, one of the more sinister landmarks of recent history in Haiti. The events of the Duvalier years are tentatively looked at in the epilogue.

I am grateful for the invaluable assistance of Frère Raphael and Frère Lucien of St Louis de Gonzague who placed their library at my disposal. I am also indebted to all those Haitians – writers, critics and friends – whose suggestions and information clarified many of the dark areas of Haitian history. I would also like to express my gratitude to Dr Bridget Jones, Dr Beverly Ormerod and the late Professor Coulthard without whose guidance and encouragement the original thesis would never have been accomplished. My further thanks, too, go to my wife who painstakingly typed the manuscript.

J. M. D.

University of the West Indies
Mona, Jamaica

Acknowledgements

The author and publishers wish to thank the following who have kindly given permission for the use of copyright material

René Dépestre for extracts from his poems from *Etincelles* (1945) and *Gerbe de Sang* (1946).

Société de Gérance Pour l'Edition et la Diffusion du Livre, (SOGEDIL) Paris, for extracts from the poem *Guinée* by Jacques Roumain, (Editeurs Français Réunis).

A. Watkins Inc., New York, for the poems *Sainement, Grand'rue* and *l'Atlas à Menti* by Philippe Thoby-Marcelin.

Chronology 1915–1961

Year	Internal Political Events	Literary Events	External Events
1915	American Occupation		World War 1 (1914–18)
1918	Caco uprising		Dadaist movement
1920	Visit of J. W. Johnson and founding of *L'Union Patriotique*	Price Mars begins a series of lectures later published in *Ainsi Parla l'Oncle*	Harlem Renaissance begins
1924			Surrealist movement
1925		Roumer's *Poèmes d'Haiti et de France*	
1927	Roumain's return	Appearance of *La Trouée La revue Indigene* and *Le petit Impartial*	
1928		*Ainsi Parla l'Oncle*	
1929	Strike at Damiens		
1930	Election of President Vincent		
1932			*Legitime Défense*
1933			Hitler comes to power
1934	End of Occupation and Founding of Communist Party		Damas, Césaire and Senghor publish *L'Etudiant Noir*

Year	Internal Political Events	Literary Events	External Events
1935			Italy invades Ethiopia
1936	Roumain exiled		Spanish Civil War
1937	Thousands of Haitians massacred in Santo Domingo		Léon Damas' *Pigments*
1938		Appearance of *Les Griots*	
1939	Roumain leaves France for the U.S.	Roumain's *Bois d'Ebène*	World War II and Césaire's *Cahier . . .*
1941	Election of President Lescot, *campagne anti-superstitieuse* and Roumain's return.		
1942		Visit of N. Guillen	
1943		Visit of A. Carpentier	
1944	Roumain dies	Visit of A. Césaire and publication of *Gouverneurs de la rosée*	
1945		Visit of André Breton; appearance of *La Ruche* and *Etincelles*	End of World War II
1946	Lescot overthrown and election of President Estimé		
1947		Brierre's *Black Soul*	Founding of *Présence Africaine*

Year	Internal Political Events	Literary Events	External Events
1948			Senghor's anthology of Black French poets
1950	Estimé overthrown and President Magloire elected		
1955		Alexis's *Compère Général Soleil*	
1956	Magloire resigns		First Congress of Negro-African writers; Césaire resigns from Communist party
1957	Election of President F. Duvalier	Alexis's *Les Arbres Musiciens*	
1959			Cuban revolution
1960	Dépestre leaves for Cuba		
1961	Alexis is murdered		

1 A Survey of the Nineteenth Century

I. Genesis of a National Consciousness

In Aimé Césaire's reconstruction of Henry Christophe's court in *La Tragédie du Roi Christophe*, the court poet Juste Chanlatte is made to recite the following ode to Haitian rum:

> Quels doux roseaux dans ces plaines jaunissent!
> J'entends au loin cent pressoirs qui gémissent.
> Du jonc noueux le nectar exprimé
> Brille à mes yeux, en sucre transformé[1]

> [What sweet reeds ripen in the yellowing plains!
> I hear in the distance the sigh of a hundred presses.
> From the knotted stalk the nectar squeezed
> Glitters before my eyes, transformed into sugar.]

In order to satirise the imitativeness and awkward attempts at refinement among Christophe's nobles, Césaire presents in this illustration of the poetry of the time, the application of French Classical conventions to patriotic ideals. The national drink is celebrated as deriving from *doux roseaux* and *jonc noueux* in strict adherence to the Classical notions of *bienséance* and preciosity. What we have here is the widely accepted stereotype of nineteenth-century Haitian writing – imitative in its literary technique and exhibitionist in its nationalism.

Césaire's comment on early Haitian poets does not go beyond this brief satire, but it does indicate the fundamental literary dilemma of the nineteenth century. A distinct and resolute political consciousness on one hand is expressed by anonymous literary voices. Far from being *pionniers* as most anthologies tend to categorise them, the early poets are disappointing as creative writers for their celebrations of nationalist fervour consistently reveal the stranglehold of French Classicism.

It was not, however, simply a matter of yielding to the demands of Classical form. The wars that preceded Independence in 1804 had ruined one of France's richest colonies and in the face of socio-economic crises that followed independence and the illiteracy of the ex-slave population, literary matters were of secondary importance. Indeed if literature were to have a role at all, it would be within the political context of the post-Independence period. For instance, the prevailing conception of literary activity was as a purely didactic and propagandist exercise. This is evident in the following motto that was devised for one of Haiti's first literary journals – *L'Abeille Haytienne* (1817–1820):

> L'épée et les talents doivent n'avoir qu'un but
> Que chacun à l'Etat apporte son tribut.

> [Artistic and military talent must only have one aim
> Each must make its contribution to the state.]

Nineteenth-century literary figures were for the most part military and political men who conceived of their writing in terms of the larger national purpose. The issue of national survival in a hostile environment was so urgent at this time that there was little room for the detachment and contemplation that could produce sophistication in the treatment of certain political themes. Literature was simply another means of showing solidarity or divulging a particular point of view. Art as political gesture made for a narrow range of themes and encouraged a certain stylistic conformity. What we have here is a dramatic illustration of the way in which political crisis could encourage a certain aesthetic conservatism in literature. Such a situation would be repeated much later during the American Occupation when writers for a while suspended aesthetic considerations for the immediate cause of political engagement.

One of the best known poems of this period of *littérature de combat* is 'Hymne à la liberté' by Antoine Dupré – about whom little is known except that he was a soldier. This poem shows the extent to which the revolution of 1789 was the source of political as well as literary inspiration for the Haitians. It bears a striking resemblance to the 'Marseillaise':

Haiti, mère chérie
Reçois mes derniers adieux
Que l'amour de la patrie
Enflamme nos neveux.
Si quelque jour sur tes rives
Reparaissent nos tyrans
Que leurs hordes fugitives
Servent d'engrais à nos champs.[2]

[Haiti, cherished mother
Receive my last farewell
May love of the motherland
Inspire our children.
If some day on our shores
Former tyrants appear
Let their fleeing numbers serve as manure for our fields.]

This poem is a clear example of the themes that inspired these early poets – national solidarity, denial of tyranny and so on. But it can also be seen as literature so closely concerned with specific ideological needs that there was little concern with artistic originality. This unimaginative rhetoric would cease to be significant when the crisis was over.

There are numerous examples of pseudo-classical verse in which Greek mythological allusions, periphrasis and French Classical prosody abound. For instance the poem 'L'Union' written in 1820 to promote a feeling of solidarity after the civil war of Pétion and Christophe contains the following lines:

Ecartons loin de nous la Discorde ennemie
    Que des fils de la liberté
Sous les drapeaux de Mars la troupe réunie
    Se livre à la fraternité.[3]

[Let us distance ourselves from hostile Discord
Let the sons of freedom
Their troops reunited under the banner of Mars
Devote themselves to brotherhood.]

If these writers are to be considered *pionniers* it must be in the limited sense of being representative of the beginnings of a national and historical consciousness in Haitian writing rather than as providing a real artistic legacy for future literary generations. To avoid too dismissive an attitude to these poets one must keep in mind the strong temptation for the total identification of the writer with political reality in the first flush of victory after 1804. Also one should not dismiss too lightly the limitations imposed on these writers by the rigid and exclusive rules governing literary acceptability during the Classical period. Greater assurance and originality would come only when the threat of French invasion as well as political crises had diminished and with the advent of the Romantic movement that would promote diversity of expression among individual writers.

However, in this time of urgent political issues which were ultimately destructive to the literary imagination, an important Haitian voice emerged which gave a clear indication of the nature of the political consciousness of the early nineteenth century. Le baron de Vastey, self-taught secretary to King Christophe, was the most important ideological figure in early Haitian history. An extremely clever man, he had an acute awareness of the nature of the colonial system and the way in which various forces were used to maintain such a system – for instance, the Catholic Church:

> These priests would forever tell us in their sermons that whites were superior to us; they preached respect, submission and kindness towards whites; they consoled us when we were tortured and punished, by telling us that it was necessary to suffer and endure the pains of this world to ensure happiness in the next . . .[4]

These sentiments which could easily belong to any militant négritude writer of the mid-twentieth century, were expressed by de Vastey in 1816.

His most famous work was *Le Système Colonial Dévoilé* (1814) in which he treated such themes as the extermination of the autochthonous people of Haiti and the strange legacy of the colonial past. His work has a much truer and more authentic ring than that of the poets of the time. In his prose we have evidence of the kind of ideological vision that would be retained at various levels of intensity throughout Haitian literary history. He was preoccupied with the question of national survival and in his writings we have the prototype of the voice of protest that would predict the end of the materialist Western World during the American Occupation: 'Decadent Europe weary after centuries of enlightenment and civilisation will return to barbarism . . . until time and circumstance should so unite and create new elements that will recall her to civilisation.'[5]

Unlike many of his contemporaries who had turned to poetry, de Vastey, using a strict prose form could easily avoid the temptation of Classical allusions in his deliberations on the historical legacy of injustice. This particular form, indeed, seemed better suited to this period of political uncertainty. The problems of political poetry become even more apparent when what at best could be called inspired plagiarism, from an aesthetic point of view, gave way to *littérature commandée* among Haitian writers.

This degeneration of Haitian writing into court poetry and propaganda for the various presidents of Haiti was detrimental to contemporary poetry and would be considered a major lapse in integrity by later generations – particularly at the turn of the century. The lesson to be learnt from this phenomenon was that the relationship between art and politics was a very complex one. The concept of poetry as political gesture, the identification of poets and political causes – prevalent in this early period – would eventually lead to a situation where art would fall victim to post-Independence politics.

The early *littérature de combat* at least laudable in its intentions was the product of an ideologically unified Haiti. It expressed a vision of national sovereignty and a violent rejection of the colonial past which were products of early nationalist fervour. With the threat of French invasion gradually receding and the outbreak of civil war between Christophe and Pétion – representing black and mulatto interests respectively – this early idealism was not sustained but became an easy casualty of this social and political division within Haiti. What we now see is a poetry still filled with laboured Classical allusions but now glorifying the exploits of Haiti's presidents. Artistic independence and integrity had been betrayed by those closely allied to political platforms or purely seeking political favour. For instance, the following example of an ode to Pétion shows this mercenary attitude to the poet's role. This example of *littérature courtisane* was supposedly read aloud to the president:

Généreux protecteur dont le puissant génie,
Voulant régénérer notre chère patrie,

Appelle, dans son sein, les arts et les talents
Dont aime à se nourrir l'esprit de ses enfants
Agréez le tribut que notre âme sincère
Offre au grand Magistrat qui nous tient lieu de père[6]

[Generous protector whose powerful genius,
Wishes to regenerate our dear motherland
Summons to its bosom creative talents
With which the spirit of his children yearns to be nourished
Accept the tribute that our sincere soul
Offers to the great Leader who serves us as a father.]

Even Dupré who earlier celebrated the birth of the Haitian Republic, began to dedicate flattering lines to Pétion, 'philosophe, guerrier, prudent législateur', and describe Christophe as a 'tigre ensanglanté'.

This tendency was to continue into the 1930s, actively encouraged by President Boyer. However, it is also during Boyer's regime with the comparative peace of that period and the influence of French Romanticism that a younger generation of Haitian writers would begin to have reservations about their predecessors and seriously reflect on the question of literary originality.

Boyer's presidency (1820–1843) represented a period of unprecedented political calm, the increasing recognition of Haitian independence by other countries (e.g. France in 1825), and was to be the only time that the entire island of Hispaniola would be politically unified. It was also a very significant period for the evolution of Haitian society, for it was under Boyer that the mulatto élite consolidated its strength socially and politically. Also historians such as Joseph St Rémy began their biased versions of Haitian history, praising the leaders of the mulatto élite and discrediting black leaders. The cultural plurality of Haiti, which distinguished the urban mulatto élite from the rural ex-slaves, now worsened into what Leyburn calls a caste system. This rift is apparent in ethnic, religious, linguistic and educational terms. On one hand an educated, French-speaking and Catholic class of mixed blood and on the other, a creole-speaking, largely black peasantry who worshipped their voodoo deities.

This particular trend in Haiti's history provoked a response among a small group of intellectuals at the time. They had the time to reflect on cultural, and in particular, literary questions. Their position was based on protest against Boyer's inability to arrest the fragmentation taking place in Haitian society and the limitations of cultural activity in Haiti. What interests us is their literary *prise de position* which was inspired by French Romantic literary theory. It represents the blueprint for an indigenous literature, – which would only be seriously taken up during the American Occupation – and must have been one of the first manifestations of literary indigenism in the New World.

French Romanticism, with its emphasis on cultural diversity and artistic individualism, did much to liberate the Haitian creative imagination. French Classicism had imposed on earlier writers a high degree of literary conformity to confining artistic ideals. The rigid rules of preciosity were independent of time and space. Now under the liberating influence of Romanticism greater latitude and consequently greater possibilities for improvisation were permitted for the writer –as an individual and the product of a specific milieu.

Two fundamental notions now enter the mainstream of literary theorising in Haiti. Firstly, there was the basic admission of the autonomy of the writer, and the necessity for the independence of the creative imagination. Only under such conditions could true authenticity be found. (This stood in stark contrast to the literary sycophancy of *poésie commandée*.) The second concept follows closely on that of artistic individualism and revolved around the validity of finding artistic inspiration in *any* of the features which constituted the national culture. This tendency promoted an awareness of the various manifestations of Haitian culture–particularly that of the peasantry and represents the beginning of a search for *La Muse Haitienne* or the folk culture. Occasional original features only dimly perceived in the impersonal rhetoric of earlier writers would now receive greater attention as these intellectuals planned their literary renaissance which would defy the torpor and fragmentation so apparent in the outside society.

This group which has been termed the 'generation of 1836' published two newspapers – *Le Républican* and then *L'Union* – founded in 1836 and 1837 respectively, and both forced to disappear after a few years because of political censure. This reaction on the part of Boyer indicates the nature of the impact this group was having on the society and the fierce resistance from official circles. The pages of the newspapers show evidence of lively discussion between the editor and the public on both literary and non-literary matters. The former saw themselves as an embattled avant-garde dedicated to Haiti's survival in a hostile world and painfully aware of the officially encouraged cultural desolation of Haiti. In the face of Boyer's increasing mistrust of any intellectual activity they saw themselves as 'une poignée de soldats hardis et aventureux' which would create a spirit of national regeneration.

The preoccupations of this group were not solely literary. For instance, they were against excessive economic dependence on the metropolitan powers and also very conscious of preserving a record of Haiti's history. Emile Nau, one of the founders of this group, in his *Histoire des Caciques* (1854) described himself as 'always actively concerned with the importance of saving Haiti's history from oblivion'.[7] Generally they were no less assertively nationalistic than de Vastey, for example, and the question of a Haitian identity in all spheres of activity was important to them. For instance, the question of Africa was raised by the historian Beauvais Lespinasse who termed Haiti 'Africa's oldest daughter'. It is also in their attitude to literature and culture that they represent an unprecedented *prise de conscience* among Haitian writers.

In the most important literary declaration of the group, Emile Nau in 1837 proceeded to look with some detachment at literary activity in Haiti. He found the imitativeness and anonymity of the early nationalist outpourings cause for alarm. In a clearly articulated appeal for an indigenous literature, Nau began with a rejection of the pseudo-classical rhetoric of the past:

> The idea of writing these lines occurred to us after reading on several occasions a number of attempts at poetry; this poetry in general is characterised by a lack of inspiration and imagination, to which are added mythological allusions in the nineteenth century! . . . There could well be a reason for Racine to use mythology . . . For you poets of Haiti no such reason will ever exist.[8]

This did not signify a total rejection of European literary movements by Nau. His position was based on a kind of literary eclecticism which would free the Haitian writer from blind imitation but avoid the possibility of literary provincialism: 'The imitation of the styles and techniques of European poets is more unpleasant and sterile here than anywhere else; our poets must not side with any school; they must pay close attention to all of them and belong to none.'[9] Consequently even though Nau saw inevitable links with the metropolis in terms of literary movements and language, he explicitly stated that themes and sentiments should be drawn from local sources. This position reflected the new possibilities and freedoms that came with Romanticism. Indeed, the theories of literary relativity advanced by Mme de Stael are evident in Nau's prescriptions for a Haitian literature determined by the national experience. The creative imagination of Haitian writers was to be linked 'to the beliefs and sentiments of the age and particularly of the country'.[10]

Here we see the beginning of a preoccupation with *La Muse Haitienne*, which would be echoed again and again in Haitian literary manifestos. It is centered on a crucial drift away from the immutable and universal concepts of Classicism towards an emphasis on the diversity of national cultures. The latter was defined in 1836 as a product of the cultural *métissage* which constituted the *génie national* of Haiti. The particular advantage of Haiti's cosmopolitan background was offered by Nau as proof of Haiti's cultural uniqueness:

> We are quite like the American, transplanted and stripped of traditions, but there is in the fusion of the European and African cultures which constitutes our national character, something that makes us less French than the American is English. This advantage is a real one.[11]

Nau sees Haitian society in terms of a creole hybrid rather than fragmented and plural. The product of such creolisation, if explored, would result in literary authenticity. Nau in his article speculated as to the possibilities of such a literary language, 'a little sunburnt in the tropics':

> One of the benefits of civilisation will be to naturalise the French language in our culture. It is up to those aspiring poets to do from now a specialised and profound study of this. It will not be a question of taking the language ready-made from the best exponents; it will be necessary to modify it and adapt it to our local needs.[12]

Even though Nau did not elaborate on this point concerning the link between language and culture, he anticipated (through his insistence on the fact that language was not neutral but the product of a particular system of values) the later, more sustained analysis by such writers as Frantz Fanon as to the cultural values that language imposes on writers.

The generation of 1836 took the question of literature very seriously – as did every other intellectual gathering in Haiti's history. Literature was not just another manifestation of culture but the ultimate proof of a refined and civilised Haitian culture. The emphasis given to the humanities at this early stage indicates how crucial this question was to the nineteenth century and would later explain an essential feature of anti-American feeling during the Occupation. Nau stated quite clearly the significance of literary activity within the national process of survival and as an integral part of the defence of the black race against the stereotype of brutishness and babarity:

> How wonderful it will be when Haiti is represented in each literary genre. We like sometimes, in moments of silence and meditation, to dream of her brilliantly adorned in all the arts, in the distant future. Happy are the generations that will witness this future splendour.[13]

The actual artistic achievement of this movement is less impressive than its literary theories. Its main contribution to Haitian writing lay in the attempt to reverse the sterile tendency towards court poetry and to establish the possibility of treating in a more personal way certain features of the Haitian landscape and national experience. Naturally, there were still many who, in defiance of the spirit of Romanticism, persisted in simply copying themes and sensibility from their French conterparts. For instance, Pierre Chenet, a minor literary figure of the 1830s, declared:

> Lamartine, Hugo, sont des dieux immortels:
> ils ont reçu ma foi, je sers sur leurs autels[14]
>
> [Lamartine, Hugo, are immortal gods
> I have pledged myself to serve at their altars]

Yet one can see signs of the ornatè and hackneyed uniformity of the *pionniers* yielding in the 1830s to a more promising exploration of the potential for evolving a distinctive Haitian 'voice'. Coriolan Ardouin and Ignace Nau, two of the more innovative poets of the period revealed these new possibilities in their work.

Coriolan Ardouin could be said to have anticipated Nau's appeal for artistic authenticity. He died in 1835 when he was twenty-three years old and the movement of 1836 was just being born. He left several poems scattered in various journals (later collected by Emile Nau) but here we have an honest attempt to defy the tendency to glorification of political leaders. Ardouin was much more preoccupied with the tragedy of his own life and sense of universal melancholy which he had inherited from French Romanticism.

Never was an individual more predisposed, because of personal experience, to echoing the melancholy and fatalism of French Romanticism. Ardouin had tuberculosis; his child died soon after being born and his wife quickly followed. In this respect he was close to Lamartine in terms of sentiments and even vocabulary. This oppressive sense of fatalism, mortality and his own isolation, is seen in numerous laments which more or less echo the following theme:

> Mais nous qui ne brûlons que de la pure flamme,
> Mon ami, notre monde est le monde de l'âme.
> Tout n'est que vanités, que misère et douleurs,
> Le coeur de l'homme juste est un vase de pleurs.[15]

> [But we who are only consumed with a pure passion
> My friend, our world is the world of the soul
> All else is pure vanity, misery and grief
> Man's heart is a vessel of tears.]

In spite of the similarity to orthodox French Romanticism, it would be unfair to dismiss Ardouin's work as purely derivative. There is certainly in his work that personal quality and confessional tone that give it a more authentic ring than the earlier pseudo-classical declamation. Indeed, this pervasive sense of the tragic is even applied to Haitian history. No longer do we have the monotonous glorification of the heroes of Independence but a solemn contemplative attitude to this period. In treating Dessalines Ardouin offers the following fatalistic observation:

> Si contre des écueils sa barque fit naufrage
> Et qu'il s'ensevelit sous un triste linceul,

C'est qu'il faut que d'un ciel la clarté se ternisse,
Que le flot se mêlant au sable se brunisse[16]

[If his ship foundered on the rocks,
And he was buried beneath a sad shroud,
The fact is that the sky's brilliance must grow dim,
The waves mingled with the sand grow dark]

Equally attracted by human tragedy and drawn to dealing with various themes in Haitian history, Ardouin treated the theme of slavery in 'Le Départ du Négrier'. The poem is both a real attempt to visualise the injustice of this particular experience as well as one that suffers from too delicate, even too consciously 'poetic' an evocation of the scene. In the opening lines one has a sense of the scene being almost artificially described at twilight. The colours suggesting the injustice and carnage and the bird of prey, the cruel fate of the Africans:

Le vent soufflait quel ques nuages
Empourprés des feux du soleil,
Miraient leurs brillantes images
Dans les replis du flot vermeil.
On les embarque pêle-mêle,
Le négrier immense oiseau
Leur ouvre, une serre cruelle
Et les ravit à leur berceau![17]

[The wind was blowing, some clouds
Made purple by the fires of the sun
Reflected their glistening images
In the ripples of the reddened waves.
They are embarked helter-skelter
The slave ship, an immense bird
Opens its cruel claws
And snatches them from their birthplace!]

Nevertheless, the poem has a sense of assurance and evokes in its final vision the true significance of the cruelty of slavery. In his quiet and solemn manner Ardouin does not launch into invective about the injustice of the slave trade but creates a sense of the mutual destructiveness of the experience, thereby suggesting the eternal cycle of man's inhumanity to man:

> Car à la nef qu'importe
> La rive qui l'attend
> Insensible elle porte
> Et l'esclave et le blanc![18]

> [For what does it matter to the ship
> Which shore awaits them
> Insensitively it sails along
> With both white slaver and enslaved.]

Much more so than Ardouin, Ignace Nau was a direct product of the theories of 1836. His life was almost as tragic and tormented as that of Ardouin and he died in 1845 when he was thirty-seven years old. His work is outstanding, particularly because it is almost certainly the first conscious response to theories of literary indigenism. He published in *Le Républicain* and *L'Union* and his attention was drawn not only to poetry but there are some short stories published in the 1830s which are quite remarkable in their attempt to use local material.

His verse shows the obvious effects of the literary manifesto put out by his brother Emile. He was primarily a nature poet and his poems reveal a synthesis of the Romantic themes of nostalgia and melancholy and the landscape of Haiti. Naturally, some of the clichés of French Romanticism are present in his work – 'l'horizon lointain', 'votre oeil de pur cristal', 'les bardes du ciel', 'l'airain'. However, this world of delicate fantasy is fused with Nau's own meditations on the flora and fauna of Haiti. In 'Les Pipirites', he describes how the chirping of the birds creates a private sense of beauty – contrasting 'Angélus des bois' and 'l'airain':

> Vous êtes l'Angélus des bois qui me réveille
> Et fait chanter mon coeur aux concerts du matin.
> Oh! Combien votre voix est plus douce à l'oreille
> Que le bourdonnement sinistre de l'airain![19]

> [You are the Angelus of the woods that awakens me
> And makes my heart sing to the harmonies of the morning
> Oh! How your voice is sweeter to the ear
> Than the sinister hum of fate!]

This blending of the tendency to brooding pantheism in the Romantic movement with the realities of the Haitian landscape, is central to all Nau's nature poetry. Another interesting theme found in Nau's work derives from the feeling of exile experienced during a visit to France. The poem 'Basses-Pyrénées' is inspired by a sense of nostalgia and in its own delicate way is the prototype of later poems by numerous black writers who would treat the feeling of alienation and isolation experienced in Europe. He lyrically evokes his separation from 'le sol de la patrie' with:

Et me voilà jeté, moi, triste passager,
Sans amour, sans amis sur un sol étranger
Attendant du retour l'heure lente et tardive.
Ce ciel est trop désert, ce soleil sans rayon . . .

Qu'il est resplendissant et d'azur et de feu
Le ciel de ma patrie, et si vaste et si bleu![20]

[And here I am, sad voyager, abandoned
Loveless, friendless on a strange shore
Awaiting the moment of return that is so long in coming.
This sky is too empty, this sun without rays . . .
How magnificent and fiery blue
The sky of my homeland is, so vast and so blue!]

The contrast of 'soleil sans rayon' and 'ciel (resplendissant) de ma patrie' suggests the opposition of the vitality of Haiti with the grey inclemency of Europe – an opposition that would be elaborated on a century later in the Négritude movement.

In the theories of 1836 and the work of Nau and Ardouin we have the tentative but important efforts to repossess the Haitian landscape. This generation can be justifiably considered the true *pionniers* of Haitian writing. The various influences, literary and non-literary, that came together in 1836 made for a genuine awakening of the creative imagination and resulted in the first conscious attempt to grasp the range and complexity of the national experience in literary terms. The legacy that Romanticism and 1836 left with the Haitian writer was an acceptance of the validity of literary diversity. This was a crucial turning point in Haitian literary history as the spirit of 1836 would always exert a powerful influence on literary creativity and so check any sustained attempt at blind imitation.

Boyer's regime fell in 1843 and Haiti was to witness no lengthy period of political stability until the American Occupation of 1915. A succession of army generals and illiterates (twenty-two between 1843 and 1915) created increasing chaos. These crises reached a high point in the reign of Soulouque (1847–1859) who declared himself Emperor Faustin I. The shabby grandeur and despotism of his 'empire' produced a twelve-year nightmare for Haiti and left the country ruined and chronically unstable.

It was also in the latter half of the nineteenth century that the stereotype of Haiti as being a land of sorcery and cannibalism was firmly established. 'L'Affaire de Bizoton' in 1863 in which eight people who confessed to sacrificing a child during a voodoo ceremony were executed, received dramatic international publicity. Lurid tales of black magic were spread by Haiti's critics. One of the most grotesque accounts can be found in Spenser St John's *Hayti or The Black Republic* (1884) which contained sensational and gory episodes, appealing to the repressed fantasies of the Victorian imagination. St John's tales were not gratuitous, however. They were meant to illustrate the following stereotype:

> I have read with deepest interest Froude's 'English in the West Indies' and I can but join with him in protesting against according popular governments to these colonies. I know what the black man is and I have no hesitation in declaring that he is incapable of the art of government.[21]

In the face of such international notoriety and internal discord, literature was once more seen as preserving some of the ideals of the past as well as a means of refuting the charge of barbarity.

Some of the more important prose works written in the latter half of the nineteenth century reveal the basic preoccupations of Haitian intellectuals: Hannibal Price's *De la réhabilitation de la race noire* (1900), Louis Janvier's *L'Egalité des races* (1884) and Anténor Firmin's *De l'Egalité des Races Humaines* (1885). The defence of Haiti and the refutation of the stereotype of savagery are the fundamental aims of their works. Price launched into his defence of Haiti by declaring. 'I am from Haiti, the Mecca, the Judaea of the black race.' Firmin and Janvier are no less assertive in their polemic against Gobineau's theory of a racial hierarchy. Like Price, their attempts to prove the equality of all races made no distinctions between Africa and the Caribbean. Firmin was well aware of the fact that notions of racial superiority could not only damage the black race as a whole but could also have a divisive effect on Haitian society.

These laudable defences of Haiti and the black race did contain a certain weakness, however. Their objective was to demonstrate the potential of any race for arriving at certain abstract ideals which were the criteria for assessing humanity and civilisation. But it would be wrong to see them as precursors of the Négritude movement, in that they made little or no attempt to mention far less defend any African survivals in Haitian culture. The voodoo religion tended to be dismissed as peasant superstition and they insisted on illustrating the ways in which Haiti was no different from Europe. French culture was still very much the norm. The nature of the limitations of these writers can be seen in Firmin's introduction to a collection of poetry *Feuilles de chêne* by Paul Lochard. Lochard is praised for the fact that he is indistinguishable from his metropolitan counterparts. The observation is true enough but Firmin saw it as worthy of admiration. It proved his theory about the potential of the black race:

> M. Lochard is Haitian and more black than white . . . In reading this poetry in which this Caribbean bard has employed all the notes of his lyre, can one ever notice the strong dose of African blood that flows in his veins? Certainly not; for whether it is his syntax or his sensibility, there is nothing, absolutely nothing, to distinguish him from a French poet of the purest French stock.[22]

It is only in post-Occupation Haiti that these reservations about Haiti's Africanness would disappear. In Firmin, Janvier and Price we get a clear impression of the strong sense of indignation felt by educated Haitians their reaction to European racialism in the nineteenth century. Nevertheless, their ambivalence also shows that even though they may quite conceivably have been the only black writers who undertook such a defence in the late nineteenth century, they were, in essential ways, different from the Africanist intellectuals of the 1930s who did not so much refute Gobineau's theory of racial essences as reverse it – considering the black race and Haiti's African heritage as superior to any other race or cultural influence.

In these turbulent years there was no literary movement to succeed the theories of 1836. What does take place is an attempt by creative writers to follow the prescriptions of Emile Nau. The links with French Romanticism continued and were strengthened by sympathy shown to Haiti by Romantic poets such as Victor Hugo.[23]

In applying Nau's ideas, poets at this time tried to present a lyrical and natural evocation of Haiti. A distinct movement towards a carefree and musical verse (and away from the pathos of Ignace Nau and Ardouin) can be discerned. This desire for a new uninhibited verse which celebrated the Haitian landscape was called for in the following lines:

> O Muse, n'est-ce pas
> Gaie enfant des collines
> Que tes fines bottines
> Gênent un peu tes pas? . . .
>
> Dégraffe ton corsage,
> Respire à pleins poumons
> Le souffle pur des monts,
> L'air griseur de la plage![24]
>
> [O Muse, is it not
> Carefree child of the hills
> That your fine shoes
> Inhibit your steps a little? . . .
> Unhook your blouse
> Breathe in deeply
> The pure air of the mountains
> The intoxicating blast from the sea-shore.]

This desire for spontaneity and the elevation of the commonplace and the familiar to poetic status grew into an important tendency among these poets.

The best and most famous example of this tendency is Oswald Durand. There is little evidence in his verse of the cosmic brooding that was favoured by the French Romantics. This solemn intro- spective quality is replaced by a thorough effort at seeking artistic inspiration in every feature of the Haitian experience. As he declared in 1896:

> J'ai chanté nos oiseaux, nos fertiles campagnes,
> Et les grappes de fruits courbant nos bananiers,
> Et le campêche en fleurs parfumant nos montagnes
> Et les grands éventails de nos verts lataniers[25]

> [I have celebrated our birds, our fertile countryside,
> Our banana trees bent over with bunches of fruit
> And the logwood in flower perfuming our mountains
> And the great fans of our green palm trees]

This celebration of Haiti's flora and fauna was a vast but uneven undertaking. Durand's work, in spite of a tendency to superficiality, represents a conscious admission by a Haitian poet that the Haitian landscape could provide themes worthy of being celebrated in verse. The indigenous writers of the Occupation period were anxious to claim him as a precursor and he is still the only nineteenth century poet to have survived so well: 'It is still there that we must go to find the true face of our country. Oswald Durand is a precursor. He is indigenous.'[26]

The pervasive light and bohemian quality of Durand's poetry is evident in his *Rires et Pleurs* (1896). The literary significance of this collection is indisputable in its demonstration of the flexibility of poetry. This is not to say that the influence of French Romanticism was not evident in Durand. Quite often the women of Haiti as they appear in his verse are disturbingly close to Hugo's sensual and languishing odalisques. Sensuality is conveyed through images that suggest a certain plasticity akin to Parnassian technique:

> Rien n'est beau comme nos payses
> Au front bruni par le soleil!
> Aux dents blanches qu'on aurait prises
> Pour des perles dans du vermeil.[27]

> [Nothing is so beautiful as our countrywomen
> With their brows bronzed by the sun
> With their white teeth that could be taken
> For pearls in vermilion.]

His poem 'Idalina' is no different and Jean Price-Mars would later show the obvious similarity between Durand's voluptuous, fleshy stereotype and Hugo's 'Sara la Baigneuse':

> Le vent, entr'ouvrant sa robe
>   Montre un globe
> Double telles l'oeil peut voir
> Deux sapotes veloutées
>   Surmontées
> De deux grains de raisin noir[28]

> [The wind, parted her dress
>   To show two orbs
> Such that the eye can see
> Two velvety plums
>   Surmounted by two small black grapes]

Durand was obviously aware of the unexplored areas of the national experience which deserved to be sung by the Haitian poet. The culture of the peasantry received some attention from Durand and did not appear merely as a backdrop for a meditation on the poetic soul but was an end in itself. His evocation of voodoo rituals may appear stylised today but is unprecedented in its treatment of this sensitive area of Haitian culture. For instance, in one of these poems 'sur le Morne Lointain' the mystery of the voodoo ritual emerges in a rather distant and allusive way but the introduction of such a theme meant that the way was opened for experimentation with form and even a new poetic vocabulary drawn from this culture:

> Sur le morne lointain semé de blanches cases
> Le tambour qui rugit le chant mystérieux
> Du magique vaudou, aux divines extases,
> Où l'on immole un bouc, où l'on brise des vases
> Enivre les papas, qui battent furieux
> Le tambour qui rugit le chant mystérieux
> Sur le morne lointain, semé de blanches cases[29]

> [On the distant hillside dotted with white huts
> The drum which roars a mysterious song
> Of voodoo magic, with that divine frenzy
> Where a goat is sacrificed, where vessels are broken

Maddens the drummers who beat furiously
The drum which roars a mysterious song
On the distant hillside, dotted with white huts]

Other themes such as the sense of ambiguity associated with being a mulatto are found at this early stage in Durand's 'Le fils d'un noir'. It was essentially this desire to treat indiscriminately all areas of his experience and to revitalise the language of poetry that prompted his most remarkable and best known poem. 'Choucoune' was the first really successful effort to write poetry in Haitian creole.[30]

There is one other area of preoccupation in Durand's poetry which was shared by many others at this time and was a product of the political problems experienced by Haiti. In what can be considered the poetic equivalent to the polemic works defending Haiti and the black race, a note of earnest declamation enters Durand's verse as he attempted to re-establish the old ideals of patriotism and national consciousness. This poetry is reminiscent at times of the swelling tones and thundering rhetoric of Hugo's political verse. In 'La Mort de nos Cocotiers' he likens the death of the coconut trees to the loss of freedom and ideals in contemporary Haiti:

Non, tu ne mourras pas, o liberté–quand même,
Sous le souffle d'un vent mortel,
Nous verrions se flétrir ce palmier, ton emblême,
Nos coeurs resteraient ton autel! . . .

O mes frères, les noirs! rappelons-nous nos pères
Héros–martyrs des premiers jours,
Qui prirent corps à corps les gros colons prospères
Et les chassèrent pour toujours![31]

[No, you will not die, O freedom–even when
Blown by a fatal wind,
We would see this palm tree, your symbol, wither
Our hearts would remain your altar! . . .

O my black brothers! Let us remember our fathers
Heroes–martyrs of the first days,
Who engaged the prosperous colonisers in hand to hand combat
And got rid of them for ever!]

Many of these poems were inspired by actual incidents in Haitian history for instance the 'Batsch Affair' (in which the Haitian flag was insulted and the Germans were demanding an indemnity from Haiti), which produced the poem 'Ces Allemands'.

Such a tendency among these poets has caused this period to be termed *L'Ecole Patriotique*. It was not that any organised literary movement existed but there was a spontaneous and widespread attempt by poets to rally to the defence of their native land. Some of them were actually involved in political matters. Massillon Coicou whose *Poésies Nationales* (1892) is often cited as typical of this period, was actually executed in 1908 for taking part in a conspiracy to overthrow President Nord-Alexis. His poetry reflected the political activity that eventually cost him his life.

Coicou was singleminded as far as his attitude to poetry was concerned–it would devote itself to the national cause. He may have been a more capable artist than the early pseudo-classical versifiers, but concentration on a declamatory political verse with an immediate appeal would be a limitation in his work. It would also later be used to support those who at the turn of the century stressed the danger of a literature that was too utilitarian and narrowly nationalistic. In his *Poésies Nationales* he is unequivocal in his dedication to his native land:

> Et me voici seul! . . . Seul, sans luth, je chanterais
> Pour toi, Patrie, objet de mon culte sacré!
> Oh! pour la rendre fière, invincible, immortelle,
> Dieu pour qui je combats en combattant pour elle,
> Pour elle inspire moi; comme elle inspire moi.[32]

> [And here am I! . . . Alone, without my lute, I would sing
> For you, motherland, object of my sacred veneration!
> Oh! To make her proud, invincible, immortal,
> God for whom I fight in fighting for her
> For her inspire me! Like her inspire me.]

This epic and sonorous quality is present in his many depictions of the heroes of Independence. His desperate insistence on this glorious past is a revealing index of the turmoil in contemporary Haiti. As in the poetry of Durand we have a *poésie de circonstance* composed in response to actual incidents during which Haiti was insulted or her sovereignty challenged. However, Coicou, like many of his contemporaries who were deeply troubled by Haiti's increasing chaos, produced verse that was well-intentioned and sincere but in no way distinctive.

To these writers of *L'Ecole Patriotique* who rushed to the defence of Haiti, the role of literature within the national experience was clearly defined. History was a coherent linear process and they were progressively moving away from the colonial past to a secure independent future. Literature was situated in the vanguard of this process. They were the last generation in the nineteenth century to believe this implicitly. The following literary generation–*La Ronde*–could not share this innocent enthusiasm in the face of political chaos. History was no longer a rational force. The dominant mode at the turn of the century is irony and a less grandiose view of the writer's role.

One has the overwhelming impression that the majority of writers in the nineteenth century have a more secure and significant place in literary history than in literature *per se*. Yet this anonymous stream of minor writers and those of some stature that have been looked at, not only established certain preoccupations in Haitian literature but created the possibility of a tradition that would produce the genuinely important artistic achievements of the post-Occupation period. In a time when colonial empires were intact and other black writers revealed a quiescent and derivative sensibility in their work, Haitian writers were attempting to come to terms with their history. This debate with the legacy of the past would be later seen as an essential feature of post-colonial literatures. By the turn of the century there is evidence in the poets of *La Ronde* of the kind of literary sophistication and profound awareness of the complexity of literary creation that at least modifies the stereotype of nineteenth century writing as being purely imitative and immature. Indeed, it would be difficult to apply such a label to poets coming after the Romantic period – for even an attempt to imitate a literary movement whose main emphasis was artistic individualism was in itself a negation of imitation.

José Mariategui, in dealing with emergent literatures, proposed the following three distinguishable periods of literary creativity:

> colonial, cosmopolitan and national. In the first period, the country, in a literary sense, is a colony dependent on its metropolis. In the second period, it simultaneously assimilates

elements of various foreign cultures. In the third period, it shapes and expresses its own personality and feelings.[33]

Even though the general pattern of Mariategui's progression is a tempting scenario for emergent literatures, one would be hard put to apply such labels in a rigorous fashion to the nineteenth century. Indeed, in some of the better writers there is a creative overlapping of the national and the cosmopolitan, the indigenous and the eclectic. Also the nature of a writer's dependence was not only determined by the strength of his own talent but by the literary movement with which he was involved. A highly defined aesthetic and the demand for artistic conformity varied from one movement to another.

Overwhelming evidence of the growing complexity of literature in nineteenth-century Haiti and the sophistication of the literary imagination can be found at the turn of the century. In the writings, both creative and theoretical, of *La Ronde* we have an attempt to put all that preceded into focus. This conscious reappraisal of the strengths and weaknesses of Haitian writers is indication enough of the new authority that had crystallised in Haitian literature.

NOTES

1. Aimé Césaire, *La Tragédie du Roi Christophe* (Paris: Présence Africaine, 1970) p. 54.
2. Quoted in Pradel Pompilus and Frères de l'instruction chrétienne, *Manuel illustré d'histoire de la littérature haitienne* (Port-au-Prince: Henri Deschamps, 1961) p. 11.
3. *L'Abeille Haytienne*, 15 June–31 Oct. 1820, pp. 3–4.
4. Le baron de Vastey, *Réflexions sur une lettre de Mazères* (Cap-Henry: imp. du roi, 1816) p. 53.
5. Ibid., p. 77.
6. *L'Abeille Haytienne*, April–June 1820.
7. Emile Nau, *Histoire des Caciques d'Haiti* (Port-au-Prince: Panorama, 1963) Preface.
8. *L'Union*, 16 Nov. 1837.
9. Ibid.
10. Ibid.
11. *Le Républicain*, 1 Oct. 1836.
12. *L'Union*, 16 Nov. 1837.
13. Ibid.
14. Pierre Chenet, *Chants du barde glanés chez les Muses* (Paris: Paul Dupont, 1846) p. 192.

15. Coriolan Ardouin, *Poésies* (Port-au-Prince: Etheart, 1881) p. 21.
16. Ibid.
17. Ibid.
18. Ibid.
19. *Manuel illustré d'histoire de la littérature haitienne.*
20. *L'Union*, 18 Jan 1838.
21. Spenser St John, *Hayti or The Black Republic* (London: Frank Cass, 1971) Introduction, p. xi.
22. Preface to Paul Lochard's *Feuilles de chêne* (Paris: Ateliers Haitiens, 1901). Firmin, Price and Janvier have nevertheless acquired a reputation as fathers of Négritude. See Aimé Césaire's interview with René Dépestre, *Casa de las Américas*, no. 49, Aug, 1968, 141.
23. See *Oeuvres complètes de Victor Hugo*, Correspondence, 1849–1866 (Paris: Albin Michel, 1950):

    A Monsieur Heurtelou, redacteur du *Progrès* Port-au-Prince, Haiti, 1860: I love your country, your race, your freedom, your republic. Your magnificent and pleasant island pleases at this time free spirits; it has just provided a great example; it has broken free from tyranny p. 331

24. Tertulien Guilbaud, *Feuilles au vent*, (Paris: Leopold Cerf, 1888) p. 7.
25. Oswald Durand, *Rires et Pleurs I* (Port-au-Prince: Panorama, n.d. (original edn 1896) p. 111.
26. Jacques Roumain in *La Revue Indigène*, no. 3, Sept. 1927.
27. Durand, *Rires et Pleurs I*, pp. 20–1.
28. Ibid., p. 99. See comparison between 'Idalina' and Hugo's 'Sara la Baigneuse' in Price-Mars' *De St Domingue à Haiti* (Paris: Présence Africaine, 1959) pp. 20–30.
29. Durand, *Rires et Pleurs I*, p. 72.
30. Durand, *Rires et Pleurs II*, p. 222.
31. Durand, *Rires et Pleurs I*, p. 134.
32. Massillon Coicou, *Poésies Nationales* (Paris: Goupy et Jourdan, 1892) p. 39.
33. José Mariategui, *Seven Interpretive Essays on Peruvian Reality* (Austin: University of Texas Press, 1974) p. 191.

II. La Ronde: a Revaluation

In the year that the Americans invaded Haiti, 1915, Edmond Laforest, one of the leading poets of the literary journal *La Ronde*, tied a Larousse dictionary around his neck and committed suicide by drowning. It seemed a bizarre case of life imitating art as his contemporary Etzer Vilaire, who also collaborated in *La Ronde*, had published in 1901 a long poem entitled 'Les Dix Hommes Noirs'. This poem dealt with the themes of disillusion and futility and described the cases of nine young men who are driven to commit suicide and one who witnesses this tragedy and becomes insane. 'Noirs' in the title has no ethnic significance but rather suggests the pervasive atmosphere of gloom in the poem. The following lines in the poem could easily be ascribed to Laforest:

> Je n'ai de place ici, moi, que dans le cercueil
> On ne vit pas au sein d'un peuple en agonie.[1]
>
> [There is no place for me but in the coffin
> No one lives among a people in agony.]

Laforest's suicide was not allowed to remain merely an unhappy accident. Two relatively recent literary movements – the Indigenous school in post-Occupation Haiti and the Négritude movement of the 1930s – saw in the poet's self-immolation a convenient symbol of nineteenth-century Haitian writing in particular and colonial literature in general. The generation of *La Ronde* was stereotyped as escapist, fatally tied to French culture and morbidly fascinated by the French Symbolist movement.

As we shall later see, the stereotype of a derivative and escapist literary past became a functional part of post-Occupation polemics in Haiti. Also, the Paris based *Légitime Défense* (1932) and *L'Etudiant Noir* (1934) sought to vilify nineteenth-century writers as assimilationist and alienated in order to justify new departures in their own militant writing. The nationalist and politically committed nature of these two movements made for very rigid criteria for judging literary activity. Whatever did not conform to their new imperatives of engagement or indigenism was rejected as assimilationist. *La Ronde* became an easy target for these criticisms of elitism, intellectual abdication and cultural ambivalence that were levelled at the nineteenth century.

The pieties and received ideas of the militant thirties have become the point of departure for a whole school of literary criticism that has fixed the label of *mimétisme culturel* on the nineteenth century.[2] This has tended to obscure important and relevant issues raised in the nineteenth century particularly in Haiti where, as we have seen, a century of independence had already begun to create greater assurance and sophistication among Haitian writers.

However, ample circumstantial evidence seemed to support the conviction that *La Ronde* illustrated a blind adherence to a borrowed aesthetic, namely French Symbolism. This impression was created by the polarisation of literary activity in turn of the century Haiti into two opposing camps. This antagonism mirrored the debate between Realists and Symbolists in France. In Haiti, *La Ronde* seemed to be in favour of a cloistered aestheticism in literature and poetry in particular. The Realist cause, with its emphasis on social reality and the tendency to local colour, inherited from Romanticism, was defended by Haiti's first novelists. Seymour Pradel, a literary commentator at the time, described these two trends in a series of articles started in 1896 and entitled 'Les Deux Tendances':

> As far as literature is concerned I think we have one, I would say even two: one which is linked to our national history, which finds its inspiration there, which is purely Haitian; the other which is more drawn to the depiction of mankind, which contains broader, more universal qualities and which we will term franco or humano-Haitian.[3]

Pradel's commentary attempts to be generous to both sides but in showing *La Ronde* to be not 'purely Haitian' he only contributed to the criticism of *La Ronde's* position. The humano-Haitian school was obviously inspired by the Symbolist insistence on an anti-realist even anti-materialist approach to creativity. In contrast to which we have Haiti's novelists using the theories and conventions of the Realist and Naturalist movements in France to deal with Haitian society not as an abstraction nor in universal terms but as specifically determined by certain historical conditions. The novel would be a sociological investigation of Haitian reality.

The contrast is even more marked when we examine the literary production of these two groups. The Haitian novelists of the turn of the century had borrowed from their metropolitan counterparts a conception of the novel as a record (more precisely a mirror) of external socio-historical reality. They also attempted a creative exploitation of the legacy of indigenism from the earlier 'Romantic' period. The novel would inevitably be a product of strong regionalist qualities combined with photographic realism. Frédéric Marcelin, one of the most vocal writers of the late nineteenth century, defended the novel in these terms:

> Local colour . . . is not always highly considered by our writers. They feel it is more or less a lapse in taste, an unrepressed instinct

for the banal and the vulgar . . . (However) our literature must
be increasingly inspired by our history, by the moral and material
conditions of our world, by all the physical beauty of our country.
They must be celebrated to be loved.[4]

Along with this insistence on indigenism came an element of social
consciousness. What Zola had done for the urban poor in France,
the Haitians wished to do for their own society. This sympathy was
directed particularly towards the peasantry. What was desired was
more than local colour and sensationalism. There is evidence of a
strong emotional commitment to exposing the harsh realities of
peasant life:

> Think a little of those wretched peasants, cannon fodder for our
> fancies and passions, unwitting tools, playthings in our miserable
> quarrels. We have devastated and ruined their fields, we have
> dismembered and dislocated pitilessly their humble families, we
> have ultimately sent them to their deaths.[5]

What was created from these early attempts at prose fiction was one
of the most important genres in Haitian literature – the peasant
novel. The mimetic value of the novel form and a strong social
conscience were fundamental to the creative imagination of the
nineteenth-century Haitian novelist.

The novels of this period seem to be either political satires of one
kind or another or depictions of peasant life. For instance Frédéric
Marcelin's *Thémistocle Epaminondas Labasterre* (1901) is a parody
somewhat in the manner of Flaubert, of the pretensions of a corrupt
political demagogue.

The early peasant novels are equally interesting as precursors to
the important and successful novels of the post-Occupation period.
For instance, Justin Lhérisson's *La Famille des Pitite Caille* (1905) is
an interesting attempt at creating real originality in the novel form.
Using a narrative framework drawn from the Haitian oral
tradition, Lhérisson described the adventures of his naive *nouveau
riche* protagonist in a combination of the vernacular and standard
French. Semi-literate and of peasant origin, Eliezer Pitite Caille's
ostentation is mercilessly satirised by the revelation of his shallow-
ness and ignorance.

Along with this modest vignette by Lhérisson we have Antoine
Innocent's *Mimola* (1906) which descended directly into the

peasant experience. In this novel which deals with the use of the voodoo religion by Mme Georges to cure her daughter, we have the first attempt to capture the peasant milieu and religious rituals in prose. These are sometimes so detailed that they verge on the ethnographic. The importance of Innocent's work does not lie so much in its literary quality – since plot and characterisation are contrived and improbable at times – but in the author's attempts to come to grips with the peasant experience. Even if these first works never produced a real masterpiece, they represent important literary experiments and a serious artistic concern with the peasantry without which the persuasive peasant novels of the twentieth century would have been impossible.

In apparent opposition to the stand taken by Haiti's first novelists we have a radically different literary *prise de position* argued by those who collaborated in the journal *La Ronde*. The impression of escapism and art for art's sake in *La Ronde* was created by their adherence to Symbolist views on poetry. Like Proust, Realism to them could be no more than 'a miserable listing of lines and surfaces'. Their aesthetic would depend solely on the writer's subjectivity. The reconstruction, *not* the reflection of external reality through the literary imagination. Most of the literary proclamations in *La Ronde* stress this theme. Art must be disinterested, non-functional even to the point of being hermetic. The short-lived review *La Jeune Haiti* (1896) was the precursor to *La Ronde* and in the latter's first editorial the continuity with *La Jeune Haiti* and the plea for absolute independence in the arts are unmistakable:

From the first edition (of *La Jeune Haiti*) its wishes were clearly shown: a revival of a serious appreciation of art, a dismissal from our literature of those lapses in taste and unintelligent limitations that mar it . . . In short, art is independent; nothing must inhibit its free expression. Its only morality is in its capacity to broaden and purify our sensibility . . . taking us into a world of the imagination, filled with fantasy and dreams, where life is more noble and more pure.[6]

Solely on the evidence of such a manifesto one has the impression of a small group of intellectuals isolating themselves from reality and wanting to use the artificial sense of ideal coherence in poetry as well as the organised private fantasy of the poet as a means of shutting out the political situation in Haiti. Etzer Vilaire's proclamation

'Great truths lie in the realm of fantasy![7] suggests a literary preciosity and deliberate detachment from the real world that have been used to typify this group. This attitude seems particularly disturbing in the face of the earlier declaration by Marcelin in favour of depicting the cultural and political milieu.

The case against *La Ronde* was further strengthened by various statements that were made proclaiming the superiority of poetry and poets. The impression of elitism was easily conveyed by the sense of being misunderstood and set apart from ordinary men that prevailed in this group. Mallarmé's rather Nietzschean exhortation: 'Let the masses read their moral fables, but please do not waste our poetry on them. O poets, you have always been proud: go even further, become scornful',[8] left its mark on this Haitian generation. Vilaire's image of himself in 'Aux lecteurs de Tristesses Ultimes' corresponded to the sense of being misunderstood and victimised – a prophet stoned by the Jews, Baudelaire's 'Albatross' trapped by the sailors:

Ma vie est un miroir funèbre et réfléchit,
Sous un décor lugubre, un fantôme qui pleure . . .
Qui m'a tué si tôt? C'est vous, hommes de fiel!
C'est le monde des juifs lapidant leurs prophètes;
C'est le grand mal soufflant aux quatre vents du ciel
Le poison lent et sûr dont meurent les poètes![9]

[My life is a mournful mirror that reflects
Against a dismal decor, a weeping phantom . . .
Who killed me so soon? It is you men of venom!
It is the world of Jews who stone their prophets,
It is the evil which blows from the four corners of heaven
The slow and deadly poison from which poets die!]

To this extent *La Ronde*'s position was akin to that of the *Modernismo* movement in Latin America, with its contrived artistic posturing and other excesses that led to an impression of affectation. Poetry was to be accessible only to the initiated as is evidenced in the poetry of *La Ronde* as well as in Ruben Dario's *Prosas Profanas* (1895). In contrast to the militant and earnest style of the past, the writer was now to be a refined dilettante – not a social activist.

The accusation of cultural subservience to France that has been made against this generation could well be supported by one of the

most notorious documents to appear at the turn of the century –
d'Ussol's article in *Haiti littéraire et sociale*. This anonymous article
(d'Ussol is a psuedonym which appears to be an ironical variation of
'du sol'), set out a preposterous argument negating a national
culture and recommending a complete reintegration with France.
One is tempted to believe that it was a deliberately provocative
piece of writing which did not necessarily reflect the honest views of
any writer or group. Somehow it has been used to confirm the
assimilationist stereotype of *La Ronde* even though it never appeared
in that journal – it actually appeared in the journal of Frédéric
Marcelin. D'Ussol not only negated African retentions in the
society, calling Haiti's black population 'merchandise without a
label', but openly advocated that Haiti should become a cultural
province of France:

> Our language is French, our customs, habits and ideas are French
> and whether we like it or not, our soul is French. The very patois
> spoken by our common people, our creole, is simply made up of
> old French words piously preserved and mispronounced at will
> for the pleasure of our lazy lips and indolent ears.[10]

What seems to be a deliberately concocted article has been cited as
just another example of nineteenth-century cultural insecurity.
There is no evidence of such an extreme position on the subject by
any writer in *La Ronde*. For instance, Vilaire saw France as the final
consecration for the creativity of an intellectual élite in Haiti, but he
nevertheless insisted on the originality and uniqueness of the
Haitian contribution:

> This dream is the arrival of a Haitian élite in the literary history of
> France, the production of strong and lasting works which can
> demand attention from our intellectual metropolis; and gain
> recognition for the fact that the French sensibility flourishes in an
> orginal way in our literature, mixed with the vitality of our
> African heritage.[11]

Vilaire's notion of an intellectual élite is close to W. E. B. Dubois's
'Talented Tenth': such a group would embody a cultural ideal that
would gain respect for the nation or race as a whole. It is a plea for
cultural *métissage* not blind subservience. It is also much more
complex and reasoned a position than the uncompromising manifesto of d'Ussol.

Nevertheless the assimilationist stereotype of the nineteenth century was established and supported. It became part of a general pattern as every description of the evolution of emergent literatures follows the same scenario – from assimilationist to militant. One of the most influential voices on this question took a categorical stand on the issue: Frantz Fanon in his essay 'West Indians and Africans' declared, 'Until 1939 the West Indies lived, thought, dreamed . . . composed poems, wrote novels exactly as a White man would have done . . . Before Césaire, West Indian literature was a literature of Europeans.'[12] We have seen so far the extent to which such crude categorisation was inapplicable to the earlier Haitian writers. The case of *La Ronde* at the turn of the century needs closer scrutiny.

In looking at the whole development of Haitian writing, what becomes evident is that the unifying force in a literary tradition is not the compatibility of individual philosophies or artistic group-ings but the dominant problem the various theoretical positions are designed to solve. To this extent *La Ronde* is as much a part of the literary culture of Haiti as the more overtly Indigenist movements. The former's position, if regarded objectively, is not only intelligible as a response to the historical process but highly relevant to the current post-ideological literary scene in Haiti. *La Ronde*'s views obviously reflected certain aspects of French Symbolism but to dismiss their position as simply another case of blind imitation is to miss the complexity of their position and deny its significance.

There are two essential features discernable in the literary culture of Haiti in the nineteenth century which were destined to remain essential elements of a national literature. The first of these is the seriousness with which literature is taken – almost an inevitable reaction from a literate élite against the stereotype of barbarity constantly levelled against Haiti. Secondly, the debate with history – i.e., the negation of the colonial legacy and the desire to vindicate a free, independent Haiti – was an essential form of motivation for Haitian writers. From the pedantic but unsophisti-cated rhetoric of the early poets to the Romantic insistence on indigenism and literary individualism, the basic preoccupations remain constant. Literature was always committed to responding to a vision of history as intelligible and essentially Utopian.

Although *La Ronde* represented a shift in terms of literary sensibility, the movement was no less preoccupied with Haiti's fate and no one could contest its serious attitude to literature. What had changed was the view of how history proceeded and consequently literature's relationship to this process. The generation at the turn of the century could not believe with the same innocence as its predecessors, in a deterministic and progressive movement in history. Rather it now became a cyclical process substantiated by the collapse of authority and order in Haiti. The past was not a nightmare they could dismiss but one they were condemned to relive. Vilaire in one of his many comments on the chaos in Haiti speaks of:

> Those agonising torments through which a generation which has known martyrdom for some time, struggles, a generation overwhelmed by disillusion and suffering that seem almost hereditary, by accumulated evils, from the first hesitant beginnings to the present day when unending tragedy continues to be seen in society through the double oppression of material privation and moral anguish.[13]

'Hereditary suffering', 'accumulated evils' and 'unending tragedy' suggest an absolute sense of futility from which there was no hope of release. The Haitian writer could no longer have a secure and confident voice in face of such political absurdity. What became established was a deep sense of vulnerability and a distrust of all-embracing systems, simply of any ideology. The earlier conception of literary *engagement* could not survive this crisis intact.

The *crise de conscience* of *La Ronde* had important literary implications. In the same way that there was a perceptible shift away from a certain conception of history, similarly there was a reaction against the literature spawned by such a view. *Littérature de combat* and *poésie de circonstance* which were mainly responsible for the rhetorical and epic quality so prevalent in earlier writing were now severely criticised. Politics were now distrusted and so was the literature which served the cause of political efficacy. *La Ronde* is distinctive as a period of literary creation in Haiti as the tendency to thundering rhetoric is absent and the movement is towards the private and contemplative. Indeed, the greatest threat to the turn of the century poet was silence.

La Ronde's literary position can be most clearly defined by showing firstly what they were reacting against and then isolating what they saw as necessary for Haitian literature. The individual poets of *La Ronde* paid as much attention to Haitian literature as they did to European literary movements. Their own conclusions as to what literature should be came after a profound assessment of literary tendencies that preceded them. They seem to have been deeply disturbed by the aesthetic failures apparent in many of their predecessors. Indeed, their ultimate position on literature can be seen as a reaction against two particular literary phenomena that were evident among earlier writers – the use and abuse of local colour and the utilitarian and didactic attitude to creative writing.

As we have seen, the Romantic influence on Haitian writers had earlier encouraged the use of local colour. This was both timely and necessary as it broke the stranglehold of French Classicism on Haitian writing. Thus the celebration of local flora and fauna and the use of creolisms provided a ready solution to the problem of literary originality. By the late nineteenth century, however, such a solution was widely abused as poetry centred around a hackneyed listing of the typical features of a tropical island. It was evident that the inclusion of local customs and the vernacular did not guarantee authenticity or control over the literary medium. Indeed, this could easily lead to superficiality and could even be more quiescent and escapist than poetry which was not similarly decorated. What had become clear to *La Ronde* was that one who really belonged could dispense with local colour. As the Argentinian writer, Jorge Luis Borges, argued, local colour was no guarantee of national identity:

> Gibbon observes that in the Arabian book par excellence, in the Koran, there are no camels; I believe if there were any doubts as to the authenticity of the Koran, this absence of camels would be sufficient to prove it is an Arabian work. It was written by Mohammed and he, as an Arab, had no reason to know that camels were especially Arabian; for him they were part of reality, he had no reason to emphasise them; on the other hand, the first thing a falsifier, a tourist, an Arab nationalist would do is have a surfeit of camels, caravans of camels on every page.[14]

The position of *La Ronde* on this particular issue has been somewhat distorted by even such well-intentioned articles as Pradel's 'Les Deux Tendances' in which *La Ronde* is categorised as humano-Haitian and not purely Haitian. The truth is that *La Ronde's* position did emphasise originality but their solution was not the obvious one of regionalism. The fallacy that local colour was the key to originality was openly debated at the turn of the century:

> We survive through laziness or impotence on a small number of
> ideas, sensations and, why not say it, solemn rantings...There is in
> all Haitian poetry – at least prior to 1900 – the same annoying,
> monotonous quality; it is this quality that makes the best works
> tasteless and all equally mediocre.[15]

The contention of the poets of *La Ronde* was not that they should
surrender the right to have a distinctive voice but that their cultural
and historical uniqueness could make itself manifest without having
to resort to local colour. It is not that they despised their own
experience and folk culture – in fact, Georges Sylvain demonstrated
his belief in the versatility of the creole language in his translation of
La Fontaine's fables in *Cric-Crac* (1901). What they did object to was
the uncontrolled use of local colour to give an artificial identity to
literary works. Vilaire in his preface to *Poèmes de la Mort* strongly
condemned those who sought 'a superficial and false
originality . . . a purely local, narrow and banal kind of realism'.
For Vilaire and his contemporaries, originality lay not in the subject
chosen but in the treatment. The only guarantee of a distinctive
voice was found in the creative imagination of the poet. This is
particularly important as far as their own tendency to metaphysical
speculation is concerned, since they had to come to terms with the
possibility of using the French language to express their own sense of
dislocation in the face of the contemporary political anarchy.

La Ronde's *prise de position* on literature did not only involve a
violent reaction to the question of local colour but included an
important *mise au point* on the subject of ideology and art. The level
of political commitment among Haitian writers in the nineteenth
century is already evident. This didacticism in literature, though
well-intentioned, did create a debilitating uniformity in Haitian
poetry in particular. The debasement of this public poetry into *poésie
commandée* or court poetry clearly showed the dangers of too
propagandist a literature. The objection of *La Ronde* to this tendency
is similar to their rejection of local colour. Essentially both
movements ultimately meant the debasement of poetic language.
What *La Ronde* sought was a freeing of the creative imagination, a
flexibility and formal perfection which they saw as sadly lacking in
their predecessors. It is quite probable that the attraction of the
Symbolist movement was the latter's call for a similar independence

and purity in literary form. It is quite absurd to treat the major poets of *La Ronde* as blind imitators. The choices they made were always conscious ones. Indeed, in this particular instance, one can argue that this insistence on formal purity had conceivably more to do with a specific form of literary protest than with a desire to escape.

La Ronde was the only literary movement in Haiti worthy of the name, in that it concerned itself almost exclusively with the poetic word. These poets saw themselves as an avant-garde but essentially a literary one, having little or no ideological pretensions. These, in any case would have been almost impossible in the face of the political crises at the time. *La Ronde*'s literary manifesto revolved around two essential features – eclecticism and aestheticism – in striking contrast to the questions of *engagement* and accessibility that dominated earlier periods.

The very name *La Ronde* chosen by this generation for their journal conveys the notion of eclecticism which they saw as central to their literary credo. In the first number of the journal, Bellegarde writes 'we (ferons la ronde) will survey all ideas and individuals attempting to understand them.' Such a stand was the inevitable result of *La Ronde*'s rejection of the narrow provincialism and hollow rhetoric that had crept into Haitian poetry. If the poetic vision was to be renewed, it had to be exposed to new experiences as cosmopolitan and varied as possible. They now reserved the right to use any tradition, to improvise, to handle any experience with the same degree of irreverence. The Draconian exclusiveness that prevailed in the past yielded to an aesthetic which could draw on any tradition and in which the only guarantee of originality was the poet's perception – even reconstruction – of reality. Vilaire's 'Credo littéraire' stated:

> Eclectisme, à present tu dois régner dans l'art.
> Il nous faut tout savoir, tout sentir et tout fondre;
> Etre un, oui, mais divers et vaste. Venus tard,
> Vous n'avez pas un pré maigre et stérile à tondre . . . [16]

> [Eclecticism, at present you must reign in art.
> We must know all, feel all and absorb all;
> Be one, yes, but diverse and wide-ranging. Having arrived late
> You do not have a sparse and sterile field to harvest . . .]

Consequently the poetry of this group was not too rigidly linked to any literary movement. Romantic poetry ('Le Flibustier' written about a romantic fugitive in a style which recalls Lamartine's), Parnassian verse (Laforest's *Sonnets et Médaillons* which bestowed on him the name 'The Haitian Heredia') and writings in creole (Sylvain's translations of La Fontaine's *Fables* into creole) all attest to the new diversity and flexibility *La Ronde* desired.

This cosmopolitan tendency allied with a deep sense of insecurity that prevailed at the time created a chronic need among these writers to be recognised by foreign critics. The need for foreign consecration of their talents – some of their work was awarded prizes by the Académie Française – can be seen in Vilaire's conception of 'the arrival of a Haitian elite in the literary history of France.' This may be an example of cultural paranoia but it did have the positive side. The tensions produced from such insecurity had much to do with the objective assessment of the Haitian literary tradition and with the formulation of a literary theory that stressed formal competence.

The second important question raised was that of aestheticism and this particular aspect of their manifesto has attracted the most criticism since it seemed to suggest a gratuitious disregard for reality and encourage an 'ivory tower' attitude to art. Such a criticism is a simplification of *La Ronde*'s attitude. They were intensely concerned with defining what poetry was all about. In this they felt that the language of poetry had to be more intense, more pure than any other. They took strong objection to the fact that poetic language had become clichéd and debased because of the clumsy rhetoric and the 'réalisme étroit et banal' of earlier writers. It was the poet's duty to create a new and rare language – to purify everyday language – so that he could present a new vision of the world. This is an important technical point which had never really been raised before with such force. Poetic language – and in this they followed Symbolist literary theory – would not be involved in the process of naming and fixing reality but its most important objective would be to move away from the prosaic to create new resonances. In poetry what ultimately mattered was not reality itself but the perception of reality. This was not purely a literary question, however. It was intimately linked to the political chaos in Haiti. A literal reflection of reality was absurd in such a context. The writer could no longer have a public voice. He could only trust his own sensibility.

The nature of the adherence of three important poets of *La Ronde* – Edmond Laforest, Etzer Vilaire and Georges Sylvain –

varied according to the temperament of each individual. However, they all shared the desire for literary renewal and were haunted by the tragic events of their times. It is therefore possible to see in certain works by these poets a highly original response to Haiti's situation. This can only happen, however, if we recognise the fact that the view of historical reality as intangible and unpredictable prevailed at the time. One can then see the poetry of *La Ronde* as delicately wrought, imaginative fantasies steeped in the tragic and the absurd. To think of *La Ronde* as alienated and dilettante is to ignore the nature of their relationship to contemporary reality. As Pradel put it:

> They did not create artificial reasons for their suffering. They were sincere because their tortures were real . . . more than others, we felt the weight on our shoulders, which were crushed by it, of the regime of that time, regime of force, violence, corruption which trampled on and humiliated men's consciences.[17]

There are two kinds of responses in the poetry of *La Ronde* to the absolute sense of chaos that prevailed among them. Firstly, there are imaginative works that treat the question of Haiti's decline directly and in which the strident tone of the earlier rhetoric yields to a subdued, desperate appeal. Secondly, there are those which contain subtle intimations of the writer's dark preoccupations and which also involve a conscious use of their new ideas on poetic technique. Vilaire stressed the relationship between his creative vision and his times when he explained:

> Certain dominant ideas of an era, certain attitudes which are current in a country, create an irresistible excitement in the creative imagination . . . To conceive of a possible work of art that entirely escapes these fateful influences, would be to dream of harmonious vibrations in the air without the explosion that sets them off, a ray without the star that emits it.[18]

Poems such as 'A Ma Patrie' in *Poèmes de la Mort*:

> Je le sais, ta détresse est immense et poignante
> Nulle main n'a bandé ta blessure saignante.[19]

[I know, your anguish is enormous and painful
No hand has bandaged your bleeding wounds.]

and 'Nos Erostrates':

Vous dont l'aveugle esprit, assombrissant nos jours
　　Déchaîne sur nous la tempête;
Vous qui venez vers nous comme un vol de vautours
　　Vous pour qui le carnage est fête![20]

[You whose blind spirit, darkening our days,
Unleashes on us a storm;
You come to us like a flight of vultures
You for whom carnage is a festivity!]

both illustrate the bitterness and indignation of Vilaire's reaction to the state in which Haiti had found itself. This example of the first tendency previously mentioned, shows the extent to which the patriotic mode of the past had changed.

　　The real originality and achievement of *La Ronde*, however, lies in the second tendency – wherein they managed to create the kind of sophistication they required in their poetry while retaining the quality of desperation and uncertainty that prevailed at the time. An aesthetic based on an imagination that ranges free but one that is motivated by a fixed tragic gaze. In some of Vilaire's work, for instance, we find more than the strange, sad beauty of Beaudelaire or Poe's macabre imagination. The tragic fantasies written in turn of the century Haiti reveal a qualitative difference in the *mal de siècle* and anguish they express. For instance, Vilaire's 'Les Dix Hommes Noirs' (mentioned earlier) which treats the multiple suicides of sad, disillusioned men does contain a certain Gothic and nightmarish sequence of events reminiscent of Poe. Vilaire's fantasy is more than a pastiche of *fin de siècle* tendencies. It may have made use of some foreign conventions but it essentially expresses the deep-seated desperation and bewilderment of his generation.

　　This blending of the subjective, terrified vision and formal literary perfection is evident in poems once thought to be 'obviously' Symbolist. In the poetic experiments of orthodox Symbolists there is a desire for an impersonal aesthetic – a vision that is pure, that suggests a delicate and allusive world of subtle resonances. Because of their eclectic approach and their own sense of gloom, we find *La*

Ronde attempting to fuse the Symbolist literary ideal on to a subjective, almost Romantic tradition. Beneath the vague and fleeting there lurked a tragic sense of isolation and vulnerability. Haiti was the epicentre of some cosmic disorder. This is at once expressed in the terrified consciousness of the artist and yet contained in the controlled, fragile form of the poem. In Laforest's work an intense melancholy seems to permeate every image:

> Une danse macabre . . .
> Ou les plus fins valseurs sont des hideux squelettes,
> Ou j'entends résonner, sous les riches toilettes,
>   Les os sonores des pieds secs.[21]

> [A macabre dance . . .
> In which the finest dancers are hideous skeletons,
> In which I hear the rattle, under expensive dresses,
> Of the hollow bones of dry feet.]

The evanescent, delicate vision evoked is steeped in an atmosphere of gloom in 'Ombres dans l' ombre':

> Ou donc vont ces flottantes
> Formes lentes des femmes
> Ces formes vaporeuses
> Qui sont d'épais flocons
> D'ombre, de brumes sombres[22]

> [Where then go these floating
> Slow female spectres
> These hazy forms
> Which are thick flakes
> Of shadow, dark mists]

Vilaire in his *spleen* poems expresses the need for the infinite, for some sense of harmony and coherence. Into this ethereal aesthetic Vilaire drags his own desperation – a curious fusing of the tragic and the stylised. The overwhelming sense of the absurd makes the concept of 'l'azur' into more than a nineteenth-century cliché:

> Le temps fuit et n'a rien qui vaille un seul soupir;
> Attache une aile forte et pure à ton désir;

Jette en haut un regard nostalgique, o mon âme!
Fuis par-dessus l'azur baigné de molle flamme,
Vole plus haut, fuis, cherche une autre immensité
Va monte! Berce-toi dans la sérénité
Des plages de l'éther; va! déchire les voiles[23]

[Time flies and is not worth a single sigh;
Give strong pure wings to your desire;
Fix your nostalgic gaze on high, my soul!
Flee beyond the horizon bathed in soft flame,
Fly higher, flee, seek out another dimension
Go, rise! Cradle yourself in the serenity
Of these ethereal zones! go! break through the veils]

In attempting to articulate their vision of a world stripped of causality, uncertain and unpredictable, the poets of *La Ronde* were enacting almost an archetypal New World situation. Realising the impossibility of ordering the course of history into distinct evolutionary patterns, they attempted to express the terrified subjectivity of one witnessing the repeated and absurd cycle of history. The attempts to bring stylistic perfection to such a subjectivity gives *La Ronde* a central place in the Haitian experience. The desolate and tragic metaphysics of *La Ronde* attests to the attempt to survive in this twilight consciousness, always at the edge of tragedy. Sometimes this numbing sense of futility so dominated their poetry that we find such desperate responses as Vilaire's religious mysticism and self-pitying laments in 'Que suis-Je':

O mon Dieu! que suis-je? que suis-je?
La terre m'est toute étrangère.
J'exhale une plainte éphémère[24]

[O my God! What am I? What am I?
The earth is strange to me.
I utter a fleeting groan.]

The real creativity of the group is not found in such lapses, not in a surrender to the tragic, but in that twilight region where the creative imagination is fed by a sustained, intense vision of the contingent present.

The lack of a literal response to reality does not necessarily constitute artistic alienation. Proof of these poets' devotion to Haiti is easily seen in their activities during the American Occupation. Sylvain gave up poetry to become a journalist and leader of the Haitian nationalist movement. Vilaire's response to the American presence can be found in the prose poetry of *La Vie Solitaire:*

> Impossible to dream of denying it; this land, I am possessed by it. Could I do so without destroying my own being? . . . Now and for always I am in mourning for Haiti, taking with a painful pride my share in this national shame . . . O my God, I beg you to have pity on these people![25]

Nevertheless, because of the demands *La Ronde* made on poetic language, and their reservations about the public voice of the poet, they suffered at the hands of the militant and doctrinaire literary movements that followed in the wake of the American invasion of Haiti.

Every literary movement – and each work of art for that matter – stands in a provisional relationship to time. What may have been anathema to the ideologically blinkered movements of the 1930s could be reconsidered more objectively a few decades later. In spite of their less adventurous prosody, *La Ronde's* insistence on the importance of the poetic word and its rejection of realism and materialism as limited ways of perceiving reality are not essentially different from the main focus of the later Négritude poetry.[26] The latter may have found a more appealing ideological framework for their literary position but it essentially involved a similar rejection of a materialist, barren world in favour of the realm of the imagination. Consequently, the label of escapist that has been attached to much of the nineteenth century appears to be at least inadequate. Indeed, the literary activity of the period can be seen as a formative experience for the creativity that followed the American Occupation.

NOTES

1. Etzer Vilaire, 'Les Dix Hommes Noirs', *Poèmes de la Mort* (Paris: Librairie Fischbacher, 1907).

2. See chapter 2 of Lilyan Kesteloot, *Les écrivains noirs de langue francaise* (Bruxelles: Université libre de Bruxelles, 1965).

3. *La Jeune Haiti* Feb. 1896.

4. Frédéric Marcelin, *Autour de Deux Romans* (Paris: Kugelman, 1903) pp. 5–6.

5. Ibid., p. 25.

6. *La Ronde*, no. 10, 5 Feb. 1899, 152.

7. Vilaire, *Poèmes de la Mort*, p. 183.

8. Stéphane Mallarmé, *Oeuvres Complètes* (Paris: Pléiade, 1945) p. 260.

9. Vilaire, *Poèmes de la Mort*, p. 40.

10. *Haiti littéraire et sociale*, no. 2, 5 Feb. 1905, 29.

11. Vilaire, *Poèmes de la Mort*, 'Notice Autobiographique', p. xxxiii.

12. Frantz Fanon, *Toward the African Revolution* (Harmondsworth: Penguin, 1970) p. 36.

13. Avertissement aux 'Dix Hommes Voirs'.

14. Jorge Luis Borges, 'The Argentine Writer and Tradition', *Labyrinths* (Harmondsworth: Penguin, 1970) p. 215.

15. *Haiti littéraire et scientifique*, 5 July 1912, 326.

16. Etzer Vilaire, *Nouveaux Poèmes* (Paris: Albert Messein, 1919) p. 97.

17. *Haiti littéraire et scientifique*, 5 Jan. 1912, p. 12.

18. Vilaire, *Poèmes de la Mort*, p. 73.

19. Ibid., p. 109.

20. Etzer Vilaire *Années Tendres* (Paris: Albert Messein, 1914) p. 201.

21. *Cendres et Flammes* (Paris: Albert Messein, 1912) p. 97.

22. St Louis and Lubin, *Panorama de la poésie haitienne* (Port-au-Prince: Henri Deschamps, 1950) p. 190.

23. Vilaire, *Années Tendres*, p. 154.

24. Vilaire, *Poèmes de la Mort*, p. 40.

25. Etzer Vilaire, *La Vie Solitaire* (Port-au-Prince: Séminaire Adventiste, n.d.) p. 52.

26. The early poetry of Léopold Sédar Senghor shows the strong influence of Baudelaire's *spleen* poems. Lines such as 'Mes ailes battent et se blessent aux barreaux du ciel bas/ Nul rayon ne traverse cette voute sourde de mon ennui' in *Chants d'Ombre* (1945) recall the gloom and claustrophobia of Symbolist verse.

2 The American Occupation and the Beginning of a Literature of Protest

By the turn of the century, the political disorder that contributed to the atmosphere of gloom and futility in the poetry of *La Ronde*, had reached a state of absolute chaos. A tragic pattern was established in Haiti's political life. Unscrupulous individuals with political ambitions would raise a *caco*[1] peasant army in the countryside (usually in the north), march on Port-au-Prince plundering the country on the way and be elected president on arrival there. The first act of these presidents was to share the spoils of victory with their army – except when the incumbent president managed to escape into exile with part of the treasury. Such a state of anarchy can be dramatically illustrated by the rapid succession of revolts which managed to place six presidents in office between 1911 and 1915.[2]

Haiti by the beginning of the twentieth century can be said to have created the conditions for foreign occupation to the extent that in the chronic unrest of these years, neither the mulatto élite nor the black majority seemed prepared for the realities of political autonomy. Pauléus Sannon in his historical work on Boyer's regime published in 1904, warned of the impending fate that would befall Haiti:

> This interminable strife constitutes a serious threat to the future of the country. History teaches, in fact, that an indefinitely prolonged internal conflict could be a risk to a country which does not have at its command adequate forces which could maintain its national independence against powerful and enterprising neighbours.[3]

The mention of 'powerful and enterprising neighbours' suggests that Sannon was fully aware of the possible consequences of Haiti's lack of vigilance as well as the imperialist designs of the United States on the Caribbean. His speculation was destined to become historical fact on 28 July 1915 when Admiral Caperton ordered his marines to occupy Haitian territory. The actual pretext for the landing of United States marines was the total chaos that existed in Port-au-Prince when the then president, Vilbrun Guillaume Sam was seized from a foreign embassy where he had taken refuge and lynched by an angry mob. Fearing the worst, representatives of various legations asked the Americans, who had been keenly watching the situation for some time, to restore order. What was initially an invitation to impose stability in Haiti became a military occupation that would last nineteen years. As Sannon had feared, the collapse of stability in Haiti served United States interests handsomely.

The intention behind and the nature of the American Occupation form an indispensable background to Haiti's political and literary movements in the twentieth century. The presence of white foreigners on Haitian soil, the authoritarian nature of this presence and the pseudo-colonial contact that was established between the invaders and the native population, not only disrupted the traditional function of Haitian society but served as a grim reminder of the days of Saint-Domingue prior to 1804. Foreign military domination challenged in a crucial way Haiti's evolution over a century of independence. The stereotype of the black race's incapacity for self-government which was so vigorously fought in the nineteenth century could be adequately substantiated from the events of 1915. History had mockingly repeated itself.

The initial Haitian reaction to the Occupation varied from open collaboration on one hand to a sense of shock at what had taken place. There was no immediate widespread rejection of the American presence and an American commentator at the time does note the initial accomadation of the Americans by the urban élite: 'No Haitian could openly advocate American intervention, but there seems to have been an undercurrent of sentiment in that direction, though of necessarily uncertain proportions . . . the élite had nothing to gain by chronic disorder and instability.'[4] The majority who silently consented to the Occupation, did so either out of a naive confidence in the American motives for occupying Haiti or from a desire for stability at any cost. Dr Edouard Dépestre published in 1916 an explanation for the élite acceptance of the Occupation. In his *La faillite d'une démocratie* there is an air of

resignation to the American presence and a blind, desperate belief
in the progress and peace the Americans could bring to Haiti:

> Others will continue to think that our rights have been brutally
> violated . . . For my part, I will continue to think that our past
> up to the 28 July 1915 has justified foreign intervention.
>
> The future will tell who is right: those who have distrusted the
> loyalty and progressive programmes of the United States or we
> who have believed in these things since the beginning of the
> Occupation.[5]

Dépestre did not see his collaboration as an act of treachery but as a
compromise which would eventually restore order and prosperity to
Haiti. There were a few instances of a strong nationalist rejection of
the Americans. The most famous of these rare cases of opposition was
that of Raymond Cabèche who declared in his speech to the
national assembly that the Occupation would only produce 'Order
in disgrace; prosperity in golden chains. Prosperity we will perhaps
have. Chains we will surely have.'[6] As the Occupation continued
events were to prove Cabèche right and make a mockery of what
Dépestre thought would be the 'progressive programmes' of the
Occupation.

American motives for the Occupation were far more complex
than most Haitians realised. The latter with a naivety nurtured by
almost a century of isolation, blindly attributed purely altruistic
motives to the Americans. The reasons for occupying Haiti were a
complex mixture of economic ambitions, hemispheric strategy and
a self-righteous missionary zeal. The latter was continually cited as
the main reason for intervention. The Occupation was justified on
the grounds of bringing stability 'according to the demands of the
civilised world'[7] to a black nation that had resorted to primitivism
and anarchy. Documentaries of visits to Haiti by foreigners had
much to do with justifying the Occupation in the conscience of the
American public. Loederer's *Voodoo Fire in Haiti* and Seabrook's *The
Magic Island* are both examples of this kind of literature which,
rivalling the sensationalism of Spenser St John, provided lurid
accounts of atavistic urges and primitive rituals in Haitian society.
Some American commentators, even after the Occupation took on
a more brutal and authoritarian character, persisted in justifying
the Occupation in the name of progress and enlightenment. Arthur
Millspaugh writes:

it should be a great satisfaction to citizens of the United States that their own country has been able to render a service to a neighbour in need, and despite many temptations and difficulties, has at the end of the chapter returned an improved Haiti to the Haitians.[8]

This mixture of liberalism and prejudice concealed, however, more fundamental political and economic considerations. Schmidt, in his study of this period in Haiti's history,[9] convincingly argues that the United States at the time essentially measured national success in terms of empire – like any traditional European power – and was not really concerned with the question of democratic reform and liberal internationalism.

By the early twentieth century the American desire for hegemony in the Caribbean was already evident. In an attempt to establish an exclusive sphere of influence in the Caribbean, Cuba and the Dominican Republic were already under informal American control and Puerto Rico had been annexed. The process of consolidating the region under the American aegis was accelerated by two important events – the First World War and the construction of the Panama Canal. In the case of the former, Haiti had been forced to borrow significant sums of money from European sources, especially Germany. Theoretically Germany could effectively control Haitian territory as compensation for unpaid debts. As for the latter, the Panama Canal and the resultant change in shipping lines brought greater strategic importanace to the Caribbean Sea and the Gulf of Mexico. An American commentator at the time, William MacCorkle, advocated exclusive control of the region in the name of hemispheric stability:

It is usual to speak of the Caribbean Sea and the Gulf of Mexico as the American Seas, and to consider them as part of our life and practically within the control of this nation. It is necessary to glance at the great seas and appreciate how they and the canal are hemmed in by the islands, which would become a menace to our commerce in case of war or hostility on the part of the nations of Europe.[10]

The spirit of the Monroe Doctrine was the ultimate rationale for control of the Caribbean. This had more to do with commercial expansion than with bringing enlightenment and democracy to

Haiti. Indeed, well after the threat to hemispheric stability had passed with the end of the war in 1918, the Occupation continued. The Americans did not manage to conceal their motives for occupying Haiti and Haitian resistance to the American presence grew with the increasing mistrust of American liberalism.

American authoritarianism was evident from the outset in the suppression of any potential democratic institutions and the absolute control of the Banque Nationale, civil service and important administrative posts. These actions may have resulted from both a conviction that Haitians were incapable of managing their own affairs as well as a desire for as complete a control of the country as possible. In either case such a situation would not only deeply anger Haitians who found they had little authority in their own country but also militate against the creation of any real administrative or economic reform in Haiti. The first important indication of obvious American interference could be seen in the deliberate engineering of the election of a pliant president. The choice in 1915 was between Rosalvo Bobo, a northerner with strong nationalist views, and Sudre Dartiguenave, a senator willing to collaborate with the Americans. Dartiguenave was elected and Bobo went into exile. The same electioneering was repeated later with the acceptance of an American designed constitution and the election of Louis Borno in 1922. Consequently the most important public office in Haiti was not the presidency but that of the American High Commissioner. The Americans may have put a stop to the stream of corrupt, benighted presidents of the turn of the century but by establishing a puppet president who ruled with their advice and approval, they were preserving the same autocratic system that undermined popular democratic institutions in the past.

The rigid colonial nature of the Occupation can again be supported by the institution of the corvée law in Haiti. Finding Haiti's internal communications in a lamentable state of disrepair, the Americans revived the old corvée law which stipulated that the peasants were supposed to do six days of voluntary labour for the State. The implementation of this law was brutal and inefficient. At one stage peasants were actually roped together in gangs. Mistreated and overworked, the peasants found such intolerable conditions reminiscent of the past of slavery when their forebears were exploited by the French. By 1918 peasant resentment was widespread and soon broke out into an open uprising. This insurrection was known as the *caco* uprising and was led by

Charlemagne Péralte. He and his army of peasant irregulars waged guerrilla warfare on the American marines from 1918 until his death in 1920. As an example to others, Péralte's body was tied to the door of the army's headquarters in Cap Haitien. The ruthless way in which this revolt was put down, the very fact that Haitians were being shot on their own soil by white foreigners and the martyrdom of Péralte – crucified on the door of the 'Quartier Général' – made the Occupation intolerable even for those desperate for internal stability. Ludwell Montague, in commenting on the peasant rebellion, suggests that it caused the validity of the Occupation to be questioned not only in Haiti but in the United States as well:

> In this startling fashion Americans suddenly learned that all Haitians were not full of gratitude toward the United States government for its kindly and helpful interest in their affairs . . . two thousand Haitians had been killed on their native soil, as compared to seven marines and twenty-seven gendarmes and wild rumours of atrocities were abroad in the land.[11]

The élite may have been unsympathetic to the *caco* cause initially since the latter were so closely associated with the period of anarchy which earlier preceded the Occupation. But reports of atrocities and innocent peasants murdered began to reinforce their resentment of the colonial nature of the American presence. In 1920 their protest was supported by the N.A.A.C.P. and James Weldon Johnson, the black American writer, became an important figure in championing the Haitian nationalist cause in the United States.

Even though the 1920s witnessed growing resentment, on the part of the Haitians, of the American Occupation, there was to be no violent protest against the Americans until 1929. This period of uneasy calm that preceded the active resistence of 1929, further contributed to the tensions between Haitians and Americans. To all appearances the Americans could be said to have made overtures to the urban élite since both puppet presidents elected by them were mulatto. However, the re-establishment of the coloured élite in government control began to mean less and less in the face of obvious racial prejudices on the part of the Americans.

Cordial relations with the Haitians were severely hampered by both the American refusal to be tactful in dealing with the question of race and the Haitian sensitivity to American attitudes that ranged from condescension to open ridicule. The American administrators in Haiti made no attempt to understand the complex way in which colour and race operated in Haitian society. Ignoring the cultural as well as colour cleavage between the coloured élite and the rural peasantry, the Americans applied to all Haitians the 'Jim Crow' laws and segregation they were accustomed to in the United States. Edmund Wilson, during a visit to Haiti, remarked on the complexity of the racial question and the American inability or unwillingness to adapt to it:

> The visitor from the United States may not be prepared to grasp this feature of Haitian life. He is familiar, at home, with a discrimination which works against anybody whomever who is known to have any black blood, and he may not at first be aware of the complex internal strains of a society where everybody has more or less.[12]

The arrogance and ethnocentricity of American officials gratutiously wounded the Haitians and aroused their dormant racial and national pride. Commentators on the racial antagonisms of the twenties mention numerous incidents which contributed to racial antagonisms. The closure of the American club to Haitians is one such incident and Schmidt remarks on the way racial tension increased after the arrival of the wives of the American administrators.[13] The former were visibly prevented from having any contact with the Haitians. The charges of clumsiness in handling social relations and the superior attitude of many American officials can be further substantiated as many observers at the time remarked on the number of Southerners holding administrative posts and the overt racism practised by many of them:

> The mistake of employing in Haiti, Americans who have strong racial prejudices against the Negro has been stressed by almost every observer who has visited Haiti since the intervention . . . No American who does not care to maintain a certain amount of ordinary social intercourse with Negroes should be sent to a Negro state.[14]

Racial antagonism is probably the single most important reason why the Occupation failed in all its objectives in Haiti. Whatever reforms could have been made in the various sectors of Haitian society were effectively blocked by the American refusal to understand the nature of the Haitian problem. The Haitians for their part were less and less willing to adopt any plans the Americans suggested.

The resentment of the Americans by the élite did not remain exclusively on a racial and nationalist level. There was an important cultural dimension to these tensions. For instance, the following extract from an historical work written in the twenties attaches enormous importance to cultural distinctions between Haitians and Americans. The Occupation is seen in terms of brutish Anglo-Saxon cultural aggression against Haiti's creolised culture:

> The Occupation has one advantage – in that it forces us to understand . . . how much our black French backgrounds, our afro-latin feelings, our French culture was opposed to the crude materialism, rough anglo-saxon mentality of North-Americans, scornful of subtlety, ignorant of refinement and convinced that all civilisation is primarily materialistic.[15]

These cultural stereotypes of Anglo-Saxon materialism and an organic Afro-Latin legacy emerged from the cultural speculation of 1836 as well as the debate stimulated at the turn of the century by *La Ronde*. The contrast between the Symbolist conception of the magical world of the poet and the hollow materialism and atrophied sensibilities of an industrialised age was dramatised in the confrontation with the technocratic materialist nature of the American presence. It would also emerge in the rhetoric of the Négritude movement in Paris in the 1930s and later be exploited by the poets of the Haitian Indigenous movement. Much of the anti-American rhetoric of the 1920s makes specific reference to American culture as inhibited and debilitatingly materialistic. The main protagonist of the novel *Le nègre masqué* addresses an American officer in this way:

> Un matin, hommes mécaniques, vous serez anéantis sous les décombres de vos gratte-ciels, de vos usines. Il n'en restera rien, rien, de votre civilisation de ferraille, de ciment et de linoleum! Car vous n'avez fondé que sur la matière![16].

> [One morning, mechanical men, you will be annihilated under the rubble of your sky-scrapers, of your factories. Nothing will

remain, nothing, of your civilisation of iron concrete and linoleum! For you have only built on material things.]

In contrast to this cold, inhuman vision the main character appears as the epitome of Afro-Latin sensuousness and spontaneity:

> Roger dansait avec cette divination nègre des cadences, cette harmonie depouillée et libre, presque religieuse, laissées en lui par les siècles d'ancêtres qui avaient fait de la danse l'expression sacrée de leurs âmes.[17]

> [Roger danced with that black instinct for rhythms, that uncomplicated and free harmony, almost religious, inherited from generations of ancestors who had made of the dance the sacred expression of their souls.]

This question of cultural conflict became an explosive issue when the subject of educational reform was raised. The Americans did attempt to institute a system of vocational training and agricultural education in Haiti. To the Haitians whose embattled educational system revolved around a more 'Classical' French-oriented pattern, technological training was necessarily a debasement and subversion of their preference for the Humanities. Haiti certainly needed some kind of technical expertise but in this climate of tension such reform would be futile. Jean Brierre was very vocal on this subject in the 1930s:

> – From Cap Haitien to Cayes, adolescents were forced to face life . . . They had just translated the Aeneid or Cicero and they were told one fine day: 'All of that is useless and absurd. Go earn a living.'
> Some launched themselves fiercely into the 'struggle for life' where only profit matters but how many also kept on their lips nostalgia for the last Latin or Greek verses and that world of knowledge whose beauty had been barely glimpsed in a few books. It was disgraceful.[18]

This lyrical defence of a refined classical education gives one an insight into why Haiti produced too many poets and too few able administrators and technocrats. However, the Americans for their part contributed to the rejection of their educational reforms by their belief that classical and liberal studies were ill-suited for people of Negro origin. The question of the Negro's education had been a very vexed one in the United States as well. White liberal support for Bookcr T. Washington's school for vocational training instead of the more literary and cultural emphasis in W. E. B. Dubois's conception of education for black Americans, suggests that many Americans believed that blacks did not deserve anything else. In a cautious but pertinent observation on the question of educational reform in Haiti, Emily Balch comments: 'The Americans, on their side, are prone to regard classical and liberal studies as too expensive a luxury for a country like Haiti, a feeling that may be unconsciously accentuated in some cases by colour prejudice.'[19] The whole question of educational reform seems to be another example of the way in which the colonial and racial implications of the American presence prevented any useful changes from being implemented in the land they had occupied.

In spite of the uneasy relations between Haitians and Americans, the Occupation continued without being seriously challenged until 1929. In December of that year students at the School of Agriculture at Damiens went on strike to protest against the victimisation of one of their colleagues by an American. Sympathy strikes quickly followed and on 11 December thousands marched through the streets of Port-au-Prince in protest against the particular issue at Damiens and the Occupation as a whole. The disorder that followed this demonstration had the immediate effect of removing President Borno from power. The Americans also began to feel less and less able to check the mounting resistance generated by the nationalist cause. It was now impossible to justify the continuation of the Occupation on the grounds of internal political chaos or a threat to hemispheric security, since, through the enforced peace of the Occupation, order had been re-established and the First World War was over. The change in American policy regarding the Haitian situation was reflected in a commission of inquiry sent to Haiti in 1930. The Forbes Commission recommended that national elections be held and that steps be taken with a view to eventual evacuation of American troops. A new president, Sténio Vincent, came to power in that year and the administration of the country and the army was handed over to Haitian hands. In the United States a newly elected President Roosevelt agreed to the restoration of political independence and in 1934 the Occupation ended.

The actual events of 1929 that precipitated the end of the Occupation had essentially little to do with the traditional urban élite. As we shall see a younger and more spirited generation had decided that a violent confrontation with the Americans was the only way to resolve the problem of the Occupation. Elite resistance to the Occupation was characterised by a slow gestation and by a less direct but more dignified means of protest. Consistent with the style and restraint they cultivated as a class the majority made use of the weapon used most effectively to defend themselves in the past – the written word. They turned to journalism. A few of the more daring would organise demonstrations and advocate civil disobedience but the tendency was to turn to the printed word on the assumption that a rational protest eloquently delivered would have some effect on the Americans. Literary and political associations were formed in the 1920s to challenge the American presence. This *presse d'opposition* was fed by various nationalist groups such as *La ligue de la jeunesse haitienne, La société d'histoire et de géographie d'Haiti,* and *L'Union Patriotique* among others. The role of these newspapers was simply to mobilise the literate élite for the defence of Haiti's national interests.

The most outstanding and dedicated individual who initiated and participated actively in this form of protest is Georges Sylvain. Far from being the escapist that his generation has been criticised as being, Sylvain was one of the first to turn to journalism as a means of protest. The newspaper *La Patrie* was formed in 1915 and in an editorial of September 1915, Sylvain described the aim of the newspaper: 'Courageously, without flinching, let us continue then to defend ourselves against the threatening degradation. In refusing to surrender any of our essential rights, we will have at least, whatever happens, saved our honour.'[20]

In 1920 Sylvain's political activism took on a more vigorous form with the formation of *L'Union Patriotique.* The activities of this organisation dominated Sylvain's career: his interest in creative writing had ceased abruptly in 1915 with the invasion of the marines. His one poem written in this period was recited at the inauguration of *L'Union Patriotique.* This organisation was used to publicise all grievances against the Americans. It did not limit itself to the urban élite but had branches which reported on the state of the Occupation in the rural areas. In his inaugural speech in 1920, with the memory of the brutal suppression of the *caco* rebellion fresh in his mind, Sylvain declared 'they baptised with the name peaceful occupation this brutal attack on national sovereignty as if the bloody invasion of a country, forced to submit to martial law could be peaceful.'[21] Until his death in 1925 Sylvain was the most important figure in Haiti's *presse d'opposition*. His activism may not have caused the immediate collapse of American control but he did much to expose the horrors of the Occupation within Haiti and in the United States through James Weldon Johnson and the N.A.A.C.P. Sylvain's method of protest may not have gone beyond passive resistance but it did prepare the way for the more violent explosion of 1929.

The case of Georges Sylvain is a useful example of the effect the Occupation had on poets and literary activity as a whole. The intense literary debates of *La Ronde*, their delicate, intimate verse, yielded to a simpler and more public role for the artist. It was a transition that proved difficult for some as in the case of Etzer Vilaire and tragic for others as we have seen in the case of Laforest. Literature became an appendage to the militant journalism of the 1920s and consequently the introspection of the turn of the century was dramatically transformed into an epic, declamatory literary mode. Literature during the Occupation could be quite simply called *littérature de circonstance* in that the importance of these works was exhausted after the particular event that it celebrated or denounced had slipped from memory. Indeed the poetry of the first decade of the Occupation is a useful index to the changes in mood in Haiti and to the growth of the protest movement.

This poetry can be used to plot the progression from the initial shock created by the Occupation to the later emergence of a strident form of protest. The change can easily be seen in the early poems which reveal the darker mood of withdrawal and are an obvious contrast with the barely suppressed hysteria of the writing of the late twenties.

Haiti's poets were relatively silent during the first few years of the Occupation. However, some of those poems, inspired by early reactions to the American presence, reveal a predictable sense of betrayal and gloom. What is perhaps more interesting is the level of technical conservatism that now dominated Haiti's literary activity. In this early writing one has the impression of a deeply felt resentment that has been carefully ordered into harmonious and erudite literary forms – indeed, effectively undermined. This produces a quality of bathos and self-pity apparent in the two following extracts:

Un crêpe noir enveloppe ma lyre
Dont les refrains sont grêles et voilés
Mes rêves d'or se sont tous envolés
Et ma pensée est en proie au délire
                    (Dominique Hippolyte, 'A mon pays', 1915)[22]

[My lyre is wrapped in black crepe
Its refrains are thin and muffled
My golden dreams have all flown away
And my thoughts are a prey to delirium]

Je vis dans le présent le rancon du Passé
les bûchers présageant l'autel expiatoire
l'Avenir, sanglotant ou l'on avait dansé –
Et j'appris la grandeur sublime de l'Histoire.
                    (Christian Werleigh, 'Un jour', 1915)[23]

[I saw in the present the ransom of the Past
the sticks that foreshadowed the altar of expiation
the Future, sobbing where there had been dancing
And I learnt the sublime grandeur of History.]

Both these quotations are indicative of the mannered and self-conscious melancholy expressed by Haitian poets at this time. The grandiose clichés – 'ma lyre' and 'l'autel expiatoire' and 'la grandeur sublime de l'Histoire' – suggest a kind of escapism that quite accurately registers the initial withdrawal apparent in Haiti's writers. In striking contrast to the abrasive and irreverent verse of black writers in post-war Paris, the early literature of the Occupation meant a revival of traditional pieties in poetry.

Nowhere is this more visible than in the treatment of one of the stock poetic themes of this early period – the analogy with the pre-Colombian past at the moment of the arrival of Spain's Conquistadors. The analogy was particularly apt since both the American intervention and the Spanish conquest used the pretext of a civilising mission to mask their quest for empire. The poems which invoked this analogy uniformly presented the image of a glorious, serene, autochthonous culture brutally disrupted by alien military strength. Fed by this idealisation of the past and a tragic sense of the

ironies of history, Werleigh's 'Anacaona' lamented the first enact-
ment of foreign intrusion on Haitian soil:

> Et ton nom, Anacaona, quand je le vois,
> C'est l'histoire qui s'ouvre à mes yeux toute grande,
> C'est le Conquistador lâche et traître à la fois,
> Qui brise sous des morts les Fleurs de la Légende.[24]

> [And your name, Anacaona, when I see it,
> It is history which is spread before my eyes,
> It is the Conquistador cowardly and treacherous at the
>   same time,
> Who crushes under the dead the Flowers of Legend.]

Frédéric Burr-Reynaud in the sonnets of *Poèmes Quisquéyens* echoes
this vision of foreign intervention done in the name of christianity
and civilisation:

> Symbole de vainqueur, la grande croix chrétienne
> Etendait ses bras noirs sur l'immense horizon.
> Imposant l'esclavage au nom de la raison,
> Elle avait détrôné l'Olympe aborigène.[25]

> [The conqueror's symbol, the huge Christian cross
> Spreads its black arms across the immense horizon.
> Imposing slavery in the name of reason,
> It had dethroned the aboriginal Gods.]

The use of 'Olympe aborigène' again demonstrates the tendency
among these poets to favour an ornate, sonorous style. Burr-
Reynaud's artistic conservatism was particularly apparent in his
obvious use of Parnassian literary techniques to convey the order
and tranquillity of the pre-Colombian past. The following lines
contain a static, pictorial quality characteristic of Parnassianism:

> Les Palmiers dans l'azur qu'épouse le soleil
> Plongeant leurs javelots émaillés d'émeraude
> La lumière répand sa gemme lourde et chaude
> Met partout le bienfait de son baiser vermeil.[26]

[Palm-trees in the blue wedded to the sun
Plunging their javelins glazed with emerald
The light spreads its heavy and warm sparkle
Bestows everywhere the favour of its reddened kiss.]

This kind of verse is fortunately discontinued by the younger writers of the Indigenous movement. Nevertheless, it is interesting to see how the use of nineteenth century poetic clichés penetrated this phase of literary protest even when there was a radical change in mood and what might be called more properly a *littérature de combat* emerged.

As the protest movement gained momentum, a new kind of verse emerged. More public and more obviously nationalist and anti-American, it was far removed from the gloom of earlier writers. Published in the late 1920s, this poetry was meant to celebrate heroes (eg. Charlemagne Péralte) of the Haitian resistance or to express indignation at the continued American presence.

Georges Sylvain's poem 'Ode à la Délivrance', recited in 1920 at the founding of *L'Union Patriotique* is the prototype of this militant verse of the 1920s. The poem very violently expresses an open resentment of the Occupation:

Haiti, lève-toi! le monstre qui t'entraîne
Vers l'abîme, la honte et le deuil, aura peur
S'il voit se soulever la conscience humaine!
Fais frisonner le monde à tes cris de douleur!

[Haiti, rise up! the monster who drags you
Towards the abyss of shame and grief, will be afraid
If it sees a human conscience assert itself!
Make the world tremble at your cries of grief!

The frequent use of exclamations indicates the violent tone of the poem which must have been read as a dramatic monologue. Yet from the artistic point of view it was a poetry which must be forgiven because of its good intentions. The inflated rhetoric of this verse offers a good insight into the temperament of the generation that witnessed the Occupation and indicates a clear line of demarcation between the latter and the generation that would follow.

Technically, Sylvain's poem is a forerunner to the literary effusion that greeted strikes and mass demonstrations in the late twenties. For instance, Burr-Reynaud's *Anathèmes* is quite different from his early restrained reflections on the pre-Colombian past. For instance, 'Trahison' in this collection is a savage attack on the members of the élite who collaborated with the Americans:

> Ils rongent jusqu'aux os ta carcasse meurtrie
> Ils maculent ta face avec leurs doigts sanglants
> Et, tirant ta peau sèche, et calleuse et flétrie
> Ils, battent le tam-tam pour amuser les Blancs.[27]

> [They gnaw down to the bone your bruised body
> They stain your face with their bloody fingers
> And, stretching out your dry, callous and withered skin
> They drum away to amuse the Whites.]

Louis Henry Durand's *Trois Poèmes* is equally violent and each poem bears the date of an important event in the nationalist struggle. For example, the grandiose title 'Ave Juventos' celebrates the student strike of November 1929:

> Enfin! Voici l'éclair fulgurant dans la nuit!
> Dans l'abîme sans fond voici la clarté pure!
> Après le doute, après l'angoisse et la torture
>   Voici l'Espérance qui luit![28]

> [Finally! Here is the light flashing in the night!
> In the bottomless pit here is a pure brilliance!
> After the doubt, the anguish and the torture
> Here is hope shining forth!]

Indeed, these sonorous alexandrines are even used by a few younger poets who also registered their revulsion at the American presence. A very young Jean Brierre wrote his 'Drame de Marchaterre' to denounce the peasant massacre of January 1929:

> Devant l'envahisseur qu'ils haissent d'instinct
> Ils oublient tout à coup leur fatigue et leur faim
> Et leurs fils sans travail et leurs femmes sans robes
> Ils ne demanderont rien, rien à ces négrophobes[29]

> [Before the invader whom they instinctively hate
> They forget immediately their tiredness and hunger

And their jobless sons and unclothed womenfolk
They will ask nothing of these negrophobes]

Assertively nationalistic, even hysterical in tone, this *littérature de combat* was seen as an integral part of the anti-American cause. Indeed, this does, to some extent, explain the use of very formal and inflated literary codes to express feelings of anger and betrayal. This poetry is filled with formal nineteenth century clichés such as 'courroux', 'airain', 'sublime', 'douleurs eternelles', 'flamme impie'. Also such abstractions as 'L'Humanité', 'Patrie', 'Aieux' and 'Histoire' fill the pages of these collections. The origin of this style seems to be the political verse of Hugo's *Les Châtiments*, written in exile in the 1850s. For instance, the similarity between Hugo's 'Au Peuple' and Sylvain's exhortation to Haiti is readily apparent:

> La pâle Liberté gît sanglante à ta porte
> Tu le sais, toi mort, elle est morte . . .
>
> Ils te mordent dans ton cercueil!
> De tous les peuples on prépare
>   Le convoi . . .
> Lazare! Lazare! Lazare!
>   Lève-toi![30]

> [Pale freedom lies bloódy at your gates
> You know with you dead it is dead . . .
> They gnaw at you in the coffin!
> The funeral procession of the people is being
>   prepared . . .
> Lazarus! Lazarus! Lazarus!
>   Rise up!

As part of the nationalist cause this formal eloquence does, however, serve a purpose. Eloquence, indeed, is a way of establishing cultural associations, of moving away from factuality towards the imposition of a cultural reconstruction of events. In defending themselves against the charge of being barbaric and uncivilised Haitians used this high diction to demonstrate their intellectual legacy. Against the crude 'anglo-saxonnisme' of the Americans, they resorted to an erudite and ornate French literary code as a means of self-defence.

This was not to be the case, however, with that younger generation of the Occupation whose poetry would be irreverent even prosaic in contrast to the pedantic and stylised verse of this generation.

A treatment of literary engagement during the Occupation cannot omit the few *romans de circonstance* published, which form an introduction to certain themes that would dominate Haitian writing even after the departure of the Americans. Such fiction as was published tended to be documentary in content and less concerned with refinement of expression as was the case with poetry. Indeed, Léon Laleau, whose novel *Le Choc* was actually written in 1919, deliberately turned away from poetry to record his reactions in prose. The other important prose work of this time – Stéphen Alexis's *Le nègre masqué*, subtitled 'tranche de vie haitienne' – is also a documentary work. Both these novels anticipate Jacques Roumain's later prose pieces on the urban élite and are also some of the few novels in Haitian literature that deal with an urban situation. The Indigenous movement shifted its attention to the peasantry and revived the peasant novel which was to dominate the tradition of prose fiction in Haiti.

Both these novels set out to record the dramatic events of the Occupation. Léon Laleau's work is a particularly useful historical record from this point of view. Laleau's 'Avertissement' states very clearly: 'This is not a novel . . . Nothing but facts recorded as they were lived.'Alexis's work is more concerned with psychological attitudes in the urban middle class. In fact, the very title of the latter seems to anticipate Frantz Fanon's *Peau noire, masques blancs* and the novel despite its melodramatic form, focuses clearly on the political and racial *prise de conscience* of its bourgeois protagonist.

Both these novels reflect one of the more controversial issues of the time–the role of the traditional élite. They are sharply critical of this group and their open or tacit colloboration with the Americans. Laleau clearly presents the impotence of the élite and the frustration of the poor during the Occupation:

> Before the painful spectacle of the ignorant and embittered Masses shaking their clenched fists in the direction of the Elite . . . before this divided, fragmented Elite which, however, responded with kicks and spat its scorn at them . . . before the suffering and misery of two sections of a people, hostile to each other, the invader once more had smiled![31]

Alexis's novel is much more vehement on this subject. His main character, Roger Sinclair, condemns the indifference among the members of his class:

> Sachez qu'il n'y a pas d'élite sans vertus morales, sans courage, sans don de soi . . . et qu'en dehors de ces qualités une élite n'en est que la caricature. (p. 13)

> [Know that there is no élite without moral virtue, without courage, without self-sacrifice . . . and that outside of these qualities an élite is a caricature of itself.]

This kind of criticism, which became the subject of Price-Mars's collection of essays, *La Vocation de l'Elite*, would soon be the *raison d'être* of the young radical politico-cultural movements of the late twenties and early thirties.

Another somewhat related theme emerged with this scathing criticism of the élite. This was the need to reject the élite's cultural reverence of France to find a more authentic cultural matrix. The need for a racial mystique and an increasing distrust of rationality and a literary culture becomes an important concern for Alexis. His very cultured hero exclaims:

> On m'a appris trop de grec et de latin. Si j'étais nègre solitaire et nu dans une forêt, je serais heureux. (p. 130)

> [I have learnt too much Greek and Latin. If I was an isolated and naked negro in the jungle, I would be happy.]

There is absolutely no difference between this celebration of primitivism and that of McKay's equally disturbed Haitian intellectual in *Home To Harlem*:' I don't know what I'll do with my little education. I wonder sometimes if I could get rid of it and go and lose myself in some savage culture in the jungles of Africa.'[32] The loss of confidence in the values of the bourgeoisie led to the exploration of a widely different cultural hinterland as an alternative 'home'. This would be the hallmark of not only Haiti's literary renaissance but also of the Harlem Renaissance and the Négritude movement.

Indeed, Alexis's novel anticipates the Pan-African ideals of the Négritude movement. His main character envisages a fraternity of the coloured races which would later be the political '*raison d'être*' of the Négritude movement. This grand apocalyptic vision is not inspired by Marxist notions of the unity of the oppressed but rather by the, now almost forgotten, Russo-Japanese war (1904–5) in which for the first time an European power was beaten by a coloured race. Roger Sinclair sees this event as a prelude to the greater confrontation:

> La race blanche est en train de provoquer l'union de toutes les races de couleur, par sa dureté et ses maladresses. Une autre guerre viendra. Nous y jouerons un rôle. A la lueur de ses incendies, nous trouverons notre voie . . . Ils ont compris que les Japonais étaient des hommes lorsqu'ils les ont vus aussi méchants qu'eux. Ce sera la même chose pour nous. L'acier froid du Nippon a été plus éloquent que toutes les thèses d'égalité.
>
> (p. 17)

> [The white race is in the process of creating the solidarity of all coloured peoples, because of its uncompromising and tactless behaviour. There will be another war. We will play our part. By the light of its fires we will find our way . . . They understood the Japanese were men when they showed they could be equally wicked. It will be the same with us. Cold Nippon steel was more eloquent than all the defences of equality.]

The way was being paved for that outburst of literary and ideological activity which represents the beginnings of a modern Haitian literature. Alexis's hero, Roger Sinclair, in spite of his radical visions of racial confrontation and a rejection of his bourgeois environment is still a turn of the century figure. His romantic declaration of rebellion is expressed as: 'l'avenir est sur les genoux de Zeus!' The following generation would certainly build on his ideas but they would also attempt to change such a style irrevocably. National catastrophe warranted a revaluation of Haitian society. After 1928 the call for radical and profound changes in Haitian society would be widespread and with the birth of indigenism the break with the past would be complete.

NOTES

1. *Caco*, which is a bird of prey that lives off weaker birds, was the name given to the peasant irregulars who served as mercenaries to support various candidates for political office. In 1915 many *caco* chiefs surrendered to the marines but became active again during the peasant rebellion against the imposition of the corvée law.

2. Cincinnatus Leconte (1911–12), assassinated; Tancrède Auguste (1912–13) assassinated; Michel Oreste (1913–14), overthrown; Oreste Zamor (Jan.–Dec. 1914), overthrown; Davilmar Théodore (Dec. 1914–April 1915) overthrown; Vilbrun Guillaume Sam (April–July 1915), killed in office.

3. Pauléus Sannon, *Essai historique sur la révolution de 1843* (Les Cayes: Bonnefil, 1905) p. 4.

4. Ludwell Lee Montague, *Haiti and the United States, 1714–1938* (Durham, N.C.: Duke University Press, 1940) p. 193.

5. Edouard Dépestre, *La faillite d'une démocratie* (Port-au-Prince: L'Abeille, 1916).

6. See Dantès Bellegarde, *L'Occupation Américaine d'Haiti* (Port-au-Prince: Cheraquit, 1929) p. 9.

7. William MacCorkle, *The Monroe Doctrine in its relation to the Republic of Haiti* (New York: Neale, 1915) p. 95.

8. Arthur Millspaugh, *Haiti under American Control, 1915*–1930 (Boston: World Peace Foundation, 1931) p. 194.

9. Hans Schmidt, *The United States Occupation of Haiti 1915*–1934 (New Brunswick: Rutgers University Press, 1971).

10. MacCorkle, *The Monroe Doctrine in its Relation to Haiti*, p. 34.

11. Montague, *Haiti and the United States*, p. 233.

12. Edmund Wilson, *Red, Black, Blond and Olive*, (New York: Oxford University Press, 1956) p. 84.

13. Schmidt, *The United States Occupation*, pp. 136–7.

14. H. P. Davis, *Black Democracy* (New York: Dodge, 1928) p. 296.

15. Louis Morpeau, *L'histoire de Boisrond Tonnerre à Thomas Madiou* (Paris: Mercure de France, 1925) p. 256.
    This stereotype of the crude, racist American officer is a standard figure in the literature of the Occupation. See Léon Laleau's *Le Choc* (Port-au-Prince: La Presse, 1932), p. 207, and the character of Smedley Seaton in Stéphen Alexis's *Le nègre masqué* (Porte-au-Prince: L'Etat, 1933).

16. Alexis, *Le nègre masqué*, p. 96.

17. Ibid., p. 47.

18. Jean Brierre, preface to Robert Lataillade, *L'Urne Close*, (Port-au-Prince: La Presse, 1933) p. iv.

19. Emily Balch, *Occupied Haiti* (New York: The Writers' Publishing Co., 1927) p. 103.

20. *La Patrie*, no. 4, 1 Sept. 1915, 13.

21. Georges Sylvain, *Dix années de lutte pour la liberté: 1915–1925* (Port-au-Prince: Henri Deschamps, n.d.) p. 79.

22. Dominique Hippolyte, *La route ensoleillée* (Paris: Pensée Latine) 1927.

23. Christian Werleigh, *Le palmiste dans l'ouragan* (Cap Haitien: Séminaire, 1933) p. 70.

24. *Stella*, no. 20, 1927, 429–30.
25. Frédéric Burr-Reynaud, *Poèmes Quisquéyens* (Paris: Revue Mondiale, 1926) p. 131.
26. Ibid.
27. Frédéric Burr-Reynaud, *Anathèmes* (Port-au-Prince: La Presse, 1930).
28. Louis Henry Durand, *Trois Poèmes* (Port-au-Prince: La Presse, 1930).
29. Later published in a special edition of *Haiti-Journal*, Dec. 1945, 9.
30. Victor Hugo, *Les Châtiments* (Paris: Nelson, n.d.) p. 85.
31. Laleau, *Le Choc*, pp. 151–2.
32. Claude McKay, *Home To Harlem* (New York: Harper, 1928) p. 274.

3 The Indigenous Movement

The first evidence of a radically new sensibility in Haitian writing can be seen in Philippe Thoby-Marcelin's 'Sainement' written in February 1926, in Paris. The poem is more of a *profession de foi*, even a polemical gesture, than a strictly literary exercise:

J'ai le coeur, ce matin, plein de jeunesse,
    Tumultueux de violences.
Ma joue appuyée contre la fraîcheur
    de l'aube,
Jurant un eternal dédain aux raffinements européens,
Je veux désormais vous chanter:
    révolutions, fusillades, tueries
Bruit de coco-macaque sur des épaules noires,
Mugissements du lambi, lubricité mystique du vaudou;
Vous chanter dans un délire trois fois
    lyrique et religieux
Me dépouiller de tous oripeaux classiques
    et me dresser nu, très sauvage
    et très descendant d'esclaves,
Pour entonner d'une voix nouvelle le de profundis
    des civilisations pourissantes.[1]

[This morning my heart is bursting with youth,
    seething with violence.
My cheek resting against the freshness
    of the dawn,
Swearing an eternal scorn for European refinements,
I wish henceforth to celebrate.
    revolutions shootings and massacres,
the sound of coco-macaque on black shoulders,
the roar of the lambi, the mystic sensuality of vaudou;
to celebrate in a delirium three times
    lyrical and religious

    To strip myself of all classical finery
      and stand up naked, savage
      and very much a descendant of slaves,
    To sing with a new voice the 'de profundis'
      of rotting civilisations.]

The difference in scale and aesthetic values expressed in this poem and those of the earlier poems of the Occupation is striking. No lofty sentiments, no mythological allusions – the poem is in contrast rather informal and prosaic. The irregular typographic arrangement of the poem (which seems to vary with each publication) indicates a departure from regular versification. The title itself contains a note of irony as it is a re-definition of what it means to be sound and judicious.

'Sainement' is the beginning of an anti-rational intellectual tradition in Haitian literature. Terms such as 'plein de jeunesse', 'fraîcheur de l'aube' and 'voix nouvelle' suggest both a youthful exuberance and a strong Utopian impulse that would be characteristic of this generation. This is closely allied to the ever present subjectivity of the artist who is capable of transforming the world. There is a visibly Nietzschean quality in 'le de profundis des civilisations pourissantes'. Along with the absolute *refus* of repressive tradition (whether rigid prosody or social convention) comes the celebration of a hedonistic and uninhibited sensibility. The resulting delirium seems to provide an access to a primordial, authentic sense of self. What is articulated is the need for a complete revolution not only in political terms but also on the level of the psyche.

Marcelin's poem provides a graphic introduction to the iconoclastic spirit of the late twenties and thirties in Haiti. In fact, this period has been traditionally termed Haiti's literary renaissance but this is both a grandiose and misleading title since the past had never witnessed such a sustained and violent burst of literary activity.

It was to some extent a rather negative movement which felt that the past had only left behind the political decadence of the élite as well as dead literary codes. Both of which needed to be subverted and replaced. However, a more positive side to the movement also existed – the concern with creating literary authenticity. The aim of this irreverent generation was to make admissible in literature a range of experience that was once considered unworthy of formal poetic utterance. It was this unity of intention that distinguished this generation of Haitian writers.

The emergence of this radically new politico-literary stand among Haitian writers was facilitated by a number of factors. Naturally one of the most important of these was the Occupation itself. The continued American presence and the colonial nature of this presence, had created a real *crise de conscience* among Haitian writers and intellectuals. This sense of shame and bitterness is obviously reflected by those who were quite young in 1915. The two following statements are typical of the sense of hurt and disorientation felt by this generation:

> The generation which was twenty years old in 1915 was faced with a problem of great importance . . . assess the past in order to forge a new future. After a hundred and eleven years of independence all the national institutions had just crumbled in tragic circumstances. What was the reason for this disaster?
>
> (*La Nouvelle Ronde*, no. 2, 1 July 1925, 26)

Carl Brouard is particularly bitter and dramatic in recounting this experience:

> 28 July 1915. The American trampled on our soil. Alas! It was not only on this land conquered at bayonet point that their heavy boots marched, but also on our hearts. Although then in short pants, we understood that we were 'la génération de l'Humanité' and our eyes opened wide with sadness.
>
> (*Les Griots*, vol. 1, no. 1, July–Sept. 1938, 2)

What emerged was a deep distrust of those who, as far as this generation was concerned, favoured the American intervention – the élite. In fact, Joan Price-Mars's collection of essays *La Vacation de l'élite*[2] was published as early as 1919 and it addressed itself to the question of a fragmented ruling class and the nature of the reform necessary in Haiti. Price-Mars was one of the first to give the term *l'âme nationale* a special value in the context of the Occupation. His point of departure was clearly presented: 'It is indeed an established fact that when a people does not instinctively feel the need to create a national consciousness from the close solidarity of its various social strata . . . such a people is on the verge of fragmentation' (p. 15).

Haiti was simply a perfect example of cultural plurality with no cohesive creolising force to bind together the various disparate groups. In his analysis, responsibility for this situation lay with the élite: 'The fact is that the élite has failed in its social responsibility, that ultimately it has shown itself unworthy of its mission of representation and leadership' (p. 73). This feeling that the élite had effectively renounced its right to lead is echoed in the stereotype of a collaborationist élite found in early protest poetry. It was a conviction that could only reinforce the desire among younger Haitian writers to sever all ties with the past.

The restlessness, already in evidence in the pages of *La Nouvelle Ronde* in 1925, was fed by various external circumstances – not the least of which was the intellectual upheaval in Paris in the 1920s. Paris had become in this post-war period the epicentre of anti-establishment feeling. The disillusion and shock that followed 1918 in France created a profound distrust of traditional values both cultural and moral and led to a deliberate cultivation of absurdity, obscenity, madness and what was termed 'cretinisation'. The nihilism of Dada and Surrealism left an indelible mark on those Haitians who were students in France at the time. Marcelin's 'Sainement' bears the stamp of this absolute *refus* of tradition and the search for truth in the irrational. The liberating experience of the metropolis not only affected Haitians but was primarily responsible for such radical black student movements as *Légitime Défense* (1932). However, for Haitians it meant a violent commitment to rejecting the élite and all it stood for and an equally rigid anti-American stand. Normil Sylvain on his return to Haiti spoke effusively about this experience: 'France made me aware of myself . . . I had not until then felt my worth as a man, become aware of my existence. It oriented me.'[3]

The effervescence of the twenties is evident in some of the first poems published by these young Haitians on their return home. The apocalyptic voice of the poet evident in 'Sainement' dominates some of the early poems of both Carl Brouard and Jacques Roumain. Art and external reality have become one and their commitment to the nationalist cause was simply part of the poetic ideal of *révolution permanente*. The obvious non-conformist and idealistic spirit of this period can also be explained by the strong attraction that Nietzsche's ideas had for this generation. Roumain makes this very clear in an early interview in 1927: 'I read somewhere that Nietzsche is unbalanced. Quite the contrary. He is anything but ill. No trace of Hegelian melancholy. But a great celebration of life. Of determination. Of the Will to Power. This man has created a religion: that of the Superman.'[4] Roumain's early verse reflects this fiery idealism as in the following poems he presents himself as the vengeful *poète-maudit* resisted by ordinary men but ultimately a superior, destructive force:

> Et je rirai:
> je rirai à blanches dents
> et tout un riant;
> je vous crierai:
> "Ha, lâches, ha, chiens.
> Ha, hommes-aux-yeux-baissés,
> Faut-il que la mort
> hurle,
> faut-il que le feu
> brûle,
> faut-il que la bouche
> crache
> pour qu'en foule vous accourriez? . . .
>
> la mort venue d'au dela des mers
> qui hurle des insultes
> brûle votre patrimoime
> et crache
> son mépris blanc
> sur vos fronts noirs.[5]
>
> [And I will laugh
> I will laugh loudly
> and while laughing
> I will shout to you
> Ha, cowards, ha, dogs
> Ha, men with downcast eyes
> Must death
> scream,
> must fire
> burn,
> must the mouth
> spit
> for you to become a unified throng? . . .

> death come from across the seas
> hurling insults
> Burns your patrimony
> and spits
> its white scorn
> on your black brows.]

The allusion to the Occupation is not always apparent but the
mention of cowardice and submissiveness is an oblique reference to
the lack of rasistence among Haitians. This exaltation of the poet's
will and superiority did, in fact, have a specific political content.
Carl Brouard's equally defiant celebration of rebellion – 'Nous' –
offers an image of a dissolute bohemian existence that seems to draw
heavily on Rimbaud's ideal of the *poète-voyou* who by a 'dérèglement
des sens' attains a superior vision:

> Nous
> les extravagants, les bohèmes, les fous . . .
>
> Nous
> les écorchés de la vie, les poètes . . .
>
> Nous
> les fous, les poètes . . .
>
> Nous
> qui n'apportons point la paix
> mais le poignard triste
> de notre plume
> et l'encre rouge de notre coeur![6]
>
> [We
> the eccentric, the bohemian, the insane . . .
> We
> the poets flayed by life . . .
> We
> the poets, the insane . . .
> We
> who do not bring peace
> but the sad dagger
> of our pen
> and the red ink from our heart!]

Interestingly enough, the bizarre literary experiments and poetic fantasies of Dada and Surrealism never became part of the *prise de position* of this generation. As we shall see they limited themselves to exploiting the freedoms of *vers libre,* to creating a number of short poems constructed around a strong visual image and to the potential of oral poetry. However, they were attracted to one of the effects created by the *refus* of traditional aesthetic values. This was Europe's growing interest in cultures that were non-Western. Such an enlargement of the aesthetic horizon in Europe and particularly the interest in African art and culture found an obvious response among Haitians. *La Nouvelle Ronde* in 1925 in an article which analysed the failure in the past to create a national literature, makes the point that the only way of avoiding an imitative literature or one that simply presents local colour is to pay attention to the interest in black and African culture that existed in France:

> It is necessary at this time when exoticism rages in French literature, when Paul Reboux, Maran are studying the black soul, when it is the order of the day to speak of black art, to take pride in black music, it is necessary to analyse the Haitian soul, to strip it bare, to dissect it.[7]

The ultimate aim was a rejection of bland Eurocentric ideals for a more authentic, vital culture. In Europe, Maran's critique of Western civilisation in *Batouala* (1921) and Gide's indictment of the colonial exploitation of the Congo *Voyage au Congo* (1927) represented one area of interest in this prevailing trend. Also the cult of primitivism, in its Rousseauesque thirst for spontaneity and an anti-rational ideal, can be seen in Gauguin's escape to Tahiti and Rimbaud's journey to Abyssinia. Paul Morand's *Magie noire* (1928), for instance, was heavily influenced by this cult of black exoticism. A poem such as Carl Brouard's 'Nostalgie' in 1927 shows how these ideas had already penetrated Haitian writing:

> Tambour
> quand tu résonnes
> mon âme hurle vers l'Afrique
> Tantôt
> je rêve d'une brousse immense,
> baignée de lune
> ou s'échevèlent de suantes nudités

Tantôt d'une case immonde
ou je savoure du sang dans des crânes humains.[8]

[Drum
when you resound
my heart screams towards Africa
Sometimes
I dream of a huge jungle
bathed in moonlight
of dishevelled, sweating, naked bodies
Sometimes of a filthy hut
where I revel in blood drunk from human skulls.]

Brouard's fantasy of cannibalism and erotic 'défoulement' is clearly an indication of the nature of the interest in black culture in the twenties.

However, this interest in a racial mystique and African culture did have a more serious side to it. The Haitian desire for cultural authenticity was encouraged by both the mystico-nationalist creed of some French thinkers at this time as well as the growing number of ethnological works on African culture. Charles Maurras and Maurice Barrès in France were responsible for the theory of *enracinement* and the notion that genuine spiritual strength could only be gained from the untainted culture of the provinces. The concept of *l'âme haitienne* that is a collective cultural unconscious which gives some originality to a specific Haitian community seems to originate in the theories of spiritual and racial essences found in Barrès and Maurras. In fact, Dominique Hippolyte's *La route ensoleillée* (1927) begins with the following epigraph from Maurras, 'J'ai tout recu du sol natal . . . ' This is cited with approval in Price-Mars's *Ainsi Parla l'Oncle* (1928) whose work on Haitian folk culture uses as its basic premise the concept of racial essences. Phrases such as 'une certaine sensibilité commune à la race' and 'traits particuliers de notre race' can be frequently found in this work.

This concept of culture as being organic and not conditioned was reinforced by ethnological studies by Europeans done at the time. For instance Lévy-Bruhl's *La mentalité primitive* (1925) is frequently quoted in *Ainsi Parla l'Oncle* to support the theory of congenital racial essences. Indeed Lévy-Bruhl's theories of the differences between African intuition and European reason as well as Gobineau's ideas would later influence Senghor's conception of negritude. The anti-rational impulses celebrated in 'Sainement' were to some extent legitimised by these studies which attempted to demonstrate scientifically the uniqueness of the black soul. These theories, which encouraged Haitian nationalism and anti-assimilationist ideology in the twenties, would unfortunately survive this period to fuel racialist ideologies later on in this century.

There was one other source from which Haitian Indigenism drew inspiration. This was the Harlem Renaissance movement which was created by black American writers. The link between both these movements is a difficult one to trace, however. This is so partly because certain important figures in the Indigenous movement have claimed ignorance of the black American writing until as late as 1929[9] and also because many of the important works by black Americans did not appear until the late twenties and early thirties. The influence of black American writing, especially that of McKay and Langston Hughes, is more visible in the 1930s. Even if widespread awareness of black American writers may have been limited, there must have been at least a strong feeling of solidarity felt by the Haitians. As early as November 1906 the influential Jean Price-Mars, in one of his lectures collected in *La Vocation de l'élite*, drew attention to black American writers: 'Our black brothers have poets, remarkable musicians like Paul Lawrence Dunbar, M. Coles, the Johnson brothers etc' (p. 77).

In fact, from the early 1920s Johnson and Dubois were very active in championing the Haitian nationalist cause in the United States. Not only had the Occupation forged this link with black America but one of the main tenets of the Indigenous movement was to sever the link with French metropolitan literature and make Haitian writers more aware of other literary traditions. In an interview given in 1927 Jacques Roumain declared: 'We have completely ignored that there was in the United States, four days away from us a flourishing black poetry. And original too. Countree Cullins [*sic*] for example. Our literature is wrongly oriented.'[10] The similarities in the themes and aesthetic ideas between Harlem and Haitian writers must have made this sense of solidarity even stronger. The strong anti-bourgeois sentiment, the intense racial feeling and the desire to create an authentic black literary style through the use of folk material were common to both movements. Indeed, in the issue of *La Revue Indigène* which followed Roumain's interview. Dominique Hippolyte published a short piece on Countee Cullen and translated three of the latter's poems. A poem like 'Incident' (1925) would easily have attracted the attention of young Haitian writers:

> Chevauchant une fois dans le vieux Baltimore
> La tête et le coeur pleins de joie
> Je vis un Baltimoréen
> Fixer son regard sur moi . . .
>
> Ainsi je souris, mais il tira dehors
> Sa langue, et m'appela 'sale nègre'.
> Je vis tout Baltimore
> De mai jusqu'à décembre
> De tout ce que je trouvai là
> C'est tout ce dont je me rappelle.[11]

> [Once riding in old Baltimore
> Heart-filled, head-filled with glee
> I saw a Baltimorean
> Keep looking straight at me . . .
> And so I smiled, but he poked out
> His tongue and called me 'Nigger'.
> I saw the whole of Baltimore
> From May until December
> Of all the things that happened there
> That's all I remember.]

The prosaic nature of the poem/narrative which almost puts the bitterness of the theme into greater relief is remarkably close to the prevalent style among Indigenous writers. Hippolyte's version accentuates the narrative quality because the rhyme scheme of the original is lost in the translation into French. However, *La Revue Indigène* did not last long enough to cement this link with the Harlem writers but the influence of the latter is evident in the 1930s when Indigenism is left behind.

Early evidence of the new spirit of rebellion can be found in the pages of the shortlived monthly journal called *La Trouée* (July 1927 to December 1927). The very name *La Trouée* (The Breach) indicates the defiance they launched against what they saw as a claustrophobic environment: 'The Breach! Our battle cry . . . is that of young and ardent souls who are going to pierce through the barricades of ignorance and apathy which stifle us.'[12] They saw themselves as an embattled avant-garde who, just having returned from Europe, found the complacency of their class inhibiting.

La Trouée devoted itself to literary and cultural matters. Even though theories of an indigenous literature were not elaborated in the journal, its very first issue clearly stated what literature should *not* be: 'It is not the domain of the pedantic and the idle. We will get rid of both of these . . . It is not this bland pastiche of local colour we find in some, nor the colourless affectations of others.'[13] What literature should be was not yet clearly defined. Yet they stood for what was considered to be an intolerable permissiveness in aesthetic terms. It is in this journal that 'Sainement' is published and in fact is truly characteristic of the self-consciousness and irreverence of these early years.

The poems of *La Trouée* range from the fashionably bohemian themes of Carl Brouard to the more detached experimental poems of Jacques Roumain and Daniel Heurtelou. Brouard's 'Elégie', for instance, deliberately avoids being a lyrical song of lost love. The poem is of a simple prosaic construction and Dolores is not the traditional object of Romantic adoration:

> Dolorès
> te souviens-tu du passé,
> de nos amours clandestines,
> dans une rue calme de la banlieue port-au-princienne . . .
> Je garderai toujours la nostalgie de ce soir
> de pluie,
> ou tu fus tellement vicieuse.
> Parfois
> j'avais mal à la tete
> et tu me forcais à avaler
> – Dieu sait combien –
> de cachets d'asperine[14]

> [Dolores
> do you remember the past
> our clandestine loves
> in a quiet street of a Port-au-Prince suburb . . .
> I will always be nostalgic about that evening of rain,
> when you were so depraved.
> Sometimes I had a headache
> and you forced me to swallow
> – God knows many –
> doses of asprin]

The poem seems built around a systematic process of *dégonflage* and irony as sentimental clichés such as 'nostalgie de ce soir' and 'souvenir du passé' degenerate into the erotic and non-poetic 'vicieuse' and 'cachets d'asperine'. This quality of parody evident here was not always present in the treatment of proletarian themes. Marcelin's 'Petite Noire' is a straightforward poem of praise to a black girl:

> Et tu es noire comme tous les péchés. Mais tu souris
> Et c'est une fête des anges
> Douceur de tes regards blancs,
> Candeur de tes dents blanches . . .
> Je te chanterai, petite noire, c'est bien ton tour.[15]

> [And you are black like all sins. But you smile
> And it is an angelic spectacle
> The sweetness of your white gaze,
> The innocence of your white teeth . . .
> I will praise you in my song, little black girl, your time
>   has come.]

Whether in theme or form, *La Trouée* signified a departure from poetic tradition in Haiti.

As far as the question of poetic form is concerned the ornate and earnest poetry of the past was replaced by epigrammatic and sometimes absurd short poems which seem to be no more than chance impressions of landscape. No longer do we see the solemn meditative nature poetry of the nineteenth century but what appears to be nothing more than the quick impersonal glance of a snapshot – remote and trivial:

> Chaleur accablante
> ou tout semble dormir
> Un âne
> baigne sa croupe dans la poussière du chemin
> . . . un flamboyant
> surgit
> la savane
> tend
> sa lèvre rouge au soleil[16]

[Suffocating heat
when all seems asleep
A donkey
bathes his rump in the dust of the road
 . . . a flamboyante
rises up
the savanna
stretches
its red tongue to the sun.]

Heurtelou's 'Savane desolée' gives a quick impression of heat and lethargy and introduces a dramatic and bizarre note with the image of the red flamboyant tongue stretching towards the sun. Roumain's 'Midi' and 'Apres-midi' similarly use the resources of *vers libre* to present a collage of elliptical visual impressions, snatches of sound and filtered light. The latter shows how effectively Roumain creates a new set of expectations from a rapid enumeration of details of landscape:

Des moucherons bruissent, mandolines
minuscules. Sagaies fines
des palmiers-éventails
immobiles dans le Temps figé.
Le soleil filtre à travers les arbres, en barres
d'or. Un enfant quelque part
crie.
Chaque minute comme un siècle d'ennui
bâille.[17]

[Flies buzz, tiny
mandolins. Fine spears
of palm trees,
immobile in static Time.
The sun filters through the trees, in bars
of gold. A child somewhere
cries.
Each minute like a century of boredom
yawns.]

More than an attempt to depict heat and motionlessness, this poem can be seen as an attack on the poetic word. Its consciously prosaic and staccato tone seems to be a deliberate attempt to dislocate literary decorum. The resources of *vers libre* became a 'miraculous weapon' in this struggle to reach beyond erudite literary codes and create a new 'space' around words and so restore their original power.

By late 1927 *La Trouée* ceased to exist but it did represent the opening of the breach through which a new wave of creativity would surge. *La Revue Indigène*, which epitomised the new iconoclasm of this generation as well as their actual literary achievements, dominated the Haitian literary scene from the middle of 1927 to early 1928 and can be seen as the prototype of other similar but more strident journals (such as *L'Etudiant Noir* in Paris and *Tropiques* in Martinique) which launched a new phase of ideological ferment and literary experimentation among black writers. It is curious that this journal should have such an impact since it only lasted for six issues and did not represent a thoroughgoing ideological orthodoxy. In fact, it would be more accurate to see it as a loose alliance of partisans of new literary freedoms, so much so that thr group was at one point termed *indigeste* instead of *indigene* in order to suggest the diversity of temperaments and talents that it attracted.

Curiously enough, in the midst of the tensions of the Occupation *La Revue Indigène* appears to be noticeably apolitical or at best indirectly political. This note was apparent from the editorial of the very first number where Normil Sylvain asked the question: 'In the turmoil of our daily lives do you not think that we should agree to a moment of calon, a respite . . .'[18] This journal was to be a literary oasis distinct from the violent political *prise de position* its collaborators had also taken. To the latter cause they devoted their talents as journalists. The political organ of this generation was *Le Petit Impartial* (1927–1931) which outlasted its more precarious and shortlived literary counterpart. This newspaper documents the uncompromising nationalism of the members of the Indigenous movement. There are articles by Jacques Roumain, Carl Brouard and Emile Roumer among others. These constituted violent critiques of American imperialism, the Haitian élite and the Catholic Church. The latter were repeatedly condemned for collaborating in cultural imperialism or what was termed *l'occupation de la pensée*. It was the kind of militant journalism which, encouraging the youth and the masses to revolt, would precipitate the strikes and demonstrations of 1929. The paper, indeed, gives us an insight into the political mind of this generation in all its idealism and contradictions. Its pantheon of heroes, for instance, consists of figures as diverse as Mahatma Gandhi, the prophet of non-violence to Charlemagne Péralte, an open advocate of the tactics of violence. But these various figures all contribute to the ideological effervescence of the times – Gandhi for his closeness to the common man and his mystic anti-materialist philosophy; Price-Mars for his innovative ethnography and Péralte for his aggressive nationalism.

The inconsistencies and disparities in this generation are nowhere more apparent than in their pursuit of *La Muse haitienne* in the pages of *La Revue Indigène*. Their literary efforts ranged from carefully wrought sonnets to wild explosions of *vers libre*; from formal alexandrines to oral poetry whose form and emphases were determined only by the human voice; from delicate *spleen* poems to the unadorned exclamations of voodoo rituals. However, the members of this disparate group did manage, each in his own way, to convey an undeniable sense of place and for the first time, in an immediate and palpable way the diversity of the Haitian experience. Perhaps it was the combination of heightened sense of place created by their early exile (at school in Europe), as well as the pressures of the Occupation. Whatever the reason, the Indigenous movement brought fresh currency to the desire for cultural authenticity that had been initiated almost a century before in the pages of *L'Union*.

It is difficult to be precise in defining the concept of Indigenism. It is an abstraction which is as amorphous and elusive as the ideology of Négritude and the problem has been further complicated by the term being loosely applied to writers born after the end of the Occupation. Perhaps the best way of seizing the essence of what it stood for is to see the movement as a cluster of ideas and feelings generated by a deep-seated conviction of cultural rootlessness and dislocation felt by this generation. What was desired was more than an infusion of local colour into Haitian writing. They were, consciously or unconsciously, obsessed by the need for cultural wholeness, for the artist to be the voice of a community. Essentially Indigenism was built around this generation's preoccupation with the status of art and ritual in a world of materialism and broken continuities. Their desire was to move away from the contingency of the cultural present, to escape the alienation of the individual artist from his world and, in the process, to explore that repertoire of unconscious responses that constitutes the fabric of one's culture. This network of shared meanings would give identity to the group and be the link between the artist and his community. Sylvain's definition of literary *enracinement* bears this out: 'Literature presents the truest expression of a people's soul . . . What we are seeking – are the instinctive reactions of our sensibility to certain things.'[19]

Art would be seen in terms of the ideal of a mythical, pastoral culture where the artist was in communion with the spiritual. Sylvain, usually restrained in style, becomes lyrical as he envisages the movement away from the desecrated present to a hallowed past of a serene, whole culture, 'the time when Haitians loved each other, when it was a delight to live in our homeland, a delight enclosed in our serene landscape between our blue hills and the singing sea.[20] Such a sense of wholeness might be found in the culture of the folk. Poetry was seen as an *instrument de connaissance* which could retrieve this vital contact with a collective authentic culture by using elements of Haitian folk culture. Sylvain's prescription, however, is rather vague:

> It is the sound of the drums announcing the dance from one hillside to another, the call of the conch shell, the hoarse cry of mankind pressed against the wall, it is the vibrant, sensual rhythm of a 'meringue' with wanton melancholy, which must be incorporated in our poetry . . . Our poems are translated from the Haitian, that is the translation of states of mind which are really our own.[21]

Perhaps this desperate desire for a community, for an ethnic context was already an admission that it was almost impossible to regain such a status for their poetry. However, this desperate urge persists in the work of the major poets of *La Revue Indigène* even after this period. Whether the ideal was the community of the 'damnés de la terre' or the concept of the 'nigritie' of the Haitian soul, essentially the aim was to reinstate the poetic word as the voice of the group or tradition.

Sylvain, who was the only one in this group that one could see as a theoretician, did not elaborate his ideas any further and wrote little poetry. It is therefore difficult to assess the achievements of the diverse talents of *La Revue Indigène* in terms of his criteria. Yet they share a common 'point of departure' which was that poetry should not be used simply as political propaganda but represented a superior means of perceiving the world, 'a better insight into ourselves . . . into the mysterious world of the soul'.

However, these speculations were never closely followed in actual practice and their ideas on form and prosody at best appear sketchy. This may have resulted from an absolute refusal to prescribe literary criteria. Indeed, the only rule they all adhered to was the need to do away with any formal orthodoxy. Jacques Roumain indicated this refusal to pay homage to what he considered the sanctified, outmoded styles of the past, in an interview in 1927: 'Give to the poetic word, I ask of you, its fullest meaning . . . I voluntarily refuse to follow any rules. That bird which we call poetry, dies in captivity.'[22] Poetry must be uncluttered by literary tradition. They expected the poetic word, now set free, to have some kind of magical force. The poet's only guide was his subjectivity and the poem was judged simply by the intensity of the experience conveyed. Roumain in explaining this new aesthetic used the illustration of one of his early poems – 'Cent Metres':

I want a poem to have the vibrant force which shakes (the reader). A driving force. In '100 Metres' I did not want to paint a picture. I am not a painter. I wanted to bring to life what I had run. The frenzy, the wild impressions . . . to show the agonizing drama of this ordinary event.[23]

Their new poetics would not be based on traditional evocations of landscape or the delight in the well-turned phrase. Poetry, whose subject could be chosen at random, must now overwhelm by the violent shock of words or some bizarre fantasy. The poem had become an act of discovery.

Even though the word is never used in *La Revue Indigène* the Surrealist insistence on *délire verbal* and the setting free of the image seem to be at the base of these new demands on poetic form. Indeed, Etienne Lero, an orthodox Surrealist, would later in the pages of *Légitime Défense* make a similar demand on Caribbean poetry. What he called 'the colourful and sensual black imagination'.[24] This cry would also be echoed by Fanon's definition of a new revolutionary art – 'a jerky style full of images . . . Highly coloured too, bronzed, burnt, violent.'[25] This idea occurs in embryonic form in the pages of *La Revue Indigène*. This meant that the convention in poetry that would be singled out for special attention would be the image. As a Haitian critic said in 1934: 'the image has recaptured its throne . . . the image simply gives us better insight into reality without losing us in the labyrinth of abstract generalisations.'[26] The strong visual qualities apparent in those short 'nature' poems of *La Trouée* would now become the norm for *La Revue Indigène*. In the process of repossessing and renaming the landscape and reality of Haiti, the startling, evocative, poetic image would imbue the familiar and the commonplace with a sense of wonder. It could destroy both the conventional way of seeing reality as well as subvert traditional literary associations.

Perhaps the best way of identifying these new directions in poetry is in the context of the most introspective of all poetic genres – the *spleen* poems. These frequently occur in the pages of *La Revue Indigène* and reveal a darker side to some of the more violently *engagé* figures of the nationalist movement. For instance, short mood poems such as 'Orage', 'Insomnie', 'Calme', 'Noir' by Jacques Roumain are typical of this kind of writing. Yet these poems do not contain the usual wistful melancholy and sentimental rhetoric. In Roumain's 'Insomnie', for instance, the resources of *vers libre* are combined with concise and dramatic imagery to give a sharp impression of desolation:

> Clarté indécise
> La nuit
> entre dans la chambre, sombre voile
> brodé d'étoiles . . .
>
> Nuit interminable. Chaque heure
> s'étire monotone comme une litanie.
> Je me penche hors de moi
> pour écouter une voix
> ténue et triste comme un parfum.[27]

> [Shadowy light
> The night
> enters the room, sombre veil
> embroidered with stars . . .
> Unending night. Each hour
> is drawn out monotonous like a litany.
> I strain
> to hear a voice
> thin and sad like a perfume.]

This kind of mood poetry tended to be closely linked to the bohemian lives of these poets. An atmosphere of eroticism and debauchery is the context for Daniel Heurtelou's 'Douze et Demi'. In this poem the staccato rhythms of *vers libre* suggest the cacophany of the night club and the frank physical imagery heightens the oppressive atmosphere:

> Eructation pénible
> du saxophone
> qui crache
> dans le soir lourd
> des notes discordantes . . .
>
> Et dans le coin ombreux
> qu'illumine
> son sourire de noire,
> je tâche d'étouffer
> le spleen
> qui me tue.[28]
>
> [Painful eructation
> of the saxophone
> spitting
> into the evening heavy
> with discordant notes . . .
> And in the shadowy corner
> illuminated by
> her black girl's smile,
> I try to stifle
> the melancholy
> which is killing me.]

The form has been made far more effective by eliminating the usual clichés of pathos. A Haitian nightclub scene also becomes palpably real in Carl Brouard's 'Bouge'. This fantasy in prose builds up its effects from a montage of apparently random sights and sounds in the bar:

> Ce bouge. (Etait-ce un rêve)
> Des prostituées mélancoliques dansaient la mérinque,
> Songeant à un passé lointain . . . lointain, et leurs
> mules claquaient sur le parquet usé.
> Mélancoliques elles tournaient . . . tournaient comme

dans un rêve, aux sons d'un orchestre étrange; guitare,
grage, triangle, tambour.
Accoudé au comptoir crasseux, un ivrogne braillait
une chanson obscène.
Ce bouge. (Etait-ce un rêve)[29]

This bar. (Was it a dream)
Melancholy prostitutes danced the meringue,
dreaming of a past far . . . far away, and their
shoes clicked on the worn floor.
Melancholy they turned . . . turned
as in a dream, to the sounds of a strange band; guitar,
maracas, triangle, drum.
Leaning on the filthy counter, a drunk roared out an
                                        obscene song.
This bar. (Was it a dream)

Even in these short introspective pieces in Haiti, because of the new
range of theme and bizarre visual effects, poetry was being shifted
away from its traditional moorings. However, the full impact of
Indigenism is most obviously seen in the various tableaux of Haitian
life that were depicted. The resources of the Haitian landscape
would be used to convey that violently expressive style absolutely
vital to this new sensibility.

If Price-Mars was the intellectual force behind this generation,
Emile Roumer and Philippe Thoby-Marcelin represented the spirit
and intuition of these times. The latter indicated their *prise de position*
unequivocally in this wry observation: 'your older sister putting you
to bed/ hums/ the current fox-trot'.[30] Haiti was being lulled to sleep
by American civilisation. It was their duty to resist the spread of
Western materialism. Their most important literary achievements
come from this period and are the best illustrations of how this
generation set out to repossess *l'âme haitienne*. There were two ways
of restoring the primal innocence they wished for the poetic word.
Either innocence could be restored from the 'inside' through the
dislocation of traditional literary forms, or 'innocent' non-poetic
language could be introduced from the 'outside' and so reshape a
literary form. Roumer's desire to retain and subvert the alexandrine
puts him in the first category; Marcelin's conscious introduction of
the contingency and disharmonies of everyday reality in his work
makes him part of the second. It is tempting to see in Marcelin's

poetry in particular, the influence of Apollinaire's dictum – 'exalter la vie sous quelque forme qu'elle se présente'. Also we find in much of Marcelin's work an attempt to present raw snatches of life to the extent that rigid perspective or any hint of stylisation are removed. The poem 'Grand rue' presents a collage of impressions and sounds – unrelated but creating a kaleidoscope of movement and colour:

                                        Klaxons
                                        buss
                                        foule
                                        bourrique
                                        paysannes
Sous de grands-chapeaux-de-paille
Le marché et ses bruits colorés
Tohu-bohu
            pêle-mêle
Les maisons neuves sont blanches
Et carrées
Il ne faut pas rêver dans la rue
Les chauffeurs te l' apprennent gentiment à leur manière
compè ou fou?
                                        Locomotive
                                        cloche
                                        HASCO –5
Le convoi beugle
30 wagons de canne-à-sucre
Défilent.[31]

[Horns
buses
crowd
donkey
peasant women
Under huge straw hats
The market and its coloured noises
Hurly-burly pell-mell
The new houses are white
And square
You must not dream in the street
The drivers gently remind you in their own way

man you mad?
Locomotive bell HASCO –5
The train bellows
30 wagons of sugar cane
file past.]

Marcelin was also very aware of the question of poetic register and how one could combine the visceral tones of Haitian creole with free verse. In 'L'Atlas a menti' he presents the situation of a peasant who looks at an atlas and cannot understand why Haiti is a tiny dot on the map:

Ciel-papier-buvard
L'avion est une vilaine tache
    mobile
qui trace des loopings
Bouqui tresse une natte de latanier
Et Roumer étudie la géographie
    O Bouqui
crache le chique de ton mépris
O chante une 'boula'
    et crève l'assotor
        et danse la chica
'Dehie mones gain mones
Hein?
Et lan cate-la
Blancs-yo fait Haiti
                piti
                piti
                con-ça.'[32]

[Blotting-paper sky
The airplane is an ugly moving blotch
making loops
Bouqui weaves a mat
And Roumer studies geography
    O Bouqui
spit out your chew of scorn
O sing a 'boula'
    and burst the 'assotor'
        and dance the 'chica'

'Behind one hill there is always another
Not so?
And on the map
The whites make Haiti
   little
   little
   like that.']

The poem can best be read as a stream of associations almost as naive and arbitrary as those of a primitive painting. It contains allusions to peasant scepticism about the map (ciel-papier-buvard) as well as nonsense rhyme (o chante une boula . . . danse la chica) and snatches of peasant speech. On the surface a light poem on peasant distrust but it does also extend the range of language possible in poetry and recreate a temperament peculiar to Haiti. Marcelin was one of those who could see how excessive lyricism and stylisation had created many bland representations of Haiti in the past. The rhythms of free verse and the random impressions permissible in this new unrestricted style were manipulated to convey a certain immediacy and deliberately raw texture in his poetry.

Emile Roumer is one of the more enigmatic figures of the Occupation. His insistence on his own idiosyncrasies makes it difficult to see him as a member of any literary or ideological group. Perhaps the loose fraternity of *La Revue Indigène* suited him perfectly. No illustration of his originality is clearer than his poetry at this time. In a period of literary experimentation Roumer chose to retain the alexandrine. He combined this normally formal metric pattern with an enormous range of subjects and vocabulary. Behind it all one always senses an indomitable sense of humour.

Roumer did not need a movement to focus his ideas on creating a Haitian aesthetic in poetry. His most important collection of poetry – *Poèmes d'Haiti et de France* was published in 1925 and so easily predates the appearance of *La Revue Indigène*. Roumer's early poetry, however, gives us little indication of the strength of his poetic talent. His anti-American poetry, for instance, does not go beyond the earnest but unoriginal *profession de foi* of the twenties. For instance, 'Le Testament' is characteristic of this phase of stately but banal alexandrines:

J'ai perdu ma jeunesse et le rêve sauvage
de tomber dans la rue une nuit de carnage

> J'ai perdu tout espoir on cet effort suprême
> de libérer mon sol d'une infâme tutelle[33]

> [I have lost my youth and the savage dream
> of being cut down in the road in a night of carnage
> I have lost all hope in this supreme effort
> to liberate my land from an ignominious yoke]

In fact, whenever Roumer is tempted to fierce *engagement* in his poetry, the verse becomes again a strident but dull declaration of intentions. His more recent *Le Caiman étoilé* (1963) makes us aware of this weakness.

It is in Roumer's apolitical verse that his real strengths as a poet become apparent. Defiantly retaining the alexandrine he set out to create a new lyricism that would be undeniably Haitian. A quick comparison with the use of an old-fashioned lyricism by a few timid poets of the twenties clearly brings out Roumer's originality. For instance, André Liautaud serenades the hills of Kenscoff:

> O Beaux Soirs de Kenscoff! veillée autour de nattes
> Alors que le brouillard est comme un coutelas[34]

> [O Beautiful evenings in Kenscoff! Vigil around the mats
> While the fog is like a cutlass]

If this is contrasted to Roumer's own evocation of landscape, the latter's inventiveness and control of form are readily apparent. 'Impression d'août' is filled with fleeting sensual imagery and an effective use of synesthesia. This suggestion of colour, sound and smell is sharply disturbed by the last lines which almost undermine the pastoral serenity:

> Un spécial parfum de mangues qui fermentent.
> l'odeur du sol humide et l'arôme des menthes
> sous les manguiers touffus où ronfle le gérant
> près de l'étroit ruisseau dont l'eau clair se rend
> sous les jasmins en fleurs. Des boys à leur marelle
> criaillent dans l'allée; un vol de sauterelle
> met une lueur bleue au rouge des gravois.
> Soudain le type grogne avec un gros renvoi
> de gaz et fait partir de proches libellules
> tandis que les rosiers ont des roses qui brûlent.[35]

[A special perfume of mangoes fermenting
the smell of the wet earth and the aroma of mint
under the dense mango trees where the owner snores
near to the narrow stream whose clear water passes
under the jasmine in flower. Boys playing hopscotch
shout in the alley; a flight of grasshoppers
places a blue light on the red rubble
Suddenly the man snorts with a great belch
of gas and chases the nearest dragonflies
while the rose bushes have roses that burn]

The shock value of the final lines shows both Roumer's refusal to be too tightly bound by formal prosody as well as his pervasive sense of humour. In fact, Roumer probably went as far as one can go in breaking up the alexandrine into a series of dramatic pauses and random observations. 'Paysage au rhum' in spite of the regular metre is broken by abrupt shifts in perspective:

Les abeilles ont pris, bruissantes, leur vol
doré. Le soleil brûle . . . Aucun souffle frivole
ne caresse les fleurs à la base des murs
massifs . . . Repos . . . [36]

[The bees have taken, noisily, their golden
flight. The sun burns . . . No frivolous breath
stirs the flowers at the base of their walls
massive . . . sleep . . .]

The use of enjambement and the almost elliptical syntax shows how close he is to his contemporary Marcelin, how much Roumer belonged to this time of literary experimentation.

The Indigenist ambition was to create a literature so exclusively and uniquely Haitian as to make it almost inaccessible to others. Roumer made the most sustained attempt in poetry to convey the peculiarities of *l'âme haitienne*. His most successful effort in this regard is the peasant declaration of love – 'Marabout de mon coeur'. The poem can be read on two levels – an irreverent, even gross parody of Petrarchan verse and an equally successful evocation of female sexuality in Haitian terms. Translation of the poem reduces it to nonsense but in its original form it makes fun of the Petrarchan cult of pure, asexual adoration of the beloved. In contrast to the courtly love tradition, Roumer's use of hyperbole is overwhelmingly sexual in its associations. But more importantly, Roumer also exploits a particularly Haitian convention in poetry –the comparison of women to fruits or various dishes (rather than to flowers). Oswald Durand is a precursor in this respect and Roumer fills his lines with the most erotic and savoury dishes that are both an amusing rejection of poetic decorum and wickedly play on the more risqué associations of Haitian creole. In the last line, for example, both 'fesse' and 'victouailles', because of the sibilant sounds suggest the sizzling of hot oil and 'boumba' (which normally means a cauldron) clearly evokes the creole word for the human bottom.[37]

> Marabout de mon coeur aux seins de mandarine,
> tu m'es plus savoureux que crabe en aubergine,
> tu es un afiba dedans mon calalou,
> le doumboueil de mon pois, mon thé de z'herbe à clou
> Tu es le boeuf salé dont mon coeur est la couane
> l'acassan au sirop qui coule dans ma gargane.
> Tu es un plat fumant, diondion avec du riz,
> des akras croustillants et des thazars bien frits . . .
> Ma fringale d'amour te suit où que tu ailles;
> ta fesse est un boumba chargé de victouailles.[38]

> [My beloved 'Marabout' with breasts like tangerines
> you are more delicious than crab in eggplant,
> you are the meat in my *calalou*,
> the dumpling in my peas, my aromatic
>   herb tea,
> You are the salt beef stored in the fat of my heart
> the syrup drink that flows down my throat.
> You are a steaming dish, mushroom cooked
> with rice,
> crisp fritters and fried fish . . .
> My hunger for love follows you everywhere,
> your bottom is a cauldron stuffed with food.]

Both Roumer and Marcelin, each in his own way, embodies the true spirit of Indigenism as it existed in 1927. Both sought a new poetics to recapture the whole range of the Haitian experience. But Indigenism was never static and consisted of a number of varying, even contradictory patterns. During the Occupation Haitian nationalism, the *raison d'être* of Indigenism, sought various points of orientation. Among the various myths that informed Haitian nationalism were the glorious and untainted pre-Colombian past; the heroic struggle of 1804; the legacy of cultural refinement and literary taste inherited from their Latin culture and the most influential alternative to emerge in the late twenties–Africa. The possibility of seeing Africa as a cultural matrix was promoted in Indigenism because of its interest in the various components of folk culture. It would, however, outlive this early phase to become one of the most dominant ideologies of the twentieth century in Haitian intellectual and cultural life.

Africa was the most attractive of the myths of modern Haitian national feeling because of the lure of cultural authenticity. African survivals were clearly present in the folklore and religion of Haiti's peasantry – Haiti's cultural heartland. Also the emergence of an interest in the African past meant the coming to fruition of Marcelin's 'éternel dédain aux raffinements européens'. It meant the rejection of rationalism and Western culture and the retrieval of an exclusively ethnic world of the senses.

Most of the poets of *La Revue Indigène* tended to gloss over the theme of Africa in their poetry – with one exception. Carl Brouard was the first of this generation openly to celebrate the Africanness of Haitian culture in 1927. The most bohemian and dissolute member of this generation, Brouard saw the emergence of Africa as an attempt to correct the imbalance that existed in Haitian culture. He declared, 'It is ridiculous to play the flute in a country where the national instrument is the powerful assotor drum.'[39] The alien flute against the authentic voodoo drum – Brouard's words were prophetic as this would become in another decade the basis for the ideology of ethnic authenticity.

However, in 1927 Brouard's few poems celebrating Africa are inspired by the sensual, erotic stereotype of his 'Nostalgie'. For instance, the poem 'Ma Muse' puts together similar ideas of Africa and sensuality. She is a somewhat perverse vision of unrestrained emotion:

> Ma muse
> est une courtisane toucouleur
> des dents blanches
> une cascade de fous rires
> des sanglots profonds jusqu'à l'âme

une tumulte sonore
de bracelets et de verroteries[40]

[My muse
is a Toucouleur prostitute
with white teeth
a cascade of mad laughter
deep heartfelt sobs
a sonorous rattle
of bracelets and glass beads]

As is consistent with Brouard's early Africanist poetry, one senses an everpresent *refus* of the bland, repressed Eurocentric ideal in his evocation of colour, spontaneity and eroticism. In the voodoo religion Brouard found the 'défoulement' that his restless spirit needed. His early 'Hymne à Erzulie' also reflects his preoccupation with female sexuality:

Déese anthropophage de la Volupté
et des richesses
aux robes nuancées des couleurs de l'arc-en-ciel . . .

O toi
qui tends les désirs comme des cordes!   p.93
O dix mille fois dedoublée
qui dans le monde élastique et mol des rêves
chaque nuit de jeudi
Ouvre à tes amants les secrets de tes flancs
et l'odeur de ta chair[41]

[Man-eating goddess of pleasure
and wealth
with robes tinged with the colours of the rainbow . . .

O you
who stretch desire like cords
O repeated ten thousand times
who in the elastic and soft world of dreams
each Thursday night
opens to your lovers the secrets of your thighs
and the odour of your flesh]

The poem continues as a graphic celebration of the flesh – a sexual 'dérèglement des sens'.

Even though interest in Africa and Haiti's Africanness would later develop into an independent ideological position, Indigenism permitted it to develop because of the fundamental *refus* it entailed as well as its link with the masses of Haiti. In fact, it all comes back to the essential quest for a community to which the Haitian poet could belong. What the members of *La Revue Indigène* had in common was the belief that literature should not be a hermetic and exclusive activity but part of a shared homogeneous culture. The need to democratise literature and the most inaccessible of all the genres– poetry–would be the legacy of Indigenism that permeates much of modern poetry in Haiti.

In another decade the Indigenist school was already outmoded and abandoned. Those who collaborated in this venture either stopped writing completely by the end of the Occupation or took positions in the ideological debate that followed. The debate between those who opted for Marxism as an explanation for Haiti's problems and those who saw national regeneration in terms of ethnic authenticity. If they shared any common feature, it was the dream of a polyvalent literary culture inherited from Indigenism. The Marxists saw themselves as the vanguard of a proletarian culture as opposed to the 'alienated elitist artist'. René Piquion, in his Marxist phase, typifies the sentiments of this group: 'The proletarian writer or artist is above all a fighter. Each day . . . He must light the way of the proletariat and their leaders.'[42] Brouard, who firmly rejected Marxist ideology, was one of the theoreticians of the Africanist movement in Haiti. He saw the Haitian artist as a 'troubadour' or *griot* perpetually in contact with the people and their culture. He did not explicitly emphasise the revolutionary class struggle but rather the intuition that links artist and community:

Art in the service of the People has not yet been seriously envisaged, although among us, the only possible, viable Art emerges from them . . . Sometimes I have the chance to read poems to an illiterate audience. The effect is fascinating. Certainly, they did not understand much, but they perceived the essential beauty . . . All imaginations are open to the idea of beauty in the Platonic sense. It is not a matter of intelligence but of intuition.[43]

Socialist realism as well as ethnocentric ideology committed the literary word to the same role – not in the service of literary tradition but in the name of accessibility. For instance, Brouard's poem 'Vous' could be seen as the prototype of the new stripped-down literal poetic mode. More than simply being aggressively populist in its appeal, it reinforces the idea of the poem as a collective voice – a product of the new aesthetic democracy:

> Vous
> le gueux
> les immondes
> les puants:
> paysannes qui descendez nos mornes avec un
> gosse dans le ventre . . .
> Vous
> tous de la plèbe
> debout![44]

> [You
> the destitute
> the filthy
> the stinking
> peasants who descend the mountains
> with a child in your bellies . . .
> you
> all the people
> stand up]

Later Jacques Roumain, by then a Marxist and ideologically opposed to Brouard, would use a remarkably similar dramatic monologue:

> Eh bien voilà;
> nous autres
> les nègres
> les niggers
> les sales nègres
> nous n'acceptons plus
> c'est simple
> fini
> d'être en Afrique

en Amérique
Vos nègres[45]

[Well, here we are
the negroes
the niggers
the dirty niggers
we no longer accept
it is simple
all over
to be in Africa
in America
your niggers]

Indigenism meant a sharp departure from literary convention and the emergence of a new authority and creative effervescence in the arts. It also signified the end of Haiti's isolation in cultural terms. Indigenism never became narrowly provincial. Jacques Roumain, in particular, was forever insistent on the need for opening Haiti's literary horizons: 'I think that our predecessors have been too exclusively preoccupied with a few French writers whose reputation reached them. They were completely uninterested in the happenings in world literature. In the twentieth century one is a citizen of the world.'[46]

Hence it is not surprising that the literary masterpiece that eventually emerged from the movement of Indigenism should have as its hero someone who could embody both the provincial and the cosmopolitan, the traditional and the progressive. Manuel in Roumain's *Gouverneurs de la rosée* epitomises the ideals of Indigenism. These were reinforced in the 1920s by the exhortations of visitors like Paul Morand who could see in the 1920s the beginnings of an international black literary *prise de conscience*. The introduction to his Haitian anthology states the need to link Haiti's problems with those of a world-wide black community: 'aux efforts littéraires de toute votre race, de Chicago à Madagascar'.

The Occupation was a cruel experience for Haiti but without it, it would be difficult to imagine the exuberant and daring spirit of the twenties. It would be difficult to envisage a *crise de conscience* of such proportions and the kind of national feeling created, so different from the tragic sense of belonging of *La Ronde*. It was in many ways a degrading experience, but it created modern Haitian literature.

NOTES

1. *La Trouée*, no. 1, 1 July 1927, p. 21.
2. Jean Price-Mars, *La Vocation de l'élite* (Port-au-Prince: Edmond Chenet, 1919). Page numbers quoted from this edition.
3. Normil Sylvain, *La Trouée*, no. 2, 1 Aug. 1927, 55.
4. *La Revue Indigène*, no. 3, Sept. 1927, 105.
5. Jacques Roumain, *Appel* (Port-au-Prince: Pierre-Noel, 1928).
6. *La Revue Indigène*, no. 2, Aug. 1927, 71.
7. *La Nouvelle Ronde*, no. 2, 1 July 1925, 30.
8. *La Trouée*, no. 4, 1 Oct. 1927, 119.
9. Naomi Garret, *The Renaissance of Haitian Poetry* (Paris: Présence Africaine, 1963) p. 77.
10. *La Revue Indigène*, no. 3, Sept. 1927, 103–4.
11. *La Revue Indigène*, no. 4, Oct. 1927, 154.
12. *La Trouée*, no. 1, 1 July 1927, 1.
13. Ibid.
14. *La Trouée*, no. 6, 24 Dec. 1927, 185.
15. *La Trouée*, no. 3, 1 Sept. 1927.
16. Ibid.
17. Ibid.
18. *La Revue Indigène*, no. 1, July 1927, 2.
19. Ibid., pp. 3–4.
20. Ibid.
21. *La Revue Indigène*, no. 2, Aug. 1927, 53.
22. *La Revue Indigène*, no. 3, Sept. 1927, 106.
23. Ibid.
24. Etienne Lero, 'Misère d'une poésie', *Légitime Défense*, no. 1, 1932, 12.
25. Frantz Fanon, *The Wretched of the Earth*, (Harmondsworth: Penguin, 1969) p. 177.
26. Arthur Bonhomme, 'La nouvelle generation littéraire', *Les tendances d'une génération* (Port-au-Prince: Collection des Griots, 1934) pp. 152–3.
27. *La Revue Indigène*, no. 3, Sept. 1927, 111.
28. *La Revue Indigène*, no. 4, Oct. 1927, 166.
29. Paul Morand, *Anthologie de la poésie haitienne indigène* (Port-au-Prince: Modèle, 1928) p. 8.
30. Ibid., p. 60.
31. Ibid., p. 62.
32. Ibid., p. 63.
33. Published in a special edition of *Haiti-Journal*, Dec. 1947.
34. Morand, *Anthologie de la poésie*.
35. Emile Roumer, *Poèmes d'Haiti et de France* (Paris: Revue Mondiale, 1925).
36. Ibid.
37. A commentary on this poem is offered by one of Roumain's characters in *La proie et l'Ombre* (Port-au-Prince: La Presse, 1930) p. 19.
38. *Haiti-Journal*, Dec. 1947.
39. *La Revue Indigène*, no. 2, Aug. 1927, 70.
40. Ibid.

41. *La Revue Indigène*, nos. 5–6, Jan.–Feb. 1928, 201.

42. René Piquion, 'Pour une culture prolétarienne', *L'Assaut* (La voix de la génération de l'occupation), Mar. 1936, 86.

43. *Les Griots*, vol. 2, no. 2, Oct.–Dec. 1938, 155.

44. *La Revue Indigène*, no. 2, Aug. 1927, 72.

45. Jacques Roumain, 'Sales nègres', *Bois d'Ebène* (Port-au-Prince: Henri Deschamps, 1945).

46. *La Revue Indigène*, no. 3, Sept. 1927, 103.

4 The Way Through Africa: A Study of Africanism in Haiti

> Fictions can degenerate into myths whenever they are not consciously held to be fictive. In this sense anti-Semitism is a degenerate fiction, a myth . . . Myth operates within the diagrams of ritual, which presupposes total and adequate explanations of things as they are and were; it is a sequence of radically unchangeable gestures[1]

The rise of Africanist ideology in Haiti is a classic example of the way a yearning for the ideals of national liberation and cultural autonomy could congeal into politically absolutist solutions. According to Frank Kermode's definition this meant the degeneration of literary fiction into the 'sequence of radically unchangeable gestures' implied by myth. The emergence of the Griot movement in the 1930s and its theories of racial determinism provides the link between literary activity and authoritarian politics that emerged in post-Occupation Haiti.

The Griot movement, traditionally seen as the product of certain tendencies within Indigenism (namely the rejection of Europe and the growing interest in folk culture and Africa), is in some essential ways quite different from the Indigenous movement. The question of Africa and *l'âme haitienne* is one instance of this difference. Africa in the 1920s was a symptom of Haitian nationalism. It symbolised a certain permissiveness and freedom of the creative imagination that fed both the spirit of anti-Americanism as well as the need for literary experimentation. By the thirties, however, the theme of race and Africa had degenerated into a stock set of literary postures, a rigid rhetoric which meant a sharp departure from the loose literary alliance of Indigenism. The following examples of Africanist verse reveal the extent to which narcissism and paranoia had become closely allied to the theme of race in poetry:

> Here I was poor little nigger exiled in my own country
> head bare
> coatless
> belly empty
> on this shadow-filled asphalt of Port-au-Prince
> . . . and the black of my ebony skin blended with the
> shadows of the night
> and no one could see me.[2]

There is a sinister ring to this sense of victimisation. Duvalier's sentiments are echoed in the equally maudlin and confessional 'Tambour racial' by Maurice Casseus:

> Do not believe that down here your place is reserved
> in the daylight
> of happiness
> No, no
> The day, the sun are not for you
> not for you
> Seek your refuge in the night
> The great darkness receptive to other shadows.[3]

In spite of the use of free verse, this is not a poetry inspired by random imagery or the dislocation of the poetic word. It is contrived and rhetorical using symbols with fixed values and meanings, as is seen in the repeated use of night and shadows. The darkness is not a symbol of creativity but an extension of that 'original' night of the hold of the slave ship:

> The damp night feels groaning in it
> The creaking, sombre form of the slave ship
> Of the slave ship which, on the weary sea,
> Is the cradle of a race and its tragedy.[4]

To the Indigenous poets the poem was an act of discovery, a sustained effort to create new perceptual fields through literary improvisation. In the thirties Africanism made poetry an adjunct to ideology, to a racially determined historical 'truth' that permeated all areas of Haitian culture – history, the arts, folk culture and politics.

The Griot movement did not immediately follow Indigenism (the journal *Les Griots* was not published until 1938), but was facilitated by certain ideas and influences that emerged in the 1930s. The most important of these is interest in race which existed at this time. The study of African survivals and the ethnic uniqueness of Haitian culture is directly linked to the anti-rational tradition that is evident in Indigenism. Ethnological works which supported the myth of the organic and instinctive features of African culture are directly responsible for the racialist obsessions and Messianism of Africanist ideology.

We have already seen how European anthropologists had characterised African culture as intuitive and spontaneous. By the thirties a number of studies of African survivals in Haiti, particularly in the voodoo religion supported such 'scientific' theories of an anti-rational racial essence. Price-Mars's *Ainsi parla l'oncle* which contributed to the fierce national pride of the Indigenous writers was possibly even more influential after the end of the Occupation. In many ways a timely and convincing revaluation of Haitian folk culture, *Ainsi parla l'oncle* did use as its point of departure the notion of a racial mystique. In treating peasant culture Price-Mars carefully glossed over the misery and disastrous poverty of rural communities and instead speculated about the 'substratum psycho-logique d'où dérive la mystique nègre'. This work went beyond merely legitimising the African elements of Haitian culture. It implied the existence of an authentic black essence which would later encourage the ideology of Africanism. As early as 1928 Carl Brouard, destined to be one of the theoreticians of *Les Griots* emphasised this feature in Price-Mars's work: 'After all voodoo is our only claim to originality. It is the definite guarantee of a national architecture, literature, a national mysticism.'[5] Price-Mars's insistence on the need to recognise ethnic origins was repeated in other ethnological works. Dr J. C. Dorsainvil's *Vodou et Névrose* (begun as early as 1913) is perhaps a more cautious study of voodoo than *Ainsi parla l'oncle* but also relies heavily on the concept of racial essences. Terms such as 'métaphysique raciale' and 'habitus nerveux racial' are used to explain features of various religious rituals.

The ethnologists may have used race as a means of explaining areas of Haitian culture but no one was as extreme in his speculations about a racial mystique as the self-styled 'esoterist' Dr Arthur Holly. Holly refused to see Haitian culture as a creolisation of various influences. Dorsainvil and Price-Mars both acknowledged the importance of cultural *métissage* but Holly saw Haitian culture as simply an African culture. His *Les Daimons du culte voudo* presents Haitian man as the product of atavistic urges and mysterious ethnic forces: 'We are Afro-Latins. But our Latin civilisation is only on the surface; the ancient African elements in us are far reaching and live on and controls us to the extent that quite often we are moved by its mysterious powers . . .'[6]

It is difficult to imagine that such eccentric theories could have been taken seriously in the thirties and used to demonstrate the need for racial authenticity. Much of the blind acceptance of such theorising could be explained, however, by the problem of class and colour in Haiti, and the ambitions of a growing black middle-class. Jacques Roumain in *La proie et l'ombre* (1930) makes a wry comment on the way in which theories of Haiti's African heritage had permeated the society. It may be a deliberately absurd use of the theory of ethnic survivals but it does hint at the way in which this ideology is ironically linked to very Western, bourgeois ambitions: 'All Haitians are either lawyers or doctors. An ancestral survival . . . simply that: in the African tribe those who officiated at palavers and sorcerers were highly considered.'[7] Theories of racial authenticity both implied that the traditional mulatto élite was ill-suited to control a black state and legitimised the right for Haiti to be ruled by a black élite. An emergent black middle-class in Haiti saw in this ideology the rationale for a black cultural dictatorship. The groundwork for Duvalier's doctrine of a nationalist/négritude mystique was laid in post-Occupation Haiti.

The focus on questions of race in the thirties was further intensified by the increasing influence of black American writers. This link with the Harlem Renaissance was important enough to be noted by Morisseau-Leroy in his novel *Récolte*: 'The young men of "Le Phalanstère" felt solidarity with the youth of Europe and Asia, Africa and Latin America. They knew by heart the verses of Langston Hughes translated by René Piquion.'[8] The Indigenous movement expressly wanted these links to be cultivated and the interest in black American writing was a result of this attempt to widen Haiti's horizons politically and culturally. What is especially interesting is the particular emphasis that was given to the Harlem writers.

Jean Price-Mars was one of the most vocal in stressing the need to strengthen ties with black American culture. This sense of fraternity was not simply a literary bond. To Price-Mars the Harlem writers were another instance of the way in which blacks of the diaspora had retained their ancestral heritage. *L'âme haitienne* and the *valeurs nègres* of black Americans shared the same anti-rational responses and an identical intuitive sense of reality. As early as 1932 Price-Mars had begun to elaborate the idea of a Pan-African presence, a homogeneous neo-African culture common to all peoples of African descent: 'But if Africa is its distant source, is it not possible to retrieve something of this penetrating intuition, of this freshness of inspiration and this sensual realism in the members of the race transplanted in America.'[9]

Naturally the Harlem writers did share certain racial themes with Haitian writers. The rediscovery of Africa and the stereotype of an instinctive, spontaneous ethnic presence could certainly be found in Afro-American writing at the time. Indeed we have noted before how the theme of the 'tragic mulatto' – torn between European rationalism and African sensuality – was common to both Claude McKay and Jacques Stéphen Alexis (cf. p. 61). However, the Harlem movement was not exclusively concerned with the theme of primitivism. It was also a protest literature which attempted to articulate the cause of the disadvantaged in American society. This area of concern was seldom brought into prominence by Haiti's 'Africanists'. Instead it was the black American evocation of a racial mystique that attracted them. This is most apparent in the treatment of Langston Hughes's work in the thirties in Haiti.

Price-Mars in his articles on the 'Renaissance Nègre', in the United States chose one of Hughes's poems for translation. 'Notre Pays' typifies the emphasis that was given to Hughes's poetry by Haitian intellectuals. The final stanza sums up the nostalgia for an uninhibited and sensual world that is the theme of the poem:

> Ah! Nous devrons avoir un pays d'allégresse
> D'amour et d'allégresse, de vin et de chanson,
> Et non pas ce pays où la joie est péché[10]

> [Ah! We should have a land of gladness

Of love and gladness, of wine and song,
And not this land where joy is a sin.]

René Piquion, who became the most dedicated translator of
Hughes's poetry, emphasised the same racial stereotype in Hughes's
verse. In the pages of *La Relève* in the early thirties, Piquion
published his translations which all contained strong racial
sentiments. For instance the sense of historical injustice directed
against the black race in:

J'ai été victime
Au Congo, les Belges m'ont coupé les mains.

Je suis Nègre
Sombre comme la Nuit
Sombre comme les ténèbres de l'Afrique, ma Mère.[11]

[I've been a victim
The Belgians cut off my hands in the Congo.

I am a Negro
Black as the night is black
Black like the depths of my Africa.]

Or the theme of alienation and fierce racial pride in:

Tous les tam-tam de la brousse
    retentissent en moi
Et la lune des jungles, ardente, sauvage
    éclaire mon âme
J'ai peur de cette civilisation
    si colossale
    si âpre
    si froide.[12]

[All the tom-toms of the jungle
    beat in my blood
And all the wild hot moons of the jungles
    shine in my soul
I am afraid of this civilisation
    so hard
    so strong,
    so cold.]

In his critical work on Hughes *Un Chant Nouveau* Piquion made explicit what interested him in the Afro-American poet's work. It was the sterotype of *art nègre* which demonstrated the ethnic uniqueness of the race:

> The negro possesses a sense of rhythm. It runs through his nerves as it were. When the drum beats sound in the clearings of the African jungle, when the choir of 'hounsis' sing out the chants of the voodoo religion in the plains of Haiti, when in the sugar plantations of Cuba, the coffee fields of Brasil popular musicians perform the 'son' and the 'rumba', the spectators of negro origin feel the same thrill . . .[13]

Hughes's poetry was an illustration of the theory of a shared *génie nègre*, a monolithic Pan-African ideal that encompassed all black art regardless of language or nationality. Statements by Piquion as to the features of this shared essence reveal the absurdity of some of this speculation about a racial aesthetic. For instance, 'vers libre seems to be the natural mould for the black poet'. Perhaps Hughes was, consciously or not, 'misread' for the purposes of Africanist ideology in Haiti.

This seems particularly apparent when we consider that the cult of the primitive was only a phase in Hughes's early poetry. For instance, by 1938 his *A New Song* was a hymn to Marxist revolution and makes no special plea for *valeurs nègres*. By the late thirties Hughes was prominent among those writers who took a strong anti-Fascist stand in the Spanish Civil War. Piquion stated quite categorically in 1934 that dictatorship was 'reason and will linked with Force in the service of Nature'.[14] He was not noted for his ideological consistency but Piquion would later find a role in Duvalierism, having lost interest in the militant Marxism of Hughes's later work.

The need to assert a racial identity and the attendant belief in a *style nègre* became central to the Africanist position in the thirties. The dominant notion was that style in literature was ethnically ordained. Two early reviews of Roumain's *La proie et l'ombre* in the thirties show how highly favoured the idea of a 'racial style' was in literary circles. Edner Brutus saw Roumain's style as a manifestation of Haiti's Afro-Latin heritage: 'something of that sad laughter of the black race and the special characteristics of a mixture of afro-latin cultures.'[15] Carl Brouard praised Roumain for the special racial qualities in his style: 'This style is racial. It is complete, lively, taut with anguish, filled with a profound poetry, which wells up from underneath.'[16] This notion of a 'racial style' was a vague, ill-defined abstraction which could best be described as 'committed automatic writing'. It would be fed by the unconscious and by a lack of literary inhibitions but directed towards certain ideologically acceptable themes such as anti-bourgeois sentiments, ancestral Africa or peasant culture.

In contrast to the absence of a closely defined poetics in Indigenism, much effort is spent in the thirties in defining a black prosody. In *Les tendances d'une génération* Arthur Bonhomme goes into great detail to identify the inadequacies of Indigenism and define the features of an authentic racial style. Features of the *âme nègre* vaguely perceived in Indigenism will now be honestly explored in Bonhomme's view: 'Poetry, more and more, was drawn back to its original source, as close as possible to its mysterious origins in the subconscious. It then became a sudden gush from the depths of man. It lost itself in the unreal.'[17] The exploration of the creative unconscious that first appeared in the Indigenous poets would now lead to an ethnic ideal, 'the music inherent in the black soul, that strange music which recalls the savage murmur of the wind across the quivering bush, the roar of savage animals penetrating the oppressive mystery of the desert . . .'[18] This conclusion is supported by Morisseau-Leroy who very explicitly links his ideas on poetry to ethnological works on African culture: 'Let the study of African art, researched in depth thanks to the work of ethnologists and confronted with the manifestations of the Haitian soul in popular songs create for the poet a means of expression that is racially appropriate!'[19] What is striking about such theories of racial determinism in the arts is that it is fundamentally non-literary. At best Morisseau-Leroy cast the writer in a subordinate role, that of the instrument of culture. The *mode d'expression racial* described leaves out of account the individual creative imagination and instead stresses a formal esthetic orthodoxy. What soon emerged as a highly defined ethnic preciosity had completely usurped the privileged role of the creative imagination that existed in the twenties. Morisseau-Leroy's prescription for the 'true Haitian poet' reveals how a new authoritarianism had permeated Haiti's literary culture: 'The true Haitian poet will adopt an African prosody with parallelism and repetition, racially authentic techniques . . . techniques through which we will manage to retrieve in poetry the rhythm of black music.[20]

It would be wrong, however, to believe that all poetry that dealt with racial themes fell prey to these theories of racial poetics. The legacy of Indigenism and the interest created in the power of the poetic word still stimulated genuine creativity among certain writers who treated folk culture and race in their poetry. The best example of this continuing spirit of creativity is Jacques Roumain's poem 'Sur le chemin de Guinée', inspired by the peasant belief that after death the soul returns to its ancestral home in Guinea. The sombre, meditative mood of 'Guinée', emphasised by the repetition of the first line, 'C'est le lent chemin de Guinée', is quite different from Brouard's frenzied bohemian folk poetry:

C'est le lent chemin de Guinée
La mort t'y conduira
Voici les branches, les arbres, la forêt,
Ecoute le bruit du vent dans les longs cheveux
d'éternelle nuit.[21]

[It's the slow road to Guinea
Death takes you there
Here are the boughs, the trees, the forest,
Listen to the rustle of the wind in the long hair of eternal night.]

Indeed on closer scrutiny we find that Roumain has attempted something far more complex than a poem about folk customs. On the literal level the poem as in the early verse of Senghor treats the theme of the prodigal son's return home. As in Senghor's verse this return is more than an ethnic or religious rite. It also signifies the restoration of the poet's vision. In both cases the return of the prodigal signifies not only an intense communion with the numinous but is an allegory of the poetic act:

C'est le lent chemin de Guinée:
Il ne te sera pas fait de lumineux accueil
Au noir pays des hommes noirs:
Sous un ciel fumeux, percé de cris d'oiseaux
Autour de l'oeil du marigot
Les cils des arbres s'écartent sur la clarté pourissante
La t'attendent au bord de l'eau un paisible village et
La case de tes pères et la dure pierre familiale
Où reposer ton front.

[It's the slow road to Guinea:
No bright welcome will be made for you
In the dark land of dark men:
Under a smoky sky, pierced by the cries of birds
Around the eye of the river
The eyelashes of the trees open on the decaying light
There, await you beside the water a quiet village and
The hut of your fathers and the hard ancestral stone
Where you will rest your head.]

The 'case de tes pères' and 'la dure pierre familiale' both indicate the prodigal's final attainment of a state of grace. But this final stage also suggests the opening of the traveller's eyes, by implication the creative imagination, 'Autour de l'oeil du marigot/Les cils des arbres s'écartent'. To Roumain Africa was not a stock mythical symbol but a 'literary fiction' that could focus his attention on the nature of poetic creativity.

The traveller's journey towards this sacred state can also be seen as an increasing immersion into the world of the senses. The intensity of sound for instance, progresses from the 'bruit du vent' to 'les ruisseaux grelottent' to a world shattered by the shrill cries of birds. The Indigenist preoccupation with freeing the poetic image is also apparent as Roumain evokes this flight into a hallowed, sensual world. For instance, the 'ciel fumeux' and 'clarté pourissante' of the last lines strongly suggest the twilight of creativity common to both Baudelaire and Senghor. The use of synesthesia in the strange juxtaposition of images of 'l'oeil du marigot', 'cils des arbres' and 'clarté pourissante' suggests the complete liberation of the senses from the constraints of a fallen, profane past – the retrieval of an artistic as well as religious state of grace.

Roumain remains unique in the folk poetry of the thirties. It is not that folklore was not the source of poetic inspiration. On the contrary, the thirties seem exclusively preoccupied with this theme. Few, however, managed to treat peasant ritual with any originality. A random sampling of some of the minor writers of this period shows the extent to which a rigid, *précieux* element had begun to establish itself in the treatment of folk themes. In the early 1930s, for instance, Charles Pressoir and Louis Hall published *Au rythme des coumbites* (1933) and *A l'ombre du mapou* (1931) respectively. In contrast to Roumain's successful poetic reconstruction of peasant superstition in 'Guinée', these collections reveal a superficial and uncreative use of folk material. What is also evident is an ethnic affectation which created a new pedantry in literature. For instance, Haitian peasants are referred to as 'les fils de l'Afrique'; voodoo as 'la religion de Guinée' and possession as 'l'ivresse sainte'. We are also faced with a glossary of approved vocabulary for suggesting *l'âme noire* – 'mystique', 'sensuel' and so on. Pressoir's heavy handed sonnet 'La Religion de Guinée' is far removed from Roumain's poem:

> Partout, le vaudou règne, en plaine, à la montagne,
> S'annexant plusieurs saints du culte catholique,
> Près des lois des pays où l'on porte la pagne
> Marie et Erzulie en le hounfort rustique.[22]

> [Everywhere voodoo reigns, on the plain, in the mountain,
> Incorporating several saints of the Catholic cult,
> Alongside the laws of the land where loin cloths are worn
> Mary and Erzulie in the rustic temple.]

Along with the treatment of African survivals and folk culture, one of the more popular themes of the thirties is that of the tragic mulatto. This stereotype of the divided mulatto psyche we have seen emerging in the protest literature of the Occupation in its preoccupation with an Afro-Latin identity. The basis for this concept of cultural conflict can be found in the polarisation of myths of Africa and Europe – instinctive and uninhibited on one hand, repressed and cerebral on the other. The use of the words 'l'ancêtre hirsute' by Claude Fabry in 1937 immediately evoke the former stereotype and is an elaboration of the anti-rational tendency in Marcelin's 'Sainement':

> Et je ne sais pourquoi
> je voudrais être ce soir
> l'ancêtre hirsute
> qui, jadis dans le mystère de la brousse
> dansait, ignorant, libre et nu.[23]

> [I do not know why
> I would like to be this evening
> the hairy ancestor
> who in the mystery of the bush
> once danced ignorant, free and naked.]

This stereotype reappears in countless works of the period and is usually associated with the theme of conflicting cultural legacies.

Even Jacques Roumain who carefully avoided the theme of race in much of his verse felt compelled to treat this notion of the divided self. Again we see his talent for converting a potentially banal subject into striking poetic images. His 'Quand bat le tam tam . . . 'relies on images of water to convey a sensual liquid consciousness reaching for an authentic racial identity. The use of the river as a cohesive symbol in the poem is particularly effective. The water suggests continuity and, like blood, the preservation of ancestral links. The dark water also evokes the unknown, *mare tenebrarum*, into which the soul ventures. In the end the same symbol is versatile enough to provide Roumain with a strong visual image of purification and rebirth as the white scum is cast off along the banks:

Ton âme, c'est le reflet dans l'eau murmurante ou
    tes pères ont penché leurs obscurs visages
Ses secrets mouvements te mêlent à la vague
Et le blanc qui te fit mulâtre, c'est ce peu
    d'écume rejeté, comme un crachat, sur le rivage.[24]

[Your soul is the reflection in the murmuring water over which
    Your fathers bent their dark faces
Its secret movements unite you with the tide
And the white man who made you a mulatto, is the speck of
    foam abandoned, like spit on the shore.]

The best known treatment of this theme does not come from Roumain, however, but from the latter's contemporary Léon Laleau. His short poem 'Trahison' has become a predictable inclusion in anthologies of black writing. This poem has been traditionally read as a personal testimony to the problem of reconciling two distinctly different cultural legacies. However, it is difficult to ascribe this kind of self-consciousness to Laleau since he constantly avoided using popular themes and the *lieux communs* of his time in his verse. In 1933, for example, he strongly criticised what he called the 'perpetuelle et juvénile trahison des clercs' because this generation put verse 'au service de ses idées sociales. Elle la descendit à la taille de la politique.'[25]

What is more important is that the regular versification in 'Trahison' makes it less than the earnest confessional poem it is supposed to be. Laleau treated poetry as a game, a clever distraction. For instance, a supposedly 'Indigenist' poem like 'Concert Dominical' is more like a private joke:

> Le chef d'orchestre étrenne un neuf képi
> Et porte un nom chimique: Occide.
> Le timbre des glaciers s'offre un répit
> Le cuivre d'un alto s'oxyde.[26]

> [The band leader sports a new hat
> and bears a chemical name: Oxide.
> The tinkle of glass comes tô a halt
> The brass of an alto-sax oxidizes.]

Consequently it would be inconsistent for Laleau to treat literally an ideological theme of the thirties. What is present in 'Trahison' is more than the Senghoresque sense of *déchirement culturel*. Laleau is concerned less with the problems of the colonial *assimilé* than with using the rhetoric of the time to reflect on the problem of poetic creation:

> Ce coeur obsédant qui ne correspond
> Pas avec mon langage et mes coutumes,
> Et sur lequel mordent, comme un crampon,
> Des sentiments d'emprunt et des coutumes
> D'Europe, sentez-vous cette souffrance
> Et ce desespoir à nul autre égal
> D'apprivoiser, avec des mots de France,
> Ce coeur qui m'est venu du Sénégal?[27]

> [This obsessive heart which does not relate
> To my language and my customs,
> And on which bite, like a spike,
> Borrowed sentiments and European customs
> Do you feel this suffering
> And this unequalled despair
> In taming, with words from France,
> This heart which has come to me from Senegal?]

The 'coeur obsédant' as opposed to 'sentiments d'emprunt' would suggest the traditional stereotype we have already seen. Yet the poem seems to reach beyond such a commonplace to suggest the problem of the poetic word. Language unyielding and uncooperative in the face of poetic inspiration is an equally plausible interpretation of 'Trahison'. Sartre, in his introduction to Senghor's *Anthologie de la nouvelle poésie nègre et malgache* (in which 'Trahison' is included) also saw more than the *Angst* of the *assimilé* in the poem. He suggests 'this feeling of failure before the language is at the source of all poetic experience'.[28]

The fact is that Laleau is quite distinctive in the 1930s as one of the few to take the theme of race lightly. In the Griot movement of the late thirties we see how the essentially poetic fiction of Roumain and Laleau leads to a rigid ideological *prise de position*. The first indication that a formal ideology would emerge from the speculation about racial determinism can be found in *Les tendances d'une génération* (1934). This collection of essays represented the feelings of some of those who later formed *Les Griots*. The preface is written by Price-Mars and effusive praise for him is everywhere evident. Price-Mars had legitimised the idea that was the *raison d'être* of this movement – the mystique of race. Lorimer Denis indicates quite clearly the importance they attached to 'le génie de la race' by defining it as: 'All that we specially feel before the eternal unknown . . . that indescribable obscure mystery that takes hold of us, we children of Africa . . .'[29] Brouard would later create the word 'nigritie' to describe the mysterious impulses that were considered unique to the black soul.

The lure of racial authenticity was a phenomenon associated with all the important black literary and cultural movements in the thirties. However, Haiti's case is a rather special one because in no other movement was racial authenticity treated in such an obsessive way. Also it was a phase in other cultural ideologies but it became a permanent *prise de position* in Haiti that would bring black Fascism to power in 1957. The explanations for this are diverse but all have to do with the specific nature of Haiti's history. On one hand it was closely related to class and colour conflicts in Haiti and a black middle-class striving for legitimacy. Duvalier's essays on Haitian history reveal this quite clearly. For instance, his conclusions in 'Le problème de classes à travers l'histoire d'Haiti' and 'La mission des élites' all demonstrate the way in which blacks have been politically disadvantaged in Haiti: 'The bourgeois elite repressed the middle class or the black representatives of the major class in such a Machiavellian manner that the latter eventually rejected the status of outcast to which they had been relegated'.[30] The arguments for the political ascendancy of a black elite were closely allied to the growing interest in ethnology and the customs of the peasantry. An authentic black nation needed an authentic culture and religion. Price-Mars was idolised by this generation because of his pioneering work in this area. He may not have intended *Ainsi parla l'oncle* as the blueprint for political ideology but it provided the basis for speculation about a racial essence in Haitian culture.

The blind acceptance of these racial theories may also be related to ideological myth-making which has always been present in Haiti's history. In times of national crisis history appears as an arbitrary, contingent force and the turn of the century in Haiti made history appear to be a mocking, absurd phenomenon. In the period of reconstruction that followed the Occupation the temptation was to react against the radical insecurity of the past and through ideology make the world intelligible. Roumain's Marxism attempts just this and in a more sinister way Africanism was an answer to the yearning for 'total and adequate explanations'. Indeed, Fascism itself, fed by Africanist theory, offered a formal elegance which would provide a vision of order and security as well as create an ideologically comprehensible system and unity in Haiti's history. In their defence of political authoritarianism, the Griots always stressed this element: 'At the present time one must back either the Communists or the Fascists. On one hand the supporters of order and discipline; on the other the supporters of disorder and atheism . . . '[31]

History would no longer be a random series of events but could be explained and its future prescribed. Africanism could thus fulfil the emotional needs of the thirties. The inevitable totalitarian element in Africanism is present in the very name that was chosen for the movement. *Les Griots* suggests not only the privileged poet/magician in the tribal community but also a closed hierarchical world. Carl Brouard's 'Que sont les Griots' looks for parallels to the Griot in other cultures. He turns to medieval France and Islamic culture both of which suggest rigid, organised social systems and a fixed role for the artist. The Griot movement constantly looked back to a romanticised, mythical past, to a world of spirituality and order in which man was reconciled with nature, the black equivalent of 'la Vieille Hellade'. In keeping with this preoccupation with order the artist was given a special role. They were a superior caste, feared and hated by ordinary men: 'When the *Griots* pass by, men and women spit as a sign of scorn, for they are poets and sorcerers and men fear the mysterious . . . they form an exclusive caste.'[32] This may simply be a perversion of that Nietzschean element that was present in early Indigenist verse. Indeed, the concept of the Griot could well be Brouard's image of the poet as a superior force in 'Nous', now given an ethnic and religious context.

Les Griots (October 1938–March 1940), a 'scientific and literary journal' was launched as the organ of the Africanist movement. Lorimer Denis, François Duvalier and Carl Brouard were amongst the directors of this quarterly and they strongly influenced the course it took. The journal was never scientific nor literary in any serious way. It was not literary in the way that *La Revue Indigène* was. It did not provide a forum for artistic discussions or literary experimentation. In fact, very few articles on literature appear in its pages. It could only be called scientific because of the occasional article of medical topics and the numerous essays on ethnology and folklore and the pseudo-scientific language used. But these investigations into Haitian culture were very limited because they single-mindedly set out to demonstrate the Africanness of Haitian man: 'All our efforts from independence to today have concentrated on the systematic repression of our African heritage both in literary and in socio-political matters, our actions must now lead us to a revaluation of this racial factor . . . '[33]

They were not, for the moment, very interested in questions of economics or even politics. Haiti's problem was psychological and cultural and their aim was to detect the authentic 'bio-psychological elements' in Haitian culture. Such a concern with identity may have begun with Haitian nationalism but this excessive emphasis on race ultimately denied the existence of a Haitian nation. To *Les Griots* culture was organic, a congenital acquisition. Consequently the creolising process in Haitian society, the effects of historical conditioning were all denied in favour of the African element in Haiti. The use of a concept such as *notre moi fondamental* presupposes a subconscious retention of primordial impulses. Much of their speculation was concerned with this area of cultural retention demonstrating ultimately that African man is sensual and intuitive: 'he seems to aspire towards an attainment of communion with the eternal order of the world and to participate emotionally in universal life.'[34] They used folk religion and ritual to demonstrate just this. The conclusion was that authentic Haitian culture was African and was the culture of the black majority in

Haiti: 'this latin culture is nothing but the legacy of a small group of Haitians represented by our intellectual élite . . . our African heritage is pervasive in the majority of the Haitian people to the extent that it constitutes an anatomo-psycho-physiological substratum.'[35]

The phenomenon of literary creation also interested *Les Griots*. They attempted to formulate a racial aesthetic by drawing on the ethno-literary theories current in the thirties. Literature (and poetry in particular) was important because it could provide proof of the racial unconscious that they assumed in their ethnological studies. To *Les Griots* the writer was an unconscious creator in whose work the *geist* of the black race would surface. Poetic inspiration could provide evidence of that special sensibility unique to the Afro-Haitian soul. This link between literary creation and the unconscious is closely related to Surrealist theory and explains the presence of Magloire St Aude, Haiti's only self-confessed Surrealist, among the editors of *Les Griots*. Intuition, in fact, represented the vital connection between politics and art. In both systems it was the unconscious that counted:

> All souls are open to the idea of beauty . . . It is not a question of intelligence, but of intuition. The most ignorant peasant feels which voodoo temple is more artistic than another . . . in the same way he will docilely obey a dictatorship which works for order, truth and the common good, because those ideas are inborn.[36]

Such a point of departure for literary theory has important implications for the whole question of artistic creation. For instance, it meant that the individual talent was subordinate to archetypal, racial influences. The literary work was an ethnic artefact, composed of various culturally ordained elements. The artist was simply the instrument of these cultural impulses:

> Who could ever tell how much of the unconscious is contained in artistic creation? Vain poet, you are nothing but a simple medium. You think of something, an idea, and then you fall asleep and your subconscious begins to work. The following day you only have to take the trouble to write it down.[37]

The verse favoured by *Les Griots* complied with the belief that the folk represented the true source of creativity. But this verse was not a militant populist poetry. The prevalent quality was a pervasive mysticism and the eventual aim was to couple art and magic, poetry and ritual. The anti-intellectual tendencies of Indigenism had intensified into a desire for a total immersion in the irrational. Carl Brouard saw in the voodoo religion the kind of frenzy and unbridled fantasy that was prescribed for the Griot poet. The following syllogism ironically demonstrates the link between art and the irrational, poetry and voodoo: 'animism is profoundly poetic . . . Voodoo is profoundly animistic and you feel the intense beauty that it contains. Our poets only have to pronounce the 'Open Sesame' for the cave of wonders to be opened.'[38]

Brouard's poetry attempted to be the perfect illustration of the Griot aesthetic in literature. During the time of his collaboration with *Les Griots* Brouard moved from the uninhibited bohemian style of the 1920s to a period of desperate mysticism. His fascination with religious mysticism can be seen in his interest in Sufism, theosophy, magic, voodoo and in his later years, Catholicism. Brouard's preoccupation with fantasy and the occult is evident even in his early verse and seems to have been the result of an unstable, tormented psyche. Unique in Haitian literary history, Brouard seems to belong to the tradition of the French *poète-maudit* in his obsession with the brevity of life, his escape into a bohemian, sensual world, his insatiable curiosity and his continuing quest for salvation. Like his metropolitan counterparts at the turn of the century, he made no distinction between poetry and life and he eventually destroyed himself in his attempts to act out his fantasies in the real world. It is this side of Brouard's personality that was so compatible with the element of racial mysticism that was present in the ideology of *Les Griots*.

In contrast to the remote and detached quality in the literary experiments of the 1920s, Brouard's poems were passionate and spontaneous, so much so that they eventually became simply confessions of his nightmares and hallucinations. In Brouard we see the intensification of anti-rational, anti-establishment feelings which were first glimpsed in Marcelin's 'Sainement'. The following prose poem from 'Propos d'un idéaliste' can be seen as his *manifeste poétique*:

O world! too brutal world, I reject you for what you are. I have also shut the doors of my soul in order to contemplate Dreams which are truer than Reality, and which I will contemplate face to face, when my eyes are closed for ever.[39]

Such a preoccupation with the world of dream and fantasy is apparent in some of Brouard's early verse. For instance, a poem such as 'Fantaisie' is an attempt at disorienting the poetic sensibility. The random associations created by the sounds of words show how attracted Brouard was to removing poetry from the realm of rational organisation:

> La mer est pleine de voiles
> Le firmament plein d'étoiles
> Quel aérien gramophone
> joue le disque monotone
> de la lune
> sur la dune?
> Ce vieil air
> dans l'éther
> me verse la sentimentalité
> en thé . . .[40]

> [The sea is full of sails
> The earth full of stars
> What ethereal gramophone
> Plays the monotonous record
> of the moon
> on the dune?
> This old air
> in the ether
> pours out for me sentimentality
> in tea . . .]

This nonsense-rhyme seems to be the beginning of the poet's initiation into a poetry based on fantasy. His early attempts at evoking this state of dream seem, however, somewhat mannered and *précieux*:

> Avec les pavots volés à Morphee
> belle, m'ont endormi vos doigts de fée
> dans la tour
> de l'amour.[41]

[With the poppies stolen from Morpheus
beautiful, your fairy fingers have put me to sleep
in the tower
of love.]

Yet, along with the bohemian themes and non-conformist sentiments of his Indigenist verse Brouard continued his interest in
evoking artificial paradises. A poem like 'Partance' describes the
beginning of a journey into the world of the unconscious. 'Les
Antilles' reconstructs the Caribbean in terms of a sumptuous, exotic
fantasy:

Antilles! Antilles d'or
vous êtes d'odorants bouquets
que bercent sur la mer, les vents
alizés, îles de saphir,
où la lune baigne d'argent
les palmistes
cependant que là-bas résonne
sourd
le tam-tam.[42]

[Antilles! Golden Antilles
you are perfumed bouquets
borne on the sea by the Trade Winds
Sapphire islands,
where the moon bathes in silver
the palm trees
while down yonder resounds
muffled
the drum.]

This relation between poetry and dream was not taken lightly by
Brouard. In an early confessional poem Brouard has doubts about
his visions, about poetry's ability to provide a permanent refuge
from reality:

One summer morning, under a radiant sun and
our hearts desperate with hope we set out for
the land of Canaan . . .
But Canaan keeps getting further away.

And here we are tired. And we wonder, anxiously,
if that blue land saturated with aromatic herbs and
all dappled by the flight of peacocks is simply a mirage.[43]

Brouard's later poems, particularly those published in *Les Griots*, are
more obviously immersed in a world of mysticism. This atmosphere
is provided by the rituals and mythology of the voodoo religion. In
contrast to the delicate stylisation of his earlier vision, Brouard now
attempts to present the frenzy and delirium of his various
hallucinations. Essentially these visions contain an unbridled
sensuality communicated through the use of synesthesia. His
evocation of a voodoo deity is seen as:

> Ruisselante de blancheur, Ayda Ouédo s'avance,
> Vêtue des couleurs de l'arc-en ciel.[44]

> [Whiteness streaming, Ayda Ouedo advances,
> dressed in the colours of the rainbow.]

Or his savouring of sexual passion, strongly reminiscent of
Baudelaire's eroticism:

> Ce matin, un parfum de Kénépier en fleurs ainsi
> qu'un bourdonnement d'abeilles, pénétrèrent dans la
> chambre ou je caressais le beau corps ardoisé de
> l'aimée, tout en respirant la senteur de cannelle de sa
> chevelure. O délices![45]

> [This morning, the perfume from the 'Kenepier' in bloom
> as well as a humming of bees, entered the room in
> which I caressed the beautiful slate-coloured body of
> my beloved, while breathing the cinnamon smell of her hair.
> O Pleasures!]

What is also present in this effort to convey a quality of *expérience
vécue*' in verse, is the use of the vocabulary, ritual and mythology of
the voodoo religion and African culture. For instance, 'Behanzin a
Blida' describing the king's exile uses words like 'litham' (an Islamic
veil) and 'foulard de Badagry' (red) which have a specific cultural
context:

Les premières étoiles s'allumèrent dans le litham
du ciel. L'horizon devint de la couleur du foulard de
Badagry. Le royal exilé rêvait toujours.[46]

[The first stars brightened in the veil of the sky.
The horizon became the colour of a Badagry scarf.
The royal exile kept on dreaming.]

This is even more apparent in his poems inspired by possession. A
poem such as 'Hogoun Balindjo' is only accessible through a
knowledge of voodoo ritual. This is assumed as Brouard obliterates
the dividing line between the raw, frenzied exclamations of
possession and literary form:

> . . . une voix étrange, inoubliable, une voix qui
> semblait venir de partout et de nulle part et qui semblait
> les baigner dans un fluide sonore retentit: 'Aroo chainin
> ayo, Hogoun Balindjo, moutchés tchès.
> Ago!
> Ago!
> Marie, Elise
> A bobo, a bobo pour papa Hogoun
> Alors le vieux guerrier nago chanta:
> Houncis yanvalou
> Ohoo! Ohoo![47].

[. . . a strange voice, unforgettable, a voice which came apparently from everywhere and nowhere and which seemed to
wash them in a sonorous liquid rang out: . . .]

The more Brouard retreated from the rational and the formal in art
the fewer were his demands on his own creative imagination. The
hermetic disorder of his voodoo poetry may have served the Griot
belief in the power of the irrational over the black soul. However, it
made for a poetry that simply became either macabre confessions or
recorded ritual:

> A zombi torments incessantly, King Degonde.
> Each night, when sleep weighs on my eyelids,
> crouched on my chest, with his sharp nails,
> he tries to tear out my eyes . . . [48]

The incoherence and triviality of his work after the thirties indicate that Brouard was finally overwhelmed by his own search for the irrational. He desperately denounced the voodoo religion and turned to Catholicism in his late years. The effects of early senility and alcoholism seem apparent in this sudden change of heart. Even as early as 1942 this change is apparent:

> All this Africanism bores me. I can also
> celebrate my white ancestors. Will I ever see
> the light sky of the land of Valois . . . Let's drink
> to the memory of the King of Navarre, of the melodious
> troubadour of the 'lily white queen'[49]

This signalled Brouard's descent into final incoherence and madness but it did not mean the end of Africanism. The very ideas, that Brouard had championed in his less irrational phase, had become quite influential by the 1940s. The then president's collaboration with the Catholic church in its persecution of *Vaudouisants* in the *campagne anti-superstitieuse* as well as the entrenchment of the mulatto élite in the centres of political power made the question of folk culture and the need for racial authenticity a rallying cry for many. By the second half of this decade the influence of Négritude and *Présence Africaine* further strengthened the Africanist position.

Until the end of the Second World War the whole debate about Africanism was manifestly internal and fixed in the context of nationalist feelings expected in post-Occupation Haiti. By the late forties, however, négritude seemed to legitimise the Africanist position with the former's defence and illustration of a homogeneous neo-African culture. Haitian poets are for the first time drawn into the mainstream of the Negritude movement. Historically Haiti was a misfit among the various black colonies clamouring for independence, in the 1940s. It was this 'ache to come into the world as men' (as James Baldwin said) which had become the *raison d'être* of the ideals of negritude among emergent territories. The scars left by the Occupation are perhaps the most plausible explanation for the strong emotional attraction of negritude in the forties. A certain feeling of security could be obtained from this cult of ethnic uniformity:

> Que mon bloc, le bloc noir, un grand rocher noir,
> Domine par sa structure tout le reste du monde[50]

[When my block, the black block, a black rock,
Dominates by its structure the rest of the world]

Jean Brierre uses the same image in 'J'ai frappé le roc de ma négritude' [I struck the rock of my negritude].[51] The sense of solidarity that resulted fulfilled that need for a community which this generation desperately sought:

Tu chantes en anglais mon rêve et ma souffrance,
Au rythme de tes blues dansent mes vieux chagrins,
Et je dis ton angoisse en la langue de France.[52]

[You sing in English of my dream and my suffering,
My old regrets dance to the rhythm of your blues,
And I tell of your anguish in the French language.]

What was envisaged was a pan-African culture that transcended both national and linguistic barriers. *L'âme noire* cultivated and scrutinised so closely by *Les Griots* had now become the driving force behind an international cultural movement. The first evidence of this new ethnic fraternity in the arts was Senghor's *Anthologie de la nouvelle poésie nègre et malgache de langue française* in 1948 which included Haitian poets among its new black voices. Sartre's introduction to this work underlines the uniformity of this neo-African literature, 'From Haiti to Cayenne, one single aim: to express the black soul.'[53]

The ideology of Negritude had the effect of bringing international prestige to the Griot ideology as well as reinforcing certain conservative tendencies within Haitian poetry. Negritude not only concurred with the Griot theory about race, culture and history but actually saw among Haiti's Africanist intellectuals precursors to the Negritude movement. Certainly Price-Mars's *Ainsi parla l'oncle* was cited in this context. In literary terms Negritude meant the revival in Haiti of the ideas of the *génie poétique nègre* which had been around since the thirties. This essentially meant the sacrifice of literary individuality for a racial aesthetic. Consequently the most original literary voice in Haitian Africanism, Carl Brouard, is never championed but replaced by a number of younger poets who adhered more closely to the ideas of négritude. In some cases this meant literary imitation as the most original poetry of Negritude – that of Césaire, Senghor and Damas – was exploited as models for a new black aesthetic. Such a tendency can be seen in Roussan Camille's 'Poison dans le coeur'[54] which appears to be a pastiche of some poems from Damas's *Pigments* (1937). The very first lines evoke Damas's caustic comment on French assimilation:

> Ils m'ont mis un col blanc,
> et des gants
> pour danser la valse . . .
>
> (Camille)

> [They have dressed me in a white collar,
> and gloves
> to dance the waltz . . .]

> J'ai l'impression d'être ridicule . . .
>
> dans leur faux-col
> dans leur monocle
> dans leur melon
>
> (Damas)

> [I think I look ridiculous . . .
> in their collar
> in their monocle
> in their bowler hat.]

This theme far more appropriate to Damas than Camille (because of the former's violent critique of the French presence in Guyana) is also explored by Camille using imagery drawn from *Pigments*. For instance, Damas's use of the elliptical metaphor 'le boulevard de mon ennui', 'l'éternité de leurs boulevards à flics' to convey his feeling of isolation and personal torment is repeated in Camille's 'J'ai traîné ma faiblesse aux boulevards indifférents'.This link becomes even stronger after Césaire's visit to Haiti in 1944. René Bélance, who appears in Senghor's anthology, wrote in 1945 his *Epaule d'ombre* which draws on the fierce visionary qualities and random imagery in Césaire's *Cahier d'un retour au pays natal*:

> Je te dirai tout l'aboi des mornes,
> la plainte des ruisseaux endormis,
> inoculés par les premières aiguilles d'hélium . . .

La terre tournera autour
de nos bras polaires
et nous aurons le vertige des gravitations[55]

[I will tell of baying of the hills,
the whimper of the sleeping streams,
inoculated by the first needles of helium . . .
The earth will revolve
around our polar arms
and we will have the vertigo that comes from gravity.]

The voyage of discovery, central to Césaire's poem, is re-enacted by Bélance. To many Haitian poets of the forties Negritude meant paying literary homage to the original voices of this movement.

Whereas Indigenism can be epitomised by the Romantic insistence on the absolute freedom of the creative imagination, the effect of Negritude was an almost Classical tendency to prescribe a rigid prosody and thematic conformity for black writers. Negritude could be seen in terms of an ethnic Pléiade which legislated literary codes for the black world. Consequently certain fixed, sanctified ideas became the main source of the poetry produced. For instance, a poetic and even religious fiction which originally presented the world as profane and saw poetic utterance as a retrieval of the sacred – as is the case in 'Guinée' – is secularised and given a rigid, ideological and historical interpretation by the Negritude poets. The profane becomes the nightmare of colonial history, a catalogue of injustice and humiliation. The retrieval of the sacred is then seen as the affirmation of one's negritude, of the intuitive values of the black race. The poetry of Negritude is based on this progression – from a statement of loss through the delirium of revolt to the ultimate discovery of a new, untainted self. Each state in this scenario is evoked by a given cluster of images – not the hermetic or esoteric metaphor of Brouard but a new internationally acceptable literary code.

A number of poets too young to be part of the Indigenous movement and who were destined to fade when the generation of 1946 made its strident voice heard, provide us with evidence of the new Negritude aesthetic in Haitian poetry. René Bélance and Jean Fernand Brierre, both chosen by Senghor for his anthology, Roussan Camille and Regnor Bernard reveal the extent to which a shared pattern of symbols was imposed on their various works.

Bernard's *Nègre!!!*[56] explicitly states the dialectic of Negritude by dividing the poem into three sections: *Sur la route de l'Afrique* (stating the loss of an ancestral heritage); *Révolte* (the militant phase of negritude); *Vers la délivrance* (the ultimate vision of liberation).

In their laments over the brutal past of slavery, we see the recurrent use of symbols that are associated with the archetypal *négrier*. The epic suffering of the black race is consistently recalled by either listing the areas of the diaspora where the black race was humiliated or by using symbols of travel or movement. Jean Brierre's *Black Soul*[57] uses such a symbol to launch sections of his long poem, 'Je vous ai rencontré dans les ascenseurs' and 'A bord des paquebots nous nous sommes parlé'. The ultimately confining nature of such a rigid notion of literary Negritude becomes apparent in the repetition of symbols of the *négrier*:

> Mais dans la cale . . . la touffeur incommode fait surgir
> dans la nuit l'odeur d'autres voyages
>
> > (Bélance)[58]

> [But in the hold . . . the suffocating closeness conjures up
> in the night the smell of other journeys]

> . . . car des Négriers sont venus . . .

> et la touffeur voyageuse des cales
>
> > (Bernard)[59]

> [. . . for the slave ships came . . .
> and the closeness of those journeys in the hold.]

> > . . . cet autre voyage
> > de la lointaine Afrique
> > aux îles atlantiques
> > Tout au fond de la cale
> >
> > > (Camille)[60]

> > [. . . that other journey
> > from far-off Africa
> > to the Atlantic isles
> > in the depths of the hold]

A glossary can be compiled for each phase of this literature of international black protest. When the delirium of revenge replaces the pathos of colonial humiliation, a new, more public style emerges filled with images of aggression – 'incendies', 'volcan', 'feu', 'marée' as opposed to the brittle and fragile white world. The early critique of European materialism in Césaire and Senghor is echoed in 1942 by Brierre's 'Ecoute craquer la civilisation'.[61] The final Utopian vision is described in an equally predictable manner using images of the dawn, harvest, the rainbow and light. This rigid decorum created increasing anonymity in style among poets who adhered to it. It is only with the generation of 1946 and the questioning of *Présence Africaine* that a refreshing originality emerges among younger Haitian poets.

Whereas the poetry of Negritude flourished in the forties, it would be erroneous to think that Africanism as a political ideology was equally significant among all Haitian intellectuals. The young generation also had their idol, Roumain (who kept his distance from what he termed *affreux-latin* ideology), and his Marxist teachings as an alternative ideology. Also, the nationalism and concept of a Creole culture envisaged by Haiti's establishment made theories of race appear quite offensive. The latter group, indeed, frequently ridiculed theories of racial authenticity. For example, Sténio Vincent sarcastically described Africanism as empty posturing: 'Paris was their headquarters. But who, among them had ever thought of making a small expedition in some area of the Sudan or the Congo in order to communicate a little with the souls of our distant ancestors.'[62] Dantès Bellegarde is no less scathing in his speculation as to the eventual aim of Africanism: 'in the centre of the Americas, a Dahomean island, with a Bantu culture and a Dahomean religion for the amusement of the Yankee tourists.'[63] However, both Marxists and nationalists failed to understand the growing appeal of these notions within Haiti and certainly underestimated the political implications of such racial theories.

Racial theorising formed a part of all important black literacy movements in the twenties and thirties. But such questions usually became subordinate as the movement evolved. For instance, Langston Hughes dismissed this phase of the Harlem Renaissance quite lightly in 1950: 'Now there may have been certain false values which tended to be overstressed – perhaps the primitivism and that business of the 'color' of negro life was overdone. But that kind of exaggeration is inevitable and I doubt that any real harm was done.'[64] Even Senghor who was responsible for the diffusion of the notion of *l'âme noire* in a later *autocritique* admitted the tendency to racism in the thirties: 'This return to the ancestral past . . . the rejection of European values quickly became scorn . . . racism . . . Innocently by osmosis and as a reaction at the same time we spoke like Hitler and the colonisers, it was blood that mattered to us.'[65] In Haiti these ideas never died. Even Fascist Italy's invasion of black Africa did not motivate them to question their own racial theories.[66] It is in Haiti that negritude or its local equivalent Africanism was taken to its tragic conclusion in the politics of Duvalier.

NOTES

1. Frank Kermode, *The Sense of an Ending* (New York: Oxford University Press, 1967) p. 39.
2. François Duvalier, *Extraits des Oeuvres Ethnographiques* (Port-au-Prince: L'Etat, 1963) pp. 13–14.
3. Maurice Casséus, *Les Griots*, vol. 4, no. 4 and vol. 1, no. 1, Apr.–Sept. 1939, 534.
4. Claude Fabry, *L'âme du lambi* (Port-au-Prince: Telhomme, 1937).
5. *Le Petit Impartial*, no. 87, 13 Oct. 1928.
6. Arthur Holly, *Les Daimons du culte voudo* (Port-au-Prince: Pub. 1918–1919) p. 1.
7. Jacques Roumain, *La proie et l'ombre* (Port-au-Prince; La Presse, 1930) pp. 17–18.
8. Félix Morisseau-Leroy, *Récolte* (Port-au-Prince: Haitiennes, 1946) p. 30.
9. *La Relève*, no. 2, 1 August 1932, 15.
10. *La Relève*, no. 3, 1 Sept. 1932, 10.
11. *La Relève*, no. 12, 1 June 1933, 17.
12. *La Relève*, no. 3, 1 Sept. 1933, 15.
13. René Piquion *Un chant nouveau* (Port-au-Prince: L'Etat, 1940) p. 47.
14. *La Relève*, no. 10, 1 April 1934, 13.
15. *La Relève*, no. 4, 1 Oct. 1933, 16.
16. *Le Petit Impartial*, 9 Sept. 1930.
17. Arthur Bonhomme, *Les tendances d'une génération* (Port-au-Prince: Collection des Griots, 1934) p. 151.
18. Ibid., p. 155.
19. *La Relève*, nos. 2–4, Aug.–Oct. 1938, p. 23.
20. Ibid., p. 24.
21. Dudley Fitts, *Anthology of Contemporary Latin American Poetry* (Norfolk, Va.; New Directions, 1942) p. 290.

22. Charles Pressoir, *Au rythme des coumbites* (Port-au-Prince: La Presse, 1933).
23. Fabry, *L'âme du lambi*.
24. Fitts, *Anthology of Contemporary Latin American Poetry*, p. 29.
25. Léon Laleau, 'Les moins de trente', *La Relève*, no. 1, 1 July 1933, 23.
26. Léon Laleau, *Ondes Courtes* (Port-au-Prince: L'Etat, 1933).
27. Léon Laleau, *Musique nègre* (Port-au-Prince: Indigène, 1931).
28. S. Senghor, *Anthologie de la nouvelle poésie nègre et malgache de langue française* (Paris: Presses Universitaires de France, 1969) p. xix.
29. Bonhomme, *Les tendances d'une génération*, p. 6.
30. François Duvalier (ed.), *Eléments d'une doctrine* (Port-au-Prince: Oeuvres Essentielles, 1966) p. 326.
31. *L'Action Nationale*, no. 1350, 28 July 1936.
32. *Les Griots*, vol. 1, no. 1, July–Sept. 1938, 17.
33. Duvalier et Denis, 'L'essentiel de la doctrine des griots', *Les Griots*, vol. 2, no. 2, Oct.–Dec. 1938, 153.
34. Duvalier, 'Psychologie éthnique et historique', *Eléments d'une doctrine*, p. 158.
35. Duvalier et Denis, 'La civilisation haitienne', *Eléments d'une doctrine*, p. 203.
36. *Les Griots*, vol. 2, no. 2, Oct.–Dec. 1938, 155.
37. Carl Brouard, 'Mes entretiens avec Ariste', *Oedipe*, 10 Dec. 1931.
38. Ibid.
39. Carl Brouard, *Pages retrouvées* (Port-au-Prince: Panorama, 1963) p. 126.
40. Ibid., p. 16.
41. Ibid., p. 24.
42. *Les Griots*, vol. 3, no. 3, Jan.–Mar. 1939, 334.
43. *Libre Tribune*, 31 July 1931.
44. *Les Griots*, vol. 2, no. 1, July–Sept. 1938, 18.
45. *Action Nationale*, 4 Apr. 1935.
46. *Libre Tribune*, 22 May 1931.
47. *Libre Tribune*, 30 Dec. 1931.
48. *Action Nationale*, 8 Apr. 1937.
49. *Haiti-Journal*, 3 Feb. 1942.
50. Tony Duchemin, 'Le cri du nègre', *Optique*, no. 16, June 1955, 49.
51. Jean Brierre, 'En tombent les murailles de Chine', collected in Maurice Lubin's *L'Afrique dans la poésie haitienne* (Port-au-Prince; Panorama, 1965) p. 80.
52. Jean Brierre, *Gerbe pour deux amis* (Port-au-Prince: Henri Deschamps, 1945) p. 20.
53. Senghor, *Anthologie de la nouvelle poésie nègre et malgache*, p. xv.
54. Roussan Camille, *Assaut à la nuit* (Port-au-Prince: L'Etat, 1940).
55. Senghor, *Anthologie de la nouvelle poésie nègre et malgache*, p. 132.
56. Regnor Bernard, *Nègre!!!* (Port-au-Prince: Telhomme, 1945).
57. Jean Brierre, *Black Soul* (Havana: Lex, 1947).
58. René Bélance, *Luminaires* (Port-au-Prince: Morissett, 1941) pp. 21–2.
59. Bernard, 'Ecroulement' in *Nègre!!!*
60. Camille, 'Soutiers nègres', in *Assaut à la nuit*.
61. *Haiti-Journal*, édition speciale de Noël, 1945, 43.
62. Sténio Vincent, *En posant les jalons* (Port-au-Prince: L'Etat, 1939) pp. 153–4.
63. Dantès Bellegarde, *Haiti et ses problèmes* (Montreal: Valiquette, 1941) p. 17.

64. Langston Hughes, 'Some Practical Observations', *Phylon*, vol. xi, no. 4, 1950, 307.

65. Quoted in Thomas Melone's *De la négritude dans la littérature négro-africaine* (Paris: Présence Africaine, 1962) p. 37.

66. For a good discussion of Griot ideology cf. David Nicholls 'Ideology and Political Protest in Haiti', *Journal of Contemporary History*, vol. 9, no. 4, 1974.

5 Jacques Roumain: The Marxist Counterpoint

> ...il y a deux hommes en chacun de nous. Auprès du sportsman que je vous ai montré, exubérant de vie, il y a en moi un côté mélancolique. Ces deux hommes, dans mes actes, je les sens se heurter.
>
> *Jacques Roumain*

In the ideological ferment of the post-Occupation period it is tempting to see Jacques Roumain as simply an earnest doctrinaire Marxist whose beliefs provided an antidote to the excesses of Africanist ideology. Naturally there is much evidence to support such a view of Roumain's role in the thirties. Ever since he founded the Haitian Communist Party in 1934 and published the first Marxist critique of Haitian society *L'Analyse Schématique* in the same year, his life was marked by an unswerving commitment to this ideology – a commitment that would influence almost every decision made by Roumain until his untimely death in 1944. It explains his imprisonment and later exile in 1936, his passionate denunciation of Fascism during the Spanish Civil War, his friendship with Langston Hughes and Nicolas Guillen and ironically enough his decision to return to Haiti under Lescot's reactionary régime in 1941 (because of the latter's strong anti-Fascist stand during the Second World War).

Marxism because of its materialist and relativist explanations for social and cultural phenomena allowed Roumain to rethink and challenge many of the received ideas of his generation. It certainly provided him with the means for refuting the theories of racial determinism favoured by Griot ideology. He came closest among his contemporaries to seeing Haiti's racial tensions in their proper perspective – as simply 'l'expression sentimentale de la lutte de classes'. The same lucidity is apparent in his analyses of the voodoo religion, the Catholic Church, the peasantry and the class from which he came, the Haitian elite.

However, a closer scrutiny of Roumain's career disturbs this neat political scenario. Roumain in many ways proves to be a para-doxical figure, whose relation to orthodox Marxism as well as the ethno-cultural position of the Griot movement was a complex one. For instance, the tendency to see radical left and extreme right in Haiti as diametrically opposed can easily obscure the fact that both these positions share the same ideological beginnings in Haiti. In fact, there is little to distinguish Roumain from his contemporaries in the Occupation period in that they all shared the same anti-establishment sentiments, aggressive populism and fierce national-ism that characterised the late twenties and early thirties. Roumain's blind nationalism in this period led to an anti-rational and xenophobic *prise de position* as is evident in an article such as 'L'éloge du fanatisme' published in *Le Petit Impartial* In 1928. It shows the extent to which Roumain was as much a Maurassian at this time as the later devotees of ethnic and cultural authen-ticity.

To this must be added the fact Roumain is at his least convincing in his attempts to follow an orthodox Marxist line in his public pronouncements on the writer's role in society. His prescription for literary engagement presents the writer as an activist whose craft is harnessed to an ideological position. In Roumain's own words he simply reflects 'the complexity of the dialectic of social relations, of contradictions and antagonisms of the economic and political structure of a society at a given period'.[1] However this kind of anonymous rhetoric is not reflected in most of Roumain's writing where questions of form and the status of the individual imagination are major preoccupations. His concern with the individual will and the quest for spiritual fulfilment show the extent to which he was very much a Romantic individualist rather than an ideologue whose main interest was conformity to Marxist ideals. It was really his strong moral conscience that drove him to the secular creed of Marxism. He was not the only writer to feel that the moral truth of Marxism represented the will of History itself but to have great difficulty with the regimentation that was demanded. Ultimately Roumain emerges as a modern artist concerned with the fate of the creative imagination in a world of broken continuities.

This pattern of political activism which coexists uneasily with deep poetic longings, so entrenched as to appear at times almost independent of political intention, is evident throughout Roumain's career. This is first apparent on Roumain's return to Haiti in 1927, after completing his education in Europe. His activities in the nationalist movement at the time point to the existence of these two very different areas of interest. The passionate volubility of his early political journalism stands in marked contrast to much of the verse he published in *La Revue Indigène*, from which the sense of political urgency found in his political propaganda is absent. For instance, his articles in *Le Petit Impartial* (1927–32) consisted of numerous direct attacks on the treachery of the Catholic Church and the Haitian elite and a glorification of the non-conformity of the young and wild faith in the revolutionary potential of the Haitian masses. This led to a celebration of the ideal of violent revolt in a language not far removed from blank verse: 'Splendid epic struggle. O magnificent adventure to feel oneself surrounded by enemies and to charge their closed ranks and to emerge bloody and victorious.'[2]

This fiery rhetoric was only occasionally echoed, however, in his verse. The only poem that fully incorporates such a violent *prise de position* is *Appel* with its Nietzschean invocations (cf. page 69). For the most part Roumain's poetry published in *La Trouée* and *La Revue Indigène* in the 1920s was ill-defined ideologically. They could only be seen as 'political' in that they obviously responded to Roumain's aversion for the erudite high culture of the past in which literary creation became simply an 'occupation des pédants'. These early poems can thus be seen as products of his general anti-establishment position at the time, in that, in their understated way, they eschewed the ornate and rigid forms characteristic of the most affected nineteenth century verse. Yet, essentially, these poems present us with a sober, introspective Roumain quite unlike the image of a vengeful *enfant terrible* projected in his strident prose. They are mostly mood poems which give a sharp and usually brief impression of melancholy or quick snatches of landscape. This quiet melancholy pervades much of his early writing. A brief comparison of the poem 'Calme' and a later short story 'Fragment d'une Confession' shows the extent to which this mood was cultivated:

> Le soleil de minuit
> de ma lampe. Le temps qui fuit
> n'atteint pas ma quiétude . . .

Ma table est une île lumineuse
dans la nuit noire de la silencieuse
nuit . . .[3]

[The midnight sun
of my lamp. The passing time
has no effect on my serenity . . .
My table is a luminous island
in the blackness of the silent
night . . .]

The intimate monologue of the later short story reworks the same
theme of loneliness using a similar contrast of the light and the dark:

la fenêtre ne laisse pénétrer que la nuit, effarouchée à peine par la
lampe timide autour de laquelle elle remue comme un sombre
papillon.
    Me voici dans mon île déserte: ce plat, pale rocher de la table,
tout entouré du silence et de l'ombre[4]

[the window only allows the night to enter, hardly frightened by
the timid lamp around which it moves like a dark butterfly.
    Here I am on my desert island: this flat, pale rock of the table,
surrounded by silence and shadow]

Perhaps this early writing provides us with an insight into the
underside of a public radical Roumain. This seems most obviously
so in the occasional departure from *spleen* poems – the poems that
deal with the problem of the individual sensibility in a hostile,
uncomprehending world. It is the image of the Romantic individualist that prevails in the poems 'Le Chant de l'homme' and
'La danse du poète clown'. The theme of both these poems is the
clash between an unheeding world and the poetic consciousness –
with the latter predictably the loser:

Ainsi
vers vous je suis venu
Avec mon grand coeur nu
et rouge, et mes bras lourds
de brassées d'amour . . .
Et vos bras vers

moi se sont tendus très ouverts
et vos poings durs
durement ont frappé ma face.[5]

[So
I came to you
With my generous heart bared
and red, and my arms heavy
with armfuls of love . . .
And your arms towards
me were stretched out
and your hard fists
struck me savagely on the face.]

The nature of the confrontation is more precisely indicated in 'La danse du poète clown'. The poet rejected by his audience exacts his quiet revenge – a pure, fragile figure in a crass, hostile world:

Bondis parmi eux et danse
Avec tes jambes fines et ton coeur triste.
Danse tout autour de la piste:
aerien, mu – et lance
à leur haine l'injure
de ton sourire.[6]

[Leap into their midst and dance
with your fine legs and your sad heart
Dance around the floor:
light, naked – and fiercely respond
to their hatred with the insolence
of your smile.]

The problem is posed in terms of this deeply felt confrontation. Two possible ways of resolving the conflict are suggested in Roumain's verse. The choice was to be either the retreat into the hallowed world of the creative imagination as is suggested in the poem 'Guinée' (cf. pp. 106–7) or reach beyond this private world and yield to the demands of one's moral conscience whatever the consequences. The poem 'Miragoane' cleverly presents the latter solution to the artist's dilemma:

La chaleur de mille vies intenses
Monte brutale vers moi. Lourd
contre mon coeur, un coeur immense
bat . . .
– Là-bas, invincible, la mer
doit.[7]

[The warmth of a thousand intense lives
rises brutally towards me. Heavy against my heart, an
enormous heart
beats . . .
– Over there, invincible, the sea sleeps.]

The last line adds a note of fatalism not easily associated with the
Utopian impulse evident in Roumain's public pronouncements. It
is 'Miragoane', however, that most persuasively describes the
nature of Roumain's engagement and the pulling together of the
poet and revolutionary in him. The sentiments of this poem echo
throughout the short stories of the early period which invariably
deal with the same kind of moral crisis.

It is Marxism that attracts the political activist in Roumain in
1934 and the prelude to this conversion can be seen in the
unmistakeable self-scrutiny and dissatisfaction with the provincialism and pretensions of the mulatto élite found in two early
collections of short stories, *La proie et l'ombre* (1930) and *Les Fantoches*
(1931). Roumain's irritation with the narrow and parasitic world of
the élite evident in these works would only be later confirmed by
Marxist theory. His stories contain numerous caricatures of the
Haitian bourgeoisie. With great relish Roumain reduces his
protagonists to grotesque puppets:

Mme Ballin – 'who wraps her fat yellow like spoilt butter, in
mournful dresses which enormous cameos do not manage to
cheer up. Her head small, bony, monstrously out of proportion
with her huge body'[8]

M. Basile – 'is a perfect example of the kind of "grimaud" which
Haitians call "mulâtre forcé". . . he brings to mind, through his
hesitant gait, unbalanced, his feet too long, too slow for the jerky
movements of his arms, an enormous crustacean.'[9]

These stories show how the theory of indigenism and anti-elite feeling (because of the elite's 'conscious complicity in the Occupation'), had combined to produce a strong critique of urban society. This is even more significant for Haitian literary history in which the tradition of writing about the city is weak.

Yet, it would be a distortion to see these works as simply socio-political satire. The dominant mode is one of irony and the bleak *mise en scène* of the narrative takes us back to concerns initially raised in the early verse. The narrative voice of these works which either take the form of intimate monologues or even edited diaries, is that of a lucid, disabused sensibility but impotent in the face of the *fardeau pesant* of the Haitian milieu. The critique of the mulatto *status quo* is voiced by sensitive young men – Haitian versions of Baudelaire's 'flâneur'. Through these characters Roumain had already begun to assess the true nature of the emotional engagement of those described as 'the young Turks . . . who succumbed to the lure of plush jobs in the corrupt and dictatorial government of Sténio Vincent'.[10] These were the activists of the anti-American movement who Roumain could foresee, would eventually conform to the demands of their society.' Préface à la vie d'un bureaucrate' suggests this ironic capitulation in its very title. 'Propos sans suite' presents us with these scions of wealthy families and their voyeuristic interest in the low life of Port-au-Prince. The coming of daylight only brings a sobering awareness of their sterility, 'useless like these smashed cases, this shattered pottery scattered all over the ground'.[11]

Whereas these early stories reveal Roumain's dissatisfaction with the revolutionary posturing of the radical left of his generation, *La Montagne ensorcelée* (1931) was his response to the increasingly popular notion of *l'âme haitienne*, of the Africanists. Simply embracing the peasantry in the name of cultural authenticity was unsatisfactory to Roumain. This novella could easily have been another example of literary regionalism. Roumain's fellow collaborator in *La Revue Indigène*, Phillippe Thoby-Marcelin, made precisely this choice. His later novels, particularly *Canapé Vert* (1944) and *La Bête de Museau* (1946) were much lauded by the American critic Edmund Wilson, who saw their penchant for the bizarre and sensational as an original presentation of peasant mentality.[12] The peasant world, particularly the supernatural, would be treated differently by Roumain. It is not that this early work always avoids the lurid and melodramatic. In many ways it is heavy-handed when compared with *Gouverneurs de la rosée*. Lines like the following are by no means uncommon in the text, whether it is the grotesque caricature of hate, 'the inside of his mouth is black like an oven – the flame of his tongue can be seen flickering red'[13] or the maudlin sentimentality of:

> At the chosen time, their passionate world is silent in its isolation.
> Nothing disturbs it; all is at rest: the wind is asleep in boughs of the trees and the snake coiled under the dead leaves.
> Their shelter is the violet shadow, their bed the perfumed earth.[14]

The real innovation is that Roumain refused to view the peasant's relation with the supernatural as a literary curiosity.

He avoids this by making a careful choice in the narrative voice of the story and by a clever orchestration of the stark violence of the denouement. The narration of the text is done to a large extent by the collective voice of the community. Roumain avoids a detached third person narration by imperceptibly surrendering narration to the peasants themselves. His introduction of the character Desilus clearly illustrates this shift in narrative voice. It moves from a general tableau of peasant life to the specifies of this lonely peasant's world:

> Aujourd'hui, les hommes sont rentrés des champs pour le repas du soir. Dans chaque cabane, les femmes s'affairent autour des chaudrons . . .
> Desilus, lui, est assis sous les goyaviers. Il se repaît de leurs derniers fruits . . .
> Les jeunes noirs ne sont plus respectueux: ils disent que Desilus a l'esprit dérangé, mais les anciens ne sont pas de cet avis.
> Ainsi Tonton Jean qui est mort l'année dernière . . . répétait souvent que Desilus savait beaucoup de choses. Houng![15]

> [Today, the men have come back from the fields for the evening meal. In each hut, the women are busy around the cauldrons . . .
> Desilus is seated under the guava trees. He is filling himself with the last of these fruit . . .
> The young men are no longer respectful: they say that Desilus is deranged, but the older ones do not think so.
> So Tonton Jean who died last year . . . often repeated that Desilus knew many things. Houng!]

The only precedent for this kind of garrulous realism is Lhérisson's *La Famille des Pitite Caille* which also consciously adopts an oral tradition in the story. The choice of such a narrative view point allows the reader to become an insider in this community rather than the curious voyeur he can so easily be in Marcelin's work.

The denouement sets us straight as to how the author wants us to react to this story of misadventure in a peasant community. The ritual murder of the old woman and her daughter at the end indicates that Roumain saw peasant religion as simply a refuge for the chronic fears of a desolate peasant village. He refused to gloss over the stagnation and impotence that were part of the backward rural society in Haiti. The lingering impression left in the reader's mind is one of human tragedy:

> L'éclair s'abat en sifflant, la tête décollée roule un peu sur l'herbe.
> Tous s'enfuient, sauf Balletroy qui regarde, les yeux vides, sa machette, le cadavre, le cadavre, la machette.[16]

> [The flash slashes down with a whistle, the severed head rolls a little on the grass.
> They all flee, except Balletroy who stares, eyes empty, his machet, the corpse, the corpse, the machet.]

The message becomes even clearer by the time *Gouverneurs de la rosée* is published as there is a similar refusal to glorify the culture of *Fonds rouge* which is also afflicted by chronic impotence. In spite of all this, Price-Mars's introduction sees the work as simply a 'note émouvante de nouveauté', an example of 'une esthétique haitienne'. Roumain's apprehensions go largely unheeded in the 1930s. Such objective scrutiny could have little impact in a society desperately attempting to regain its self-esteem through pride in the indigenous culture.

The late 1930s in Roumain's life are given over to political activism. This is especially true of the period of exile from Haiti, between 1936 and 1941. The important texts of this period are certainly not literary ones. They all represent dutiful applications of Marxist theory to the specifics of Haiti and the black diaspora. However, even if these works are often unoriginal in thought they do explicitly emphasise the difference between Roumain's ideas and those of the mulatto establishment on one hand and the ethnic 'authentics' on the other. They establish more than anything else the capacity of Marxism to avoid the mystification of race and reach beyond the myopic class and colour conflict towards an objective assessment of Haitian society.

Perhaps the most striking feature of Roumain's three ideological essays *L'Analyse Schématique* (1934), *Le Grief de l'homme noir* (1939), and *A propos de la campagne anti-superstitieuse* (1942) is that they all omit the customary reference to the grandeur of the independence struggle or the humiliations of slavery and colonialism. Instead, little time is spent on brooding over the injustice of the colonial past. The following quotation shows clearly that Roumain saw the whole business of slavery as a largely economic phenomenon not a cause for acrimony: 'We will not delay ourselves with the moral side of the matter. That is only really of interest to an individual whose ancestor was a slave.'[17] With this, Roumain closes the subject. Such a document shows a marked contrast with the catalogues of injustice masochistically repeated by the Griot apologists.

The underlying themes in these texts are those of race and religion. Roumain's consistent attitude to these two vexed questions in Haitian society goes back to the orthodox Marxist approach to culture. The Marxist dialectic refutes absolutes and inevitably sees culture in relativist terms – as opposed to the ethnocentric bias of the Africanists, for example. Since culture was conditioned by certain socio-economic circumstances and not an organic process one could appreciate how it manifests itself in terms of religion and racial attitudes. For instance, the voodoo religion was both seen by Roumain as an important manifestation of national culture – specific to Haiti as well as a phenomenon that would disappear if material progress were brought to the Haitian countryside. In his critique of the *campagne anti-superstitieuse* Roumain observes that there is little to be gained by replacing belief in the voodoo gods by the fear of Hell. Voodoo was simply a product of the peasant's conception of the world. If the latter were changed the attitude to religion as a whole would also be transformed:

> We must naturally rid the Haitian masses of the shackles of superstition. But we shall not triumph over their beliefs by threatening them with violence or hell . . . If we wish to change the archaic religious mentality of our peasantry, they must be educated. And one cannot educate them without transforming at the same time their material conditions.[18]

Roumain in these texts also expressed fears as to how the myth of race could be manipulated for political purposes. In Haiti he saw it as 'the mask under which black and mulatto politicians would like to hide the class struggle'. In the southern United States it played the role of 'lightning-rod when the atmosphere is overloaded with the electricity of social tensions'. In the latter case lynching and the myth of white superiority were a means of dividing the American proletariat: 'But the lyncher is himself a victim of the act of lynching. These packs of men unleashed in pursuit of human prey are largely composed of poor whites who live under conditions which are hardly better than those of the blacks.'[19] His remarks on the Haitian situation followed the same pattern and in some ways were rather prophetic. He instinctively distrusted the nationalism of the traditional élite and also felt, as early as 1934, that a black bourgeoisie was equally capable of using racial identification in order to secure power for themselves. It is, perhaps, the earliest recognition of the importance of this group in Haitian society and certainly predicts the later use of theories of racial authenticity for specific political ends: 'The duty of the P.C.H. . . . is to alert the proletariat, the poor 'petite bourgeoisie' and intellectuals to the danger of black middle-class politicians who would like to exploit for their own ends the former's justified anger.'[20]

In this period it is the experience of exile as much as Marxism which exerts an influence on Roumain. His ability to consider the Haitian situation in non-parochial terms but rather in the context of an international system of exploitation results in part from his travels in the late 1930s. His awareness of the racial mystification of Fascism as a terrible threat to human society must have been made more acute by his moral outrage at the Spanish Civil War and the persecution of the Jews in Hitler's Germany. He became the prototype of the exiled Marxist writer that would later be reflected in the experience of Jacques-Stéphen Alexis and René Dépestre. This experience also had a marked effect on his creative writing as a change in scale is apparent in all writing that emerges from these later years. The poem 'Madrid' is our first clue to this shift from the exclusively personal or national concerns of his early work to the broader vision of his last works. The last lines of this tribute to the Spanish people reveal a grand euphoric vision unprecedented in his early writing:

> ici que l'aube s'arrache des lambeaux de la nuit
> que dans l'atroce parturition et l'humble sang

anonyme du paysan et de l'ouvrier
nait le monde où sera effacé du front des hommes
   la flétrissure amère de la seule égalité du désespoir.[21]

[here the dawn tears itself from the tatters of the night
in the horrible birth pains and the humble anonymous blood
   of the peasant and worker
is born the world in which the withered and bitter
   mark of despair shall be effaced from men's brows.]

The Spanish Civil War was an ideal situation for Roumain in that it could allow him to combine his politics with his romantic conception of individual engagement. As Stephen Spender put it, 'this was a war in which the individual still counted. It was in part an anarchist's war, a poet's war.'[22] For this short period the poet and the revolutionary were reconciled.

The last four years of Roumain's life (1941–4) meant an end to his wanderings as an exile and a return to Haiti. This was facilitated by the change of president in Haiti and the anti-Fascist stand taken by the new president, Elie Lescot. By this time Roumain is a writer of international status and certainly the most famous to emerge from the generation of the Occupation. In the comparative quiet of these years Roumain was again able to devote himself to his creative writing. The events of these years show the extent to which Roumain had gone beyond the early iconoclasm of the Occupation years and was now more interested in consolidating early gains than in idealistic revolt and also basically more capable of compromise.

Both his decision to found the Bureau d'Ethnologie (1941) and his later decision to become Lescot's chargé d'affaires in Mexico are characteristic of the later years. In the first instance it seems surprising that it is a Marxist and not a blind devotee of folklore who set up the institution. Roumain saw in this institution the possibility of breaking down traditional prejudices against Haiti's indigenous culture not by impassioned rhetoric this time but by making Haitian ethnology a respectable, scientific discipline. Marxist orthodoxy did not prove an obstacle to his interest in peasant culture. It simply meant that a degree of objectivity could be introduced to the study of the peasantry rather than the racial mystification of the Griot movement which glossed over the squalor of peasant life in the name of ethnic authenticity. His support for Lescot in spite of the latter's conservative regime, again points to the older Roumain's modified revolutionary zeal. This support became even more visible when Lescot appointed him to the Haitian embassy in Mexico. He may have found Roumain a little difficult to handle in Haiti. Roumain's decision to go, however, was influenced by the Communist Party which saw it as good strategy at the time to have prominent Marxists placed in important public positions.

Roumain's literary imagination had also undergone some important changes. The most important of these can be seen in the aesthetic volte-face that his later writing represents. Whereas Roumain's early verse was obviously a product of the modern in poetic styles in that he opted for an immediate and disabused representation of the world and his feelings, his later poetry can be seen as a more conventional, idealised presentation of his subjectivity. The former, private and marginally organised, stand in sharp contrast to the later epic, lyrical offerings of *Bois d'Ebène*, which is aimed to stimulate an international audience rather than shock the local bourgeoisie.

The euphoric humanism and veil of grandeur first seen in 'Madrid' become the dominant mode in *Bois d'Ebène*.[23] The three poems of this collection are given a symbolic unity through the image of the title. Patience, durability, inscrutability of the 'damnés de la terre' are all suggested in the symbol of ebony wood – 'ce masque de silence minéral'. The reification of man is seen in slavery and other forms of exploitation are also suggested by this wood which can be bought and sold on a commercial scale. The versatility of the image also suggests the wider context of universal revolt – the spreading upwards of the flames of a 'forêt de torches funèbres'.

The poems are unified by their utopian impulse and the Marxist imprecations they convey. Roumain, however, chooses a special idiom for each of these political poems. This ranges from the slangy, conversational 'Sales Nègres' to the shock tactics of 'Nouveau Sermon Nègre' which is again different from the lyricism and formal cadences of the title poem 'Bois d'Ebène'. Roumain with his instinctive feel for the poetic – for the lyrical line and the sustained image – is least comfortable with the dramatic monologue of 'Sales Nègres'. A form that Léon Damas masters so well in *Pigments*[24] Roumain finds alien to his sensibility. He is not the first Marxist who, driven by populist sentiment, opts for the least literary form possible for his verse. The guide to meaning in 'Sales Nègres' is not metaphor or prosody but the human voice. From the outset its register carefully avoids literary language:

> Eh bien voilà
> nous autres
> les nègres . . .
>
> nous n'acceptons plus
> c'est simple
> fini . . .
>
> nous n'acceptons plus
> ça vous étonne
> de dire: oui missié   (p. 241)
>
> [Well here we are
> the niggers . . .
> we no longer accept
> it's simple
> all over . . .
> we no longer accept
> that surprises you
> to say: yes massa]

The constant repetition of 'nègres', 'niggers', 'sales nègres' in the poem not only ensures that the message is driven home but serves as a kind of incantation which leads to the violent apocalypse at the end. However, whereas oral poetry is so effectively manipulated for protest by Damas, Roumain's poem seems longwinded and loosely constructed.

'Nouveau Sermon Nègre' exploits the symbol of Christ's suffering and the traditional Christian message of acceptance and submission in his declamation of the new revolutionary creed of the oppressed. The poem is constructed around a series of contrasting metaphors – 'Ils ont blanchi sa face noire sous le crachat de leur mépris glacé'. A desecrated Christ serves the materialistic needs of those who oppress. Roumain announces a new world, pure and hallowed, which will replace the tainted world of injustice. One of the more dramatic images of the poem predicts this transition and indicates Roumain's ability to invest an image with emotional force:

> Notre révolte s'éleve comme le cri de l'oiseau de tempête
> au-dessus du clapotement pourri des marécages . . .(p. 238)

[Our revolt rises like the cry of the storm bird
over the rotting squelch of the swamps . . .]

Roumain did object to the world of private fantasy of the Surrealists, 'balanced between the traditional poles of eroticism and dream'.[25] He, however, is indebted to them for the way in which they allowed poetic imagery to be set free.

It is the title poem which most obviously reveals Roumain's real resources as a lyrical poet of some standing. Dated 1939, it is more than a revolutionary anthem for the oppressed of the world. It is a poem of exile and dislocation – seen in terms of private experience, the black diaspora and the fate of modern man. It is a successful combination of his didactic urges and the intimate poetic voice of his early years. The most moving poem in the collection, 'Bois d'Ebène', has a quality of lived experience which is absent in the anonymous didacticism of the other two pieces. It is unique in this collection in its variations of mood as it moves from contemplation to denial towards the final visionary dawn.

The key to 'Bois d'Ebène' is, perhaps, the early folk poem 'Guinée' which represents the artist's retrieval of a state of grace. The same theme informs 'Bois d'Ebène' which can almost be seen as a sequel to the early poem. 'Bois d'Ebène' begins with man's fall from this hallowed state. The whole poem can be interpreted as a re-enactment of the Fall in secular terms. This is most obviously reflected in the theme of exile which dominates the poem and is presented in a series of images contrasting the sacred pastoral past with the profane industrial present. The poem finds Roumain accepting the Marxist notion of the solidarity of the proletariat 'reniant l'antique maléfice des tabous de sang' but rejecting a rootless materialistic present for a world of spirituality where a state of grace can be restored.

The prelude to the poem (frequently omitted in anthologies which emphasise the more ideological features of the poem) establishes the crucial break with the pastoral serenity of the past. The use of 'pluvieux', 'morne', 'brume', and 'chant funèbre' establishes a bleak *mise en scène* before departure is made explicit – 'tu partiras/ abandonnant ton village'. The threat of future exile and rootlessness is suggested by the 'foyer éteint'. The exile is never located specifically in his private experience or in ideological terms. The use of the second person singular and the lack of explicit description of landscape make the act of leaving atemporal, remote and charged with universal significance. The emotional impact of this loss and the threat of the strange odyssey ahead can almost be seen as a re-enactment of the Fall. Images of a fleeting world gradually receding suggest both profoundly felt anguish and the larger, metaphysical loss:

> la trace de tes pas dans ses sables
> le reflet d'un songe au fond du puits . . .
>
> un appel fêlé dans les herbages   (pp. 229–230)

> [the mark of your footprints in the sand
> the reflection of a dream at the bottom of the well . . .
> a broken cry across the meadows]

This evocation of the nostalgia of exile and irretrievable loss is given an explicit historical context as the poem proceeds. The specific reality of the slave trade and on a wider scale man's encounter with a profane, materialistic world are suggested by the images of a grotesque, disorienting culture which replace the fragile echoes of pastoral serenity:

> Cheminées d'usines
> palmistes decapitées d'un feuillage de fumée   (p. 230)

> [Factory chimneys
> palm-trees decapitated by a foliage of smoke]

> maigres branchages d'ombre enchaînés de soleil
> des bras implorant nos dieux.   (p. 231)

> [thin branches of shadow chained by sunlight
> hands beseeching our gods.]

The encounter of two different cultures – the pastoral and the industrial, the poetic and the materialistic – is suggested by the dislocation of natural imagery to evoke a hostile, de-humanising universe – decapitated palm trees and withered branches of arms chained by sunlight. It all comes together in the compressed imagery of:

vingt-cinq mille traverses de Bois-d'Ebène
Sur les rails du Congo-Océan   (p. 231)

[Twenty five thousand sleepers of ebony
on the rails of the Congo-Ocean.]

The 'traverses de Bois-d'Ebène' suggest human railway sleepers which permit an industrial culture to function. 'Congo-Océan' introduces the anonymous bodies of slaves stacked below decks for crossing the Middle Passage.

Roumain situates the human drama just outside the context of the revolt of negritude. His anger is not racially directed. He is articulating man's fragility in the face of the dehumanising forces of modern industrial culture. The frequently quoted 'Afrique j'ai gardé ta mémoire' is more than nostalgia for an ancestral, ethnic past. It is, rather, the desperate identification with the hallowed past lost to the exile. The 'POURTANT' in bold letters that follows simply makes this explicit. By situating his protest in broad universal terms Roumain sharply defines the difference between his position and that of Africanist ideology. The latter also saw modern materialism as incompatible with man's true needs but situates this conflict in terms of an opposition between European materialism and the authentic black soul.

The final movement of the poem centres on a radical shift in mood as strident revolt against this world that makes things of men, asserts itself. Roumain becomes the herald of the future Apocalypse that will put an end to this world. Shades of the *enfant terrible* of the Occupation years emerge as Roumain forsees the end of an epic struggle which involves all men. The 'foyer éteint' of the prelude is rekindled in the vision of fraternity that Roumain now articulates. The first person plural frequently repeated make this new solidarity emphatic:

Nous rebatirons . . .
[We will rebuild . . .]

nous foulons les décombres de nos solitudes . . .
[We trample underfoot the wreckage of our lonely lives . . .]

nous arrachons au ravin sa chevelure . . .
[we tear the hair from the ravine . . .]

nous briserons la mâchoire des volcans . . .
[we shall break the jaws of volcanoes . . .]

nous proclamons l'unité de la souffrance . . .
[we proclaim the unity of suffering]   (pp. 234–5)

The bleak, misty world of the beginning now yields to a world restored in a blaze of light. This image which underlines the renascence of the end of 'Bois d'Ebène' in 1939 was also destined to evoke the visionary climax of Roumain's last completed work – *Gouverneurs de la rosée:*

> et la plaine sera l'esplanade de l'aurore
> où rassembler nos forces ecartelées.   (p. 234)
>
> [and the plain will be the esplanade of dawn
> where our scattered forces can reassemble.]

This is echoed in the final 'coumbite' at dawn in his later novel: 'La plaine était couchée a leurs pieds dans l'embrasement de midi . . . La savane s'étendait comme une esplanade de lumière violente.'[26] [The plain lay at their feet in the burning heat of noon . . . The savanna spread itself like an esplanade of violent light.]

The humanitarian ideal and open structure of these images show how far Roumain had moved away from the narrow nationalism of his early years. Haiti's encounter with American materialism; the African's rootlessness in a disorienting, exploitative world; the poet culturally unhoused, threatened by sterility of the modern world, are all phases of the same process. This conviction becomes the point of departure for *Gouverneurs de la rosée* which re-states the basic theme raised in 'Bois d'Ebène'.

The following observations on Roumain's epic peasant novel have one feature in common. The critics Edmund Wilson and Janheinz Jahn simply see the work as a product of the author's Marxist convictions. Wilson pronounces it, 'the inevitable Communist novel that is turned out in every country in compliance with the Kremlin's prescription'.[27] Jahn does not see the novel as a piece of unoriginal hack writing but he is no less insistent on the ideological – to the extent of seeing Richard Wright's influence in the text: 'Jacques Roumain's world success, *Gouverneurs de la rosée,* which was influenced by Richard Wright lays new stress on the social side'.[28] It is difficult to see how the link with Wright could be proven since there is evidence that Roumain began writing this novel from the late thirties.[29] Furthermore, Wright's Marxist novel *Native Son* (1940) presents the main character as a statistic of white injustice, a twisted product of the inescapable, inhibiting presence of the white world. Manuel in Roumain's novel is at least a more human and positive response to the violations of the past and apparent despair of the present.

Roumain called himself a Marxist but never undervalued prose the way an orthodox Marxist would. He did not see the role of prose fiction in purely propagandist terms or as an adjunct to sociological inquiry. From what we have seen so far, literature meant for him an assertion of the individual imagination before anything else. By the time we come to *Gouverneurs de la rosée* (which was completed in Mexico in 1944) his aesthetic vision was so assured as to exist almost independently of political and moral intention.

The novel's Marxism is both explicit yet curiously unsatisfactory when examined closely. The title of the novel suggests in rather lyrical terms one of the basic beliefs of Marxism – that man is master of his own fate. This, indeed, is the kind of enlightenment that Manuel brings to the peasants of Fonds Rouge who have resigned themselves to their desolation. Manuel frequently attacks the fatalism and excessive dependence on the supernatural in his community:

> le sang d'un coq ou d'un cabri ne peut faire virer les saisons, changer la course des nuages et les gonfler d'eau comme des vessies . . . j'ai appris que ce qui compte . . . c'est la rébellion et la connaissance que l'homme est le boulanger de la vie. (p. 96)

> [the blood from a rooster or a goat cannot change the seasons, alter the course of the clouds and fill them with water like bladders . . . I have learnt that what counts . . . is rebellion and the knowledge that man is the baker of life.]

The phrase 'le boulanger de la vie' seems to echo the title of the novel but in socio-political terms. Manuel also teaches the solidarity of the oppressed in the face of the fragmentation that exists in Fonds Rouge. A feud has divided them for years but Manuel presents them with a vision of fraternity that will create a new order for all men.

Again the title is versatile enough to include this idea of brotherhood:

> nous ne savons pas encore que nous sommes une force, une seule force: tous les habitants, tous les nègres des plaines et des mornes réunis . . . Un jour . . . nous ferons l'assemblée générale des gouverneurs de la rosée.   (p. 80)

> [we do not yet realise that we are a force, a single force: all the villagers, all the men of the plains and hills reunited . . . One day . . . we will become the assembled multitude of the masters of the dew.]

The title of the novel enables Roumain to express his ideas on the impotence of folk religion and the need for a collective *prise de conscience* in Haiti. Manuel, his *porte-parole'*, is to this extent a progressive, improving force in his community – quite distinct from the characters of Roumain's early fiction, paralysed by the impotence felt in their bleak, marginal world.

However, Manuel cannot be seen as one's ideal proletarian hero. From the outset it is apparent that Fonds Rouge is a closed world and that it is difficult to see it as a universal model for proletarian revolt. The solution to Manuel's problem is implicit in the conditions that already exist – water is available, there is a fund of goodwill for Manuel on both sides and the memory of collective labour is still alive in the minds of the villagers. Manuel makes no attempt to construe his acts in larger terms. He wishes simply to settle in the village with Annaise as his wife. This leaves the question of the rapacious Hilarion unresolved at the end. Manuel's fragile achievement is regarded as a threat by the *chef de section*: 'Je ferais des recouvrements et je mettrais ma part de côté. On verra. (Oui, on verra si les habitants se laisseront faire).' (p. 215) [I will get my share and lay it aside. We shall see. (Yes, we will see if the peasants allow this to happen).] An awkward denouement, a hero with modest conventional ambitions, make the Socialist Realism of the text a little less than ideal.

A purely ideological interpretation of the text becomes even more difficult because of the form Roumain has chosen to use in telling his story. The world of the novel is not an objective and rational one of a *roman à thèse*. Roumain has shifted away from the causal, dated world of ideology to present a story that has the timelessness and inevitability of myth. For instance, Manuel's death is predicted very early in the novel during a voodoo ceremony (p. 75). It is Delira who reacts to this premonition of disaster. Later in the novel when Manuel is about to set out on his fateful journey, the god Ogoun offers a similar warning:

C'est l'image de Saint-Jacques et en même temps·c'est Ogoun, le dieu dahoméen. Il a l'air farouche avec sa barbe herissée, son sabre brandi, et la flamme lèche le bariolage rouge de son vêtement: on dirait du sang frais.   (p. 169)

[It is a picture of St James and at the same time it is Ogoun, the Dahomean god. He has a savage look, with his bristly beard, his brandished sabre and the flame licks the red patches on his clothing: one would think it was fresh blood.]

These discreet warnings have a lot to do with identifying the narrative voice of the novel. Like *La Montagne ensorcelée* it is the nervous voice of the community that is apparent here. This impression of a mythical world makes it difficult to conceive of Manuel except in terms of a figure who is larger than life – 'auréolé de mystères et de légendes'. A daring Prometheus who is punished for his act or a black Christ who sacrifices himself to redeem all men.

It is also difficult to accept the novel exclusively as a political case history because of Roumain's conscious presentation of the world in poetico-religious terms. In *Gouverneurs de la rosée* the environment is not seen in purely objective terms, a potential resource to be exploited by man. Roumain presents us, instead, with an archetypal vision of the relationship between man and nature.[30] His hero proclaims the uselessness of both Christianity and voodoo in the text but Manuel's attitude to the landscape is akin to the religious. As the 'dew' of the title suggests we are back to an elemental, sensuous conception of nature which asserts the stereotype of pastoral serenity. The drought does not simply result from peasant ignorance. It is caused because the land has been 'betrayed'. The land is frequently referred to as a woman ravaged – 'ses flancs mis à nu', 'sa peau maigre', 'l'eau tarie depuis les entrailles'. The dream of irrigating the fields of Fonds Rouge is more than just the deserved reward for collective effort. It is the restoration of that primal relationship between man and earth.

Il voyait en songe, l'eau courante dans les canaux comme un réseau de veines charriant la vie jusqu'au profond de la terre . . . toute cette terre roussie, recrépie aux couleurs de la verdure. (p. 53)

[He saw in his dream, the water flowing in the canals like a network of veins bearing life to the depths of the earth . . . this reddened earth, covered again with verdure.]

Man's fall from this world forms the prelude to 'Bois d'Ebène'. His reintegration into it is the subject of *Gouverneurs de la rosée*. The vague ancestral home lost to the wanderer in Roumain's epic poem is rediscovered in Manuel's luxuriant fantasy.

In many ways *Gouverneurs de la rosée* is a sequel to Roumain's first exploration of this genre in *La Montagne ensorcelée*. Technically that early novella depended for its effect on the documentary style promoted by the Indigenous movement. The almost audible narrative voice of this work is again present in the effect of first person narration created by the *style parlé* of the later text. The feel for authentic details of Haitian popular culture is also present in the gritty realism of *Gouverneurs de la rosée*. Such untranslatable terms as 'poule bassette' and the *double entendre* of 'je demande la permission pour une petite effronterie' have a special meaning for a creole-speaking audience.[31] The descriptions of peasant activities in *La Montagne ensorcelée* are almost a rehearsal for the extended versions that appear in the later novel. This is particularly apparent in the voodoo ceremony that occurs in both works. It is the same eye for dramatic detail and the care of the interested ethnologist that are revealed in this description of peasant ritual.

A comparison with the earlier work also permits us to understand clearly where they differ. Both prose works contain scenes in which the love of the main character is consummated. In the early novella an awkward and sometimes clichéd sentimentality intrudes: 'Une peur exquise, une faiblesse soudaine . . . Elle descend un abîme vertigineux qui se creuse en elle, une fleuve qui puise sa source dans sa chair'.[32] [An exquisite fear, a sudden weakness . . . She descends into a whirling chasm, which opens in her, a river which finds its source in her flesh.] The language of this sexual union is marked by a lyricism which simply affirms the humanness of the characters and the nature of the idyll. In *Gouverneurs de la rosée* a similar act is described in terms that avoid the sentimentality of the former.

Roumain's synthesising poetic vision in the later novel construes this union in primal terms – as a metaphor of fecundity. The figure of Annaise is extended to represent the earth itself and their union a rite of fertility: 'Elle était étendue sur la terre et la rumeur profonde de l'eau charriait en elle une voix qui était le tumulte de son sang. Elle ne se défendit pas.' (p. 133) [She was stretched out on the earth and the deep rumble of the water echoed within her a voice which the tumult of her own blood. She did not resist.] This is extended to a vision of an organic relationship between man and his world that is echoed in Bienaimé's vision of the coumbite. The prose poetry of this fantasy simply echoes the same image of the land yielding to man's sexual force:

> D'un seul coup les houes s'abattaient avec un choc
> sourd, attaquant le pelage malsain de la terre.
> – Femme-la dit, mouché pinga
> ou touché mouin, pinga-eh . . .[33]

Et le soleil soudain était là. Il moussait comme une écume de rosée sur le champ d'herbes . . . Plus caressant et chaud qu'un duvet de poussin sur le dos rond du morne . . . Ces hommes noirs te saluent d'un balancement de houes qui arrache du ciel de vives échardes de lumière. (p. 18)

[The hoes fell with a single dull thud, attacking the rough skin of the earth. – The woman said, take care you're touching me, take care. . . . And suddenly the sun was there. It sparkled like a dewy foam across the fields of grass . . . with the warm caress of down on the round back of the hill . . . These black men greet you with a swirl of hoes which snatches from the sky sharp flashes of light.]

This scene seems charged with the resonances of an erotic encounter – an elemental ritual of fertility that is finally realised by the end of the novel. The land is irrigated and Annaise becomes pregnant.

This preoccupation with spiritual fulfilment and rebirth, which has been glimpsed before in Roumain's works, brings to *Gouverneurs de la rosée* a formal symmetry of classical proportions. The extended poetic allegory of the novel creates clusters of opposing symbols which are either related to barrenness or regeneration. The dew is the key to the whole system of imagery – associated with water, dawn and a new beginning it stands in opposition to the dust, dark metaphors of a fragmented, apathetic world. At the end the relationship between the water, light and fertility is caught in the image of water as a 'mince lame d'argent' irrigating the fields.

The novel's importance is ultimately literary. Roumain had begun to see the creative imagination as providing an insight into human experience that ideology could not afford. What he began to explore in *Gouverneurs de la rosée* was not simply the nightmare of the cycle of injustice in Haitian history – a horror of the past enshrined in Griot poetics. He preferred to elaborate a vision of survival, an aesthetic of renascence in his contemplation of his native land. This is graphically presented in the image of old Delira's hand plunged into the dust at the beginning but finally resting on Annaises's swollen abdomen, where new life is stirring. Roumain's work easily transcends the vision of despair so frequently found in the Caribbean novel of protest and is perhaps the first to present the Haitian and, by analogy, Caribbean landscape with this sense of elation and poetic wonder. This concept is later explored much more intensely in the theories of 'Marvellous Realism' developed by Roumain's literary successor Jacques-Stéphen Alexis. As a writer whose life was marked by the solitude and rootlessness of exile and who was aware of the mindless carnage of the Second World War, Roumain obviously made a great emotional investment in this Adamic vision of Caribbean man repossessing and rooted in his landscape.

One of the most pervasive themes in modern literature is that of alienation and exile. The frequently articulated need for *enracinement* simply makes this fact more emphatic. Many modern writers constantly feel the need to elaborate a myth of belonging, an imaginative strategy created precisely because of their status of being culturally unhoused. Roumain is the first Haitian to belong to this band of cultural and political refugees. In this sense, Roumain as well as the poets of Negritude – Césaire, Senghor and Damas – form part of an international community of literary *déracinés* that encompasses such diverse talents as the Argentinian Borges, the Irish Beckett and the Russian Nabokov.

Consequently, Roumain's literary legacy cannot be assessed in exclusively local terms. Naturally, he had a formative influence on future generations of Haitian writers in very much the same way that the Occupation has exerted a crucial influence on his own generation. Yet, the simple fact is that *Gouverneurs de la rosée* has been translated into more than a dozen languages, gone through nine editions with Editeurs Français Réunis and inspired plays and films. Consequently, Roumain has cast a long shadow similar to the effect created by Césaire, Damas and Senghor (as was seen in the previous chapter). Roumain's novel serves as a model for those who wished either to interpret the experience of a small community in larger ideological and Messianic terms or write a novel of homecoming. Such a tribute was paid to Roumain by the Senegalese Marxist Sembene Ousmane on whom Roumain had a marked influence.

The novel *O pays, mon beau peuple*, originally published in 1957 is Ousmane's second novel and deals with the attempts of the main protagonist to save his community by courageously challenging established practices and implanting Marxist ideals. It is a work that shows obvious traces of Roumain's novel. The fact that Ousmane had not yet evolved an original literary voice and was of the same ideological persuasion predisposed him to borrowing from his literary precursor. As in *Gouverneurs de la rosée*, one of his major preoccupations was that of creating a character integrated into his community but with progressive ideas. Like Manuel, Faye is rooted in his community and overwhelmed by the 'beauté massive de la végétation'. The following epiphany to the Casamance is not uncommon in the text and obviously draws on Roumain's lyrical descriptions of Haitian landscape: 'Ah how he loved the earth, this earth, his earth . . . He compared it to a woman loving and loved. He traced the hair of her trees; the flesh of her land; the bones of her stones . . .'³³ Faye also opposes the passivity of the elders in his community and is eventually killed for his daring. His legacy is a co-operative farm and the promise of hope conveyed by his wife's pregnancy. In this novel Ousmane stands obviously in Roumain's shadow. It shows how extensive the influence is of the most important work to emerge from the Indigenous movement in Haiti.

As was the case with Roumain, Ousmane never presented the poetic *enracinement* of his hero in terms of the polemics of Negritude. For both these novelists, it remained an important literary fiction closely related to their own condition as cultural 'outsiders' during exile. Ousmane's later novels more explicitly challenge the pieties of an ethno-cultural mystique and explore more profoundly the role of the outsider in a community inhibited by tradition. It is in this way that Roumain's position can be contrasted with that of his Africanist contemporaries. Perhaps it was the essential poet in Roumain that always prized the creative heterodoxy of the twenties. His moral conscience drove him towards Marxism but his creative writing never became simply a fictional adjunct to his political convictions – whereas art gradually became an ethnic artefact for the advocates of cultural authenticity. His brief pronouncement on poetry, shortly after his return to Haiti, shows how fiercely he guarded the freedom of the creative imagination – 'this bird which we call poetry dies in captivity'.[34]

NOTES

1. Preface to Edris St Amand's *Essai d'explication de 'Dialogue de mes lampes'* (Port-au-Prince: 'Etat, 1942).
2. *Le Petit Impartial*, no. 25, 3 Mar. 1928.
3. *La Revue Indigène*, no. 3, Sept. 1927, 114.
4. Jacques Roumain, *La Proie et l'ombre* (Port-au-Prince: La Presse, 1930) p. 45.
5. *La Revue Indigène*, no. 3, Sept. 1927, 113.
6. *La Revue Indigène*, no. 2, Aug. 1927, 62.
7. *La Trouée*, no. 4, 1 Oct. 1927, 118.
8. 'Préface à la vie d'un bureaucrate', reprinted in Jacques Roumain's *La Montagne ensorcelée* (Paris: Français Réunis, 1972) p. 36.
9. Ibid., p. 45.
10. Remy Bastien, *Religion and Politics in Haiti* (Washington, D.C.: Institute for Cross-Cultural Research, 1966) p. 54.
11. Roumain, *La Montagne ensorcelée*, p. 72.
12. See the Haiti section of Edmund Wilson's *Red, Black, Blond and Olive* (New York: Oxford University Press, 1956) pp. 69–146.
13. Roumain, *La Montagne ensorcelée*, p. 155.
14. Ibid., p. 147.
15. Ibid., pp. 86–7.
16. Ibid., pp. 187–8.
17. Roumain, *Le Grief de l'homme noir* reprinted in *La Montagne ensorcelée*, p. 202.
18. Jacques Roumain, *A propos de la campagne anti-superstitieuse* (Port-au-Prince: L'Etat, 1942) p. 11.
19. Roumain, *La Montagne ensorcelée*, pp. 221–2.
20. Jacques Roumain, *Analyse Schématique 32–4*, (Port-au-Prince: Comité Central du Parti Communiste Haitien, 1934) pp. v–vi
21. Roumain, 'Madrid', (published 1937) reprinted in *La Montagne ensorcelée*, p. 251.
22. Richard Crossman (ed.), *The God that Failed* (London: Hamish Hamilton) p. 245.
23. Roumain, *Bois d'Ebène* reprinted in *La Montagne ensorcelée*. Page numbers are quoted from this edition.
24. Since Léon Damas's *Pigments* appeared in 1937, Roumain could have been influenced by it.

25. Preface to St Amand's *Essai d'explication de 'Dialogue de mes lampes'*.
26. Jacques Roumain, *Gouverneurs de la rosée* (Paris: Français Réunis, 1968) p. 218. Page numbers are quoted from this edition.
27. Wilson, *Red, Black, Blond and Olive*, p. 116.
28. Janheinz Jahn, *Neo-African Literature* (New York: Grove Press, 1969) p. 218.
29. Cf. Roger Gaillard, *L'univers romanesque de Jacques Roumain* (Port-au-Prince: Henri Deschamps, 1965) p. 14.
30. A useful article on this aspect of the text is Beverly Ormerod's 'Myth, Rite and Symbol in *Gouverneurs de la rosée*' *L'Esprit Créateur*, vol. xvii, no. 2, Summer 1977, pp. 123–32.
31. For specific comment on the language of the text see my introduction to *Masters of the Dew* (London: Heinemann, 1978).
32. Roumain, *La Montagne ensorcelée*, pp. 122–3.
33. Jacques Roumain, *O pays, mon beau peuple!* (Paris: Presses Pockek, 1975) p. 75.
34. La Revue Indigène, no. 3, Sept. 1927, p. 106.

6 Surrealism and Revolution: René Dépestre and the Generation of 1946

It is when the black proletariat . . . has access to the right to eat and the world of the imagination, a Caribbean poetry will exist only then. Etienne Léro, *Légitime Défense*, 1932

Not once during those hard years of Vichy domination did the ideal of freedom grow dim here and it is to surrealism that we owe this . . . Surrealism, taut cord of our hope. Suzanne Césaire, *Tropiques*, Oct. 1943

A harsh style, full of images, for the image is the drawbridge which allows unconscious energies to be scattered on the surrounding meadows. It is full of colour too, bronzed, sun-baked and violent. Frantz Fanon, *The Wretched of the Earth*, 1961

The moon is a drunkard   Purity a legend   The sea is only a trap   The sky a lie   Love has crossed over to the enemy camp   Enough talk   Let us create a new world with our own resources. René Dépestre, *Gerbe de sang*, 1946

In 1931 the quarrel between Louis Aragon and André Breton which divided the Surrealists, brought to light the contradictions contained in the Surrealist ideal of fusing poetry and revolution and did much to undermine the influence of this movement in Europe. Those who saw themselves as 'orthodox' Surrealists opted for the creative anarchy of *révolution permanente* and followed the 'pure' poetic experimentation of Breton and Dali. Those who saw poetic revolution in terms of political engagement followed Aragon's example. Surrealism in Europe would never recover from this schism. The crises of the Spanish Civil War and the Second World War only served to vindicate Aragon's belief that the artist had an immediate public responsibility to commit himself politically. Sartre's *Qu'est-ce que la littérature* seems to consolidate Aragon's position by voicing reservations as to the limitations of the poetic act. *Dévoiler le monde* is the motto for the *écrivain engagé* but poets 'refuse to *use* language. Now as it is in and through language conceived as a certain kind of tool that that the search for truth operates, one cannot imagine that they aim to detect the truth or to expose it.'[1]

This may have come to be seen as a simplification but it shows the extent to which the poetic theories of Surrealism had lost ground in the 1940s.

The fortunes of the Surrealist movement outside of France were, however, quite different. The four quotations at the beginning of this chapter show how Surrealism had captured the imagination of black writers in very diverse circumstances. What the latter saw in Surrealist theory on poetry and revolution was a literary aesthetic which responded to their specific artistic as well as political needs. Surrealism basically provided a tempting solution to the problems of political and most importantly psychological liberation from the metropolitan culture. Surrealist doctrine rejected the criteria for good taste and beauty which traditionally assured the cultural supremacy of the metropole. Furthermore, it shunned the fatigued rationality and inhibiting materialism of the West and actively promoted the search for spontaneity and originality in non-Western traditions – whether that of the African peasant or the pre-Colombian Indian. For instance, André Breton saw it as entirely consistent with his ideas to proclaim in one of his lectures given in Haiti, 'Mechanical progress tends to isolate man in an abstract world . . . He will have to learn everything all over again from the peasant.'[2] It is easy to see how this as an idea can be assimilated into anti-colonial polemics. Finally, it was in emphasising the bond between the poet and the revolutionary that Surrealism was at its most appealing. Poets and revolutionaries were non-conformists who altered man's attitudes to society and reality as a whole. *Transformer le monde* was a slogan they could both identify with.

Haiti had, until the late forties, resisted the full impact of this movement. It never became part of the anti-establishment and anti-American rhetoric of the thirties and could only be seen as having a small influence on *Griot* theories of the primeval unconscious. No poet – besides Magloire St Aude in his hermetic *Dialogue de mes lampes* (1941) – had explicitly experimented with or abandoned their verse to the free associations of automatic writing. Roumain's reservations about Surrealism characterise the attitude of the vast majority of the generation of the Occupation, 'It is a "machine infernale" which is anti-bourgeois but negative and anarchistic.'[3] This changed sharply by 1945 with the exposure of a new generation of writers to Surrealist theory which culminated in the arrival of André Breton himself towards the end of that year:

> Towards the end of 1945, the news that André Breton was in Haiti caught our imagination. Our enthusiasm knew no bounds when we learnt that this trip would coincide with an exhibition of the great Cuban painter Wilfredo Lam and with a series of lectures to be delivered by the famous Martinican poet Aimé Césaire . . . Surrealism was welcomed. We wished to demystify Haitian society.[4]

André Breton had arrived at the right psychological moment in Haiti. He had an overwhelming effect on the disaffected youth of 1946 who felt restless in a world made contingent by the Second World War and actively resented the reactionary politics of Elie Lescot – who had come to be seen as the Haitian version of Jarry's *Ubu roi*.

It is unlikely that André Breton would have approved of the solemn rhetoric of this hagiographic account of his arrival in Haiti, but it does reveal how powerful his presence would be among Haiti's intellectuals: 'Leonine head, mane of sunlight, god created from a thunderbolt, Breton advances. The sight of him makes one realise the beauty of the angel of revolt.'[5] This 'puissance olympienne' as Laraque later describes him, arrives in Port-au-Prince just when anti-government feeling is rife, particularly among Haiti's young writers. His first lecture was given at the Rex cinema in December of 1945 to what Gaillard calls a 'foule hétérogène' of politicians, elegant ladies, members of the Catholic clergy and local literati. It is ironic that Breton should be faced with those members of society that he despised the most. To them he was simply a French 'man of letters' and they attended dutifully. It was this speech which had an overwhelming effect on Breton's sympathisers in the cinema. So much so that Elie Lescot thought that it was Breton who had engineered the revolt that overthrew him early in 1946, and is reputed to have exclaimed a few days later 'Quant à ce monsieur Breton, il ne parlera plus!' He also seized the special edition of the student newspaper *La Ruche* which appeared in January 1946 and was dedicated to Andre Breton.

In the political and literary effervescence of 1946, the strong Utopian impulse of Marxism combined without any contradiction whatever with the revolutionary poetics of Surrealism. The defeat of Fascism and the promise of 'un renouveau du monde' in 1945 explain the idealistic political engagement of these years. Surrealist theory and Marxist politics reinforced each other. This generation felt strong sympathy with the idea that poetry could become a miraculous weapon in liberating man. This idea has remained with René Dépestre even in his most recent writing. His *Un arc-en-ciel pour l'occident chrétien* (1967) cleverly links this freedom of the imagination with the role of the voodoo god Legba, whose duty it is to open the gates to the voodoo deities and by analogy the world of unconscious forces. However, as we shall see in Dépestre's Surrealist work of this period *Gerbe de sang* (1946) Surrealism could at the very least provide a poetic language which could convey the violent frenzy of the times.

The attraction of Surrealist theory and the impact made by Breton can hardly be isolated from the effects of the Second World War. The poetry of the French Resistance also had a profound influence on this group of Haitian poets. The pages of their newspaper *La Ruche* contain sentimental tributes to Eluard, Aragon and Emmanuel whose poetry stood in the vanguard of the anti-Nazi struggle. The same Dépestre who hailed Breton's importance could now just as easily say of these poets, 'They hastened to abandon surrealism to adopt a form of expression which was more accessible to a general public.'[6] Jacques-Stéphen Alexis who collaborated with this newspaper wrote under the pseudonym Jacques La Colère which was apparently inspired by one of the pseudonyms used by Aragon during the war – François la Colère. The Resistance poets were exemplary figures to Dépestre and his contemporaries because of the way they combined political activism with the creative act. Their poetry would also have a particular significance because it meant the revival of patriotic sentiments. The same passionate idealism would be seen in the poetry of the forties. Malcolm Cowley remarked on this feature of Resistance poetry in citing the example of Aragon: 'Aragon in his poems was giving back their old meanings to words like 'love' and 'courage' and 'country' . . . and it was as if he was saying that liberty is not an orator's expression, but something worth risking one's life to restore.'[7] It was not that such an attitude to poetry was entirely new to this generation. They idolised Jacques Roumain whose own attitude to political engagement and partiality towards the epic poem that dealt with grand abstract themes they were already disposed to imitate. *Etincelles* (1945), the first collection of poetry by the young Dépestre, shows obvious evidence of the influence of both Roumain and the Resistance poets. The link with the latter is strengthened later when one of the foremost figures of France's poetic renaissance during the war – Pierre Séghers – published Dépestre's *Traduit du Grand Large* and *Végétations de Clarté* while the poet was in France in the fifties.

All these various factors contributed to the mood of restlessness and irreverence in 1946 but Haitians also had sufficient justification for radical political activity in the regime of the arch-conservative President Elie Lescot. A crisis was created in Haitian politics which Roumain had predicted in his *L' Analyse Schématique* of 1934. He felt that as soon as the American presence was removed, national unity would once more fragment into partisan politics based on class and colour.[8] The situation became explosive under Lescot as it became obvious that the traditional mulatto centres of power were once more in control. This was obvious in Lescot's actions as he was the perfect stereotype of the pro-American mulatto president. For instance, his agreement with the American controlled S.H.A.D.A. (Haitian/American Society for the Development of Agriculture) gave that company the right to expropriate peasant land for planting rubber trees. In order to subdue peasant opposition to the project Lescot sanctioned a campaign by the Catholic Church against the voodoo religion – *La campagne anti-superstitieuse* – realising that the voodoo temples could become centres of peasant revolt. The tactlessness of the Catholic Church provoked wide-spread criticism and the S.H.A.D.A. effort was a failure – thousands of acres of peasant land destroyed in the process. The revolutionary fervour of the times was easily focused on Lescot's clumsy despotism.

The overthrow of Elie Lescot in January 1946 was achieved in the name of Surrealist ideals, Marxist politics and the iconoclastic spirit of the times. Ghislain Gouraige commenting on the period largely supports this: '1946 was a revolt of young people. The war of 1939, the privation, the rejection of a tormented world, the conviction that we were backward and the evidence of our isolation created a hunger for reform . . . It was the time of the young. The time of dreams.[9] Yet, no revolt succeeds simply because of political and poetic ideals no matter how passionate. Lescot's very elitist 'nationalism', the outrage created by what was seen to be an assault by the Catholic Church on Haiti's indigenous culture as well as Lescot's accommodating pro-American policies combined to produce widespread discontent with his regime. The generation of 1946 was simply the instrument of protest created by this desire for change. The fact that the revolution of 1946 was not entirely of their making is evident in the politics of President Estimé who succeeded Lescot.

By August of 1946 when he was elected, it became obvious that the idealism of 1946 had ironically paved the way for the political emergence of Haiti's black middle-class and Africanist ideology. One of the first moves by Estimé was to outlaw the Communist Party (1948) and get the *enfants terribles* of the revolution out of the way by sending them to Europe on scholarships. Breton's presence was considered undesirable and he left by the end of 1946. The idealism of 1946 may have helped dislodge bourgeois nationalism but it ushered in a regime which gave expression to an ideology of racial authenticity. Dépestre in his later writings recognised this ironic turn of events: 'Lescot's dictatorship fell but the military apparatus of the regime remained intact . . . this failure also indicated the limitations of Surrealism in its ambition to "change the world".'[10] This bitter realisation only came to Dépestre in the 1950s. His poetry at the time conveys this sombre awareness of the fact that racialist politics had reasserted itself in Haiti. He caricatures Estimé in 1952 as a 'chacal mystique/Qui joue les houngans/Et les Christs noirs persécutés'[11] in order to maintain control over Haiti in the name of race.

Naturally the poetry of the generation of 1946 is free from this consciousness of how the revolution was to be betrayed. This generation glorified their non-conformity and the need for a violent change in Haiti's leadership. They believed in the virtue of violent change. Theirs was the last 'literary' revolution in Haiti to be conceived in such innocence. The titles of the various collections of verse produced at the time indicate the volatile passions of this generation: *Etincelles* (1945), *Gerbe de sang* (1946). *Gueules de feu* (1946), *Flammes* (1947) and *Gouttes de fiel* (1946). They conceived of their actions in terms of purposeful history. The poetic coherence imposed on Haitian politics is made clear in Dépestre's *profession de foi* in *Etincelles*:

> Je glane dans les champs ensoleillés
> des moissons d'humanité
> j'interroge le passé
> je mutilie le présent
> j'enguirlande l'avenir.[12]

> [I gather in sunlit fields
> harvests of mankind
> I question the past
> I mutilate the present
> I garland the future.]

This confidence in the poet's superior vision and his ability to shape the events of history has not been repeated so far in Haiti's literature. If it exists at all it is in the writings of Haiti's exiled poets. The tragic excesses of Duvalierism in the sixties simply produced a dazed silence among those who remained in Haiti.

The poetic fiction that fed the revolutionary zeal of this generation can easily be traced in the rhetoric that consistently reappears in their work. Louis Neptune, Dépestre's contemporary. came closest to describing the prevalent attitude to poetry when he said, 'I have no need of words which like ether can put my misery to sleep'.[13] However, little time was spent outlining a position of poetic technique. Perhaps the best word to describe this generations's literary position is eclectic. They borrowed from the Resistance poets, from Roumain's *Bois d'Ebène* and when Breton arrived, he was included in their literary pantheon. Dépestre's *Etincelles* is an obvious example of the assimilation of the epic themes of his literary predecessors as well as the revolutionary rhetoric that marked their verse. They, indeed, had created a special, sometimes *précieux* poetic diction to express their violent sentiments. For instance, 'camarades de bronze' is used to describe those who are also in the struggle; 'horizon', 'aventure cosmique', flancs de l'histoire' are closely associated with the global scale of their engagement; 'la conquête des bastilles nouvelles' and 'l' assaut de cette citadelle qui s'écroule' suggest the Apocalyptic change to a new order. Dépestre's poetry characterised a generation that made a special virtue of its youth. 'Jeunesse', 'enfant', 'poète de vingt ans' all have a special resonance in this writing. As Gouraige puts it:'The image of a dishevelled and furious Dépestre inviting men to dance on the wreckage of a rotting world was the one with which the youth in their twenties identified with.'[14]

Etincelles was strongly influenced by Paul Eluard's war poems. These form a 'pre-text' to Dépestre's first collection of poetry both thematically and in formal terms. For example, Dépestre's 'Je connais un mot' was the poem most obviously derived from Paul Eluard's 'Liberté' published in 1942. The poems closely resemble each other because similar literary devices are used to dramatise the message conveyed. In Eluard's 'Liberté' an almost incantatory quality is created by linking each verse of three lines with the words 'J'écris ton nom'. The simple lyricism of the poem gathers emotional force as the poet enumerates the ways in which this 'name' influences his life. The word that defines his life is given only at the end of the poem:

> Et par le pouvoir d'un mot
> Je recommence ma vie
> Je suis né pour te connaître
> Pour te nommer.
>
> Liberté.[15]

> [And through the power of word
> I begin my life again
> I am born to know you
> To name you.
>
> Freedom.]

'Je connais un mot' is constructed in an identical fashion drawing on the same device of repetition and creating a similar immediacy in its effect:

> Ce mot est mon avenir
> ce mot est mon amour
> ce mot est ma folie: HAITI.   (p. 5)

> [This word is my future
> this word is my love
> this word is my madness: HAITI.]

The real difference between these poems lies in the kind of poetic register used by Dépestre as opposed to Eluard's. The latter typically chooses an understated lyricism whereas Dépestre uses a thundering, declamatory style to evoke the associations of 'ce mot'. A comparison of the first verses in each poem clearly demonstrates this difference of poetic manner:

> Sur mes cahiers d'écolier
> Sur mon pupitre et les arbres
> Sur le sable sur la neige
> J'écris ton nom . . .
>
> > (Eluard's 'Liberté')

> [On my schoolboy's notebook
> On my desk and the trees
> On the sand on the snow
> I write your name . . .]

> Je connais un mot aux résonances d'ailes
> il provoque le vertige du bonheur
> il ressuscite les heures immortelles
> il gonfle le voile de mes rêves
>
> > (Dépestre's 'Je connais un mot')

> [I know a word which resounds like wings
> it creates the vertigo of happiness
> it revives immortal moments
> it swells the sails of my dreams]

The link with Eluard's poetry is also noticeable in the appeal that his discreet grasp of man's tragic grandeur had for even Dépestre. For instance, Eluard's 'La dernière nuit' uses a deceptively straightforward lyricism to capture the anonymity of death:

> Ce petit monde meurtrier
> Est orienté vers l'innocent
> Lui ôte le pain de la bouche
> Et donne sa maison au feu[16].

> [This little deadly world
> Is turned towards the innocent

Takes the bread from his mouth
And sets fire to his house]

This simple grim fact is opposed to man's capacity for renewal and
for communion with his world:

Et pourtant j'ai su chanter le soleil
Le soleil entier celui qui respire
Dans chaque poitrine et dans tous les yeux
La goutte de candeur qui luit après les larmes.[17]

[And yet I could celebrate the sun
The whole breathing sun
In each breast and in every eye
The drop of innocence that shines after the tears.]

It is this lyrical innocence that Eluard celebrates in man that
informs the long narrative poem 'Face à la nuit' by Dépestre. An
elaborate and sentimental ode to innocence defiled, 'Face à la nuit'
forcefully echoes Eluard's earlier poem to man's vulnerability:

Elle était née sur la grand'route
dans les bras du soleil
elle était née sur la grand'route
bercée par le soleil.   (p. 37)

[She was born on the highway
in the arms of the sun
She was born on the highway
cradled by the sun.]

la nuit écrasait l'enfant
et la nuit livrait l'enfant tout entière
à la prostitution
à ce métier vilain   (p. 44)

[the night crushed the child
and the night delivered the child completely
to prostitution
to that ugly profession]

It is, however, unsatisfactory to explain Dépestre's early poetry simply in terms of Eluard's war poetry. To do so would be to ignore the effect that Jacques Roumain had on this generation of writers. Numerous poems were dedicated to him and the pages of *La Ruche* are filled with quotations from his writings. The tribute to Roumain in *Etincelles* expresses this respect for Roumain emphatically. In 'Le baiser au leader' Dépestre effusively writes:

> Comrade Roumain
> you are our ideal
> you are our flame
> you are our god   (p. 18)

In literary terms it was Roumain's epic poem 'Bois d'Ebène' which had the greatest influence on the poetry of 1946. A comparison between Roumain's poem and Dépestre's 'Piété Filiale' shows how closely Dépestre followed Roumain's artistic lead. In Roumain's *profession de foi* in 'Bois d'Ebène' he asserts his commitment to his race but then directs this *prise de conscience* towards all the exploited of the earth, 'Afrique j'ai gardé ta memoire/ . . . POURTANT/je ne veux être que de votre race/ ouvriers paysans . . . '[18] Dépestre's 'Piété Filiale' can almost be seen as a gloss on Roumain's earlier work as it manages to cover exactly the same ground:

> O terre d'Afrique . . .
>
> Je veux aujourd'hui parler uniquement pour toi . . .
>
> Mais j'entends dans le lointain
> Monter la sourde clameur d'une mosaïque de souffrances
> La grondante symphonie des abandonnés
> Blonds, jaunes, noirs peu importe
> ils versent tous un sang rouge   (p. 25)

> [O Africa . . .
> Today I will speak for you only . . .
> But I hear in the distance
> Rising the muffled clamour of a mosaic of suffering
> The rumbling symphony of the abandoned
> Blond, yellow, black it does not matter
> They all shed the same blood]

The grand manner of this poem is echoed in Dépestre's Utopian vision of mankind inheriting a new cleansed world. Roumain's 'nous brassons le mortier des temps fraternels/dans la poussière des idoles' which brings his poem to a thundering close is alluded to in Dépestre's 'Confession' which ends:

> . . . dans le creuset des chaudes rencontres
> pour que ma vie
> jeune
> decidée
> jaillisse, bondissante, sur un monde écroulé.   (p. 7)

> [. . . in the crucible of warm encounters
> so that my life
> young
> resolute
> should burst forth, leaping, on this crumbling world.]

The very first poem of *Etincelles* introduces a theme which has not been explicitly treated so far. This idea is closely connected to Dépestre's interest in the Surrealist movement and recurs quite consistently in his work. Dépestre declares in 'Me Voici':

> Me voici
> poète
> adolescent
> poursuivant un rêve d'amour et de liberté.   (p. 2)

> [Here I am
> poèt
> adolescent
> pursuing a dream of love and liberty.]

The link made between 'poète adolescent' and 'rêve d'amour' takes us back to a notion of poetry as the recreation of a state of wonder, free from all inhibitions. The need to be free from a repressed consciousness is indirectly suggested in two love poems in *Etincelles*. 'Je ne viendrai pas ce soir' and 'Regret' both suggest that emotional liberation is a pre-condition to political engagement:

> ton amour ne pourra braver l'abîme
> que l'histoire a creusé entre nos routes parallèles.   (p. 16)

[your love will not be able to defy the gulf
that history has created between our parallel paths.]

This need for psychological liberation is seen as the key to both the
poetic adventure as well as revolutionary activity. The image of the
enfant terrible underpins this idea as his innocence makes him
immune from the inhibitions of ordinary reality. In a rare quiet
moment in *Etincelles* Dépestre alludes to this poetic voyage. 'Seul
dans la nuit' is more than just an intimate mood poem. It is a fantasy
that transcends the personal to suggest the daring and solitude of the
poetic quest. The typically strident tone of *Etincelles* is absent as a
world of subterranean gloom resists the poet's search for a vision.
The poem brings to mind Rimbaud's exploration of the same theme
in 'Le bateau ivre':

> Les arbres à mes côtés
> prennent des airs d'obélisques
> j'ai peur
> j'ai peur de regarder la mer . . .
> et ma barque légère, frémissante
> émerge du néant des choses immobiles
> et mouvantes
> gigantesques et puissantes
> pour tracer sur quelque page blanche
> un sillage d'espérance   (p. 31)

> [The trees beside me
> take on the look of obelisks
> I am afraid
> I am afraid of looking at the sea . . .
> and my fragile boat, trembling
> emerges from the nothingness of things static
> and moving
> immense and powerful
> to trace on some white page
> a path of hope]

The poetic vision which emerges from this voyage into the
unexplored regions of man's consciousness already responds to the
demand made by the Surrealists on the poetic imagination. This
feature becomes even more visible in Dépestre's poetry after

Breton's arrival. In *Gerbe de sang* published in 1946, the political *refus* of *Etincelles* is extended to include a rejection of reason and reality itself.

The preface of *Gerbe de sang* can be seen as a rhetorical gesture as well as an experiment in automatic writing. It both cultivates by a random enumeration of radically different nouns, a fiercely anti-poetic form and sets the tone for, the absolute *refus* celebrated in the poetry that follows:

La morale	:	connais pas
la justice	:	connais pas
les nuages	:	connais pas
le péché	:	connais pas
la gloire	:	connais pas
le sable	:	connais pas
le humfort	:	connais pas
l'enfer	:	connais pas
la radio	:	connais pas
l'émeraude	:	connais pas
la bible	:	connais pas
Napoléon	:	connais pas
le boa	:	connais pas
la brise	:	connais pas
les coquilles	:	connais pas
les seins	:	connais pas
les fous	:	connais pas
la raison	:	connais pas
verbe être	:	connais pas
les fleurs	:	connais pas

What follows does not always fulfil the promise of poetic anarchy launched in the preface. *Gerbe de sang* contains some poems dated 1945 that are obviously written in the manner of *Etincelles*. The originality of the later collection, however, lies in the adoption of Surrealist ideas to which Breton's presence had brought a fresh currency in 1946.

Many of the features loosely termed Surrealist that are associated with modern poetry can be found in *Gerbe de sang*. For instance, the title feeds certain clusters of images in the text that draw on the bizarre juxtaposition of the strange and the beautiful. The shock effect of *gerbe* which is never traditionally linked to *sang* is echoed in such phrases as 'rosée de sang pur', 'aurores saignantes' or 'rouge éclat de pollen'. The imagery of this collection is more obviously influenced by the Surrealist desire for a radical comparison of images which are as remote in character as possible. Indeed, the language of *Gerbe de sang* in general shows evidence of an enigmatic visual imagery which is deliberately ambiguous and makes few concessions to the reader's understanding. 'Plaine en proie à l'ombre' is one such example in which each time 'plaine' is repeated its associations become less conventional and more the product of a fantasy of aggression:

> Plaine à gueule ouverte bâillant son infortune au gré des saisons au gré de la menstruation des filles Plaine avec dans sa chevelure brûlée mille cris éperdus d'oiseaux pris dans le jeu de la faim comme de maigres poissons aux filets d'un maudit pêcheur.
>
> (p. 31)

> [Plain with its mouth open yawning its misfortune at the mercy of the seasons at the mercy of the menstruation of girls Plain with its burnt hair filled with a thousand cries of frantic birds caught like thin fish in the nets of a wretched fisherman.]

This cannot be seen as an entirely hermetic Surreal fantasy as the poet does allow a picture to emerge from his world of savage associations. It does reveal, though, Dépestre's discovery of a whole new poetic diction in 1946.

Gerbe de sang is particularly interesting in the way that Surrealist theory shapes Dépestre's literary and political position in this text. Sartre's *Black Orpheus* clarifies this link between radical politics and the poetic revolution:

> From Mallarmé to the Surrealists, the profound aim of French poetry appears to me to have been this auto-destruction of language . . . The European poet of today attempts to de-humanise words in order to return them to nature; the black herald is seeking to degallicise them, he smashes them together, he breaks their customary associations . . .[20]

This is clearly the case in Dépestre's poetry as he describes this conspiracy between language and the colonial world in one of his more striking images – 'la liberté à bout de souffle/bâillonnée dans la cale de l'imagination'. 'Liberté' is ambiguous enough to mean both liberation from colonial domination (suggested by 'la cale') and freedom from an inhibiting poetic tradition.

The two poems 'Royaume des mots' and 'Saison de colère' elaborate on Dépestre's need to turn away from the enslavement to dead literary language – to 'degallicise' words – and restore the poetic word to its original force. There is a clever play on meaning in 'Saison de colère' in which the need for a radical break with tradition is alluded to:

> Je me suis fait béton armé contre les vers qui nous rongent et nous dessèchent Ma peau de nègre autrefois lieu commun des supplices et des crachats voilà qu'elle est devenue un *sésame* qui ouvre des portes inviolables . . . Voilà un language comme une torche dans la poudre des passions hypocrites et des traditions rouillées . . .   (p. 61)

> [I have become reinforced concrete against the verses (worms) which gnaw and dry us up My black skin previously a commonplace of torture and spit behold has become a *sesame* that opens inviolable gates . . . Here is a language like a torch in the powder of hypocritical passions and rusted passion . . .]

The poetic imagination is freed from the inhibitions of the past and the poet can now exploit this new language to which a primordial kind of power has been restored. The primal innocence of this new poetic language is felt in:

> O mots meurtiers de nos clairs silences
> mots secourables
> je me soumets aux plus humbles parmi vous
> Feuille Sable Autel
> Crime Amour Songe rois de l'univers . . .   (p. 57)

> [O words deadly to our empty silence
> willing words
> I submit myself to the humblest among you
> Leaf Sand Altar
> Crime Love Dream kings of the universe . . .]

This dislocation of language into innocence is not a gratuitous exercise. It is the precondition to the liberation of man from all kinds of alienation and injustice: 'L'ère enchantée des dérèglements va précéder de quelques aurores celle de la libération des peuples' (p. 62) [The enchanted time of derangements will precede by a few dawns that of the liberation of men.]

This line clearly recalls Rimbaud's 'Mauvais sang' which has become one of the strongest influences on Francephone black writing.

Clear reference is made to Rimbaud's influence in 'Temps des loups', as Dépestre admits:

> Il m'est échu d'être ce poète
> héritier d'Arthur Rimbaud . . .
> je convie tous les hommes
> à être des assassins jusqu'à l'aube.   (p. 77)

> [It is my lot to be this poet
> heir to Arthur Rimbaud . . .
> I invite all men
> to be murderers until dawn.]

Here Dépestre identifies with the demonic poetic figure of 'Mauvais sang' who pours scorn on the world of convention and defiantly celebrates the purity that results from leaving civilisation behind. The poet stands aloof, despising man's enslavement to materialism and civilising values. Dépestre strikes the same pose in *Gerbe de sang* as he declares 'Le monde est un vaste remous de corps asservis'. The world and man's imagination must be stripped of this repressive crust, 'la terre amputée de son écorce pourrie', so that ultimate liberation could be achieved.

To the alienating and corrupt world Dépestre, like his predecessor, opposes the innocence and sense of wonder of childhood. The image of the child is pervasive in *Gerbe de sang* and it consistently represents the ability to perceive the marvellous:

> l'air libre de ton regard d'enfant   (p. 23)

> [the open air of your childlike glance]

nous sommes enfants . . . nos paupières n'ont point d'écluses
(p. 24)
[we are children . . . our eyelids have no controls]

Nous sommes deux enfants nouvellement
apparus sur la surface du globe . . .

nos corps tout entiers nouveaux sous
le premier soleil comme des hélices en marche
frémissent du souffle immense de l'univers   (p. 33)

[We are two children recently
arrived on the surface of the earth . . .
our bodies completely new under
the first sun like propellers in motion
quivering with the immense breath of the universe]

In this instance the corrosive perception of a decaying world is
replaced by the elation of a new beginning. His imagination yields a
whole new world to be repossessed. Here the private fantasy and the
revolutionary vision again overlap as Dépestre asserts a new dawn of
creation:

demain quand je serai Roi de mes créations
quand je serai Roi de chaque goutte de ma sueur
j'inventerai une morale pour les hommes
une vertu pour femmes
une conduite pour les gosses   (p. 77)

[tomorrow when I will be King of my creations
when I will be king of each drop of my sweat
I will invent a morality for men
virtue for women
conduct for children.]

The revolution of 1946 was built precisely on such a dream – that
of the total liberation of man. The revolutionary achievement
of 1946 may have been a literary one. It certainly was not
political.

The difficulty of reconciling the political revolution with the
poetic renaissance was posed in 1946 in the context of Surrealist

theory. Dépestre continues to be preoccupied by this dilemma. The grey uniformity and materialist goals of socialist society seem incompatible with the liberation of the individual imagination so effusively celebrated in his verse. For instance, he has had to come to terms with the terror of Stalin's dystopia. His early enthusiasms seem somewhat modified as he ruefully admits: 'And even after (the class system becomes extinct) we must still be vigilant, for it appears that progress in society is no guarantee against the recurrence of the barbarity of the past. The absolutist politics of Stalin is one of these instances of a brutal turn to the past.[21]

Until the 1940s ideological and literary issues in Haiti remained largely internal. Jacques Roumain is the only obvious exception to this tendency to parochialism that pervaded much of Haitian writing. The Second World War would dramatically change all this. The generation of 1946 had been influenced by Roumain and consistently presented Haitian problems in an international context. In contrast both the Indigenous and the *Griot* movements seem narrowly provincial. This attitude on the part of Dépestre's generation was also encouraged by the vigorous efforts of the *Présence Africaine* organisation whose activities were centred on the promotion of literary and cultural activities in the black diaspora.

This notion of a universal homogeneous black culture was attractive to a number of emergent colonial territories clamouring for political autonomy in the 1950s. The idea of a uniform cultural bloc was seen as an important strategy in their drive for independence. Haiti with its victory over the French in 1804 and its obvious evidence of African retentions in the folk culture came in for much attention. Yet, in historical terms, Haiti did not belong to this politico-cultural bloc. Haiti had not only been independent for over a century but had come to question many of the innocent simplifications of negritude ideology.

Ironically, the negritude ideology had only too well assimilated a European version of history. Both versions of history accept the success of slavery and colonisation. The literature of protest encouraged by negritude saw the past as uncreative and saw in cultural atavism a way of discovering an identity. This ideology presented culture as organic, unaffected by geographical or historical circumstances.

Haiti has not only been independent for long enough to develop a sense of a national culture but Marxism which had many adherents in 1946 emphasised culture as part of a historical dialectic. It was inevitable that the products of 1946 should challenge the simplifications of negritude ideology. Both René Dépestre and, as we shall see in the following chapter, Jacques-Stéphen Alexis were among the first voices of dissent in the fifties.

Dépestre's opposition to negritude originates in a letter written from Paris in June 1955 in which he expressed interest in the fact that the much admired poet of the French Resistance Louis Aragon was advocating a creation of a national form in French poetry. Dépestre attempts to apply Aragon's ideas to Haitian poetry. He suggests the need for national characteristics to be defined in Haitian writing: 'Aragon through his genius and the example he set, shows the direction we must take, as Haitian poets, while leaving us the responsibility, depending on the factor of individual talent, of using material foreign to the sphere of French.'[22] Indeed, there was much debate in Haiti in the mid-fifties on the question of national culture and writing in Creole. Dépestre's ideas are entirely consistent with this sequence of events in Haiti. Furthermore, the fact that he was away from Haiti made the question even more urgent to him. The threat of anonymity in his verse had begun to worry him from this time: 'My separation from Haiti, from the popular culture of my homeland, is a serious limitation on the possibilities open to me. It is the present tragedy in my poetry.'[23] This letter from Dépestre excited a critical response from Aimé Césaire who accused him of being assimilationist, in his blind following of Aragon's proposals. Césaire's poem 'Fous-t-en Dépestre, Fous-t-en, laisse dire Aragon' suggested that Dépestre was willing to surrender his originality to metropolitan literary models:

. . . Se peut-il
que les pluies de l'exil
aient détendu la peau de tambour de ta voix.[24]

[. . . Can it be
that the rains of exil
have made the skin of the drum of your voice flaccid.]

Only four years earlier Césaire in his preface to *Végétations de Clarté* had hailed Dépestre as a powerful voice in modern poetry.

Dépestre's *Introduction à un Art Poétique Haitien* was written in October 1955 in reply to Césaire's critique. Dépestre first attacked the racialist poetics of Negritude. Even though it was aimed at Césaire's criticism of his position, it can also be seen as an elaboration of Roumain's earlier attitude to racial mystification: 'They have spoken a lot about "black poetry", of "national black poetry", of "black formalism" as opposed to "white formalism", of "black cultural alienation" all elusive notions, which either are false by definition or . . . need to be reconsidered historically.'[25] The main thrust of Dépestre's argument was simple. Negritude or any monolithic notion of black culture denied the vital diversity of the various countries that make up the diaspora: 'And to speak of "black poetry" in general is a myth as confusing as the philosophical concept of negritude. It is to neglect the importance of new relations between classes which slavery have been established in each one of our countries.'[26] In spite of common beginnings national cultures had emerged. Dépestre had begun to suggest that the complex process of survival in Haiti had inevitably begun to create an authentic local culture. This refusal to view the past in terms of despair put Dépestre in the vanguard of those younger black writers who refused to share the simplification of Negritude ideology.[27] Dépestre was tentatively indicating that an important process of creolisation had taken place in Haiti. His contemporary Jacques-Stéphen Alexis would later make an even more decisive contribution to this idea.

Dépestre's life, though he was unaware of it at the time, was destined to be spent in almost permanent exile. A brief return to Haiti in 1958 and the death of Alexis in 1961 would teach him how vulnerable and ineffective the poetic imagination is in the face of totalitarian terror. In fact, his poetry from the mid-fifties onwards is marked by both the exhilaration of the poetic act and his horror at injustice in the world. His various *poèmes de circonstance* denounce the evils of this world and desperately celebrate the heroes of a new Utopian dawn. His *Journal d'un animal marin* (1964)[28] published after settling in Cuba, combines such ingratiating political poetry as 'Un Haitien parle de Cuba' with a number of more subdued, less 'official' pieces which celebrate a gentle discovery of an elemental order where spiritual fulfilment is possible. In the latter, Dépestre assumes a somewhat demiurgic role, asserting his vision in the face of his own dislocation and the void around him. In a fundamental way the key to his poetry is still the magical act of creation that was first clearly exploited in *Gerbe de sang*. His taste for revolutionary politics still originates in his poetic fictions.

The figure of the poet who appears in Dépestre's later verse is a creation of the pressures of exile. Images of separation and alienation from his 'pays natal' abound in the later years. His literary imagination is clearly that of the displaced modern writer who is not rooted like the traditional *griot* in his own community. In this he is simply the forerunner to the exiled community of Haitian writers who have fled the terrors of Duvalierism. The image of the 'petite lampe haitienne'[29] or of the 'animal marin' are examples of this sense of the instability of self-imposed exile.

One of his most important recent works *Un arc-en-ciel pour l'occident chrétien* is informed by the nostalgia of the exile. In it he uses the figure of the voodoo priest to imagine his re-insertion into his community. He becomes the medium that links the collective unconscious of his community with the world of the gods. As a priest possessed he can fulfil his desire for *enracinement* as well as satisfy the poetic demands of Rimbaud's 'dérèglement systématique de tous les sens'. As is true of his other poems of this period, he also wishes to transcend the individual act of creativity to ascribe a greater moral purpose to his role as *poète/houngan*. Consequently, Dépestre creates an original pantheon of gods that paradoxically includes heroes of Haitian Independence (who were hostile to voodoo) and earnest revolutionaries (who would have regarded it as a mere superstition). This is his way of distancing himself from the *poètes vaudouisants* of the Griot movement as the poem never becomes simply a celebration of *l'âme noire*. The very image of the rainbow is shared across cultures and Dépestre, in the final movement of the poem, embraces men of all races:

> Occident chrétien mon frère terrible
> Mon signe de croix le voici:
> au nom de la révolte
> Et de la justice
> Et de la tendresse.[30]

> [Christian West my terrible brother
> here is my sign of the cross:
> in the name of revolt
> and justice
> and tenderness]

It again underlines Dépestre's refusal to see the poetic world as exploitable in purely aesthetic terms and his dogged determination to relate his own poetic universe to the reality of revolutionary politics.

NOTES

1. Jean-Paul Sartre, *Qu'est-ce que la littérature* (Paris: Gallimard, 1948) p. 17.
2. Roger Gaillard, 'André Breton et nous', *Conjonction*, no. 103, Dec. 1966, 9.
3. Preface to Edris St Amand's *Essai d' explication de Dialogue de mes lampes* (Port-au-Prince: L' Etat, 1942).
4. René Dépestre, *Por la revolución, por la poesía* (Havana: Instituto del libro, 1969) p. 176.
5. Paul Laraque, 'André Breton en Haiti', *Nouvelle Optique*, Vol. 1, nò.2, May 1971, 126.
6. *La Ruche*, no. 1, Dec. 1945, 3.
7. *Aragon, Poet of the French Resistance*, ed. Josephson and Cowrey (New York: Duell, Sloane and Pearce, 1945) p. 6.
8. Cf. 'L'écroulement du mythe nationaliste', in Jacques Roumain, *L'Analyse Schématique* (Port-au-Prince: Comité Central du Parte Communiste Haitien, 1934)
9. Ghislain Gouraige, 'D'une jeune poésie à une autre', *Rond Point*, no. 12, Dec. 1963, 14.
10. Dépestre, *Por la revolución, por la poesía*, p. 180.
11. René Dépestre, *Traduit du Grand Large* (Paris: Pierre Seghers, 1952) p. 48.
12. René Dépestre, *Etincelles* (Port-au-Prince: L'Etat, 1945) p. 1. Page numbers are taken from this edition.
13. Louis Neptune, *Gouttes de fiel* (Port-au-Prince: Henri Deschamps, 1946) p. 1.
14. Gouraige, 'D'une jeune poésie à une autre', Rond Point., p. 15.
15. Paul Eluard, *Uninterrupted Poetry: Selected Writings* (New York: New Directions, 1975) p. 140.
16. Ibid., p. 148.
17. Ibid., p. 152.
18. Jacques Roumain, *Bois d'Ebène*, reprinted in *La Montague ensorcetée* (Paris: Français Réunis, 1972) pp. 231–2. Dépestre elaborates on his relationship with Roumain and the cultural situation in post-war Haiti in an interview published in *Trente ans de pouvoir noir en Haiti (1946–1976)* (Montreal: Collectif Paroles, 1976).
19. René Dépestre, *Gerbe de sang* (Port-au-Prince: 'Etat, 1946). Page numbers are taken from this edition.
20. Jean-Paul Sartre, *Black Orpheus* (Paris: Présence Africaine, n.d.) pp. 25–6.
21. René Dépestre, *Poète à Cuba* (Paris: Pierre Jean Oswald, 1976) p. 23.
22. *Optique*, no. 18, Aug. 1955, p. 47.
23. Ibid., p. 47.
24. Ibid., p. 50.
25. *Optique*, no. 24, Feb. 1956, p. 10.
26. Ibid., p. 10.

27. Cf. Frantz Fanon, 'Sur la culture nationale', *Les damnés de la terre* (Paris: Maspero, 1961) and James Baldwin, 'Princes and Powers', in *Nobody Knows my Name* (London: Michael Joseph, 1964).

28. René Dépestre, *Journal d'un animal marin* (Paris: Pierre Seghers, 1964).

29. This image recurs in *Journal d'un animal marin, Un arc-en-ciel pour l'occident chrétien* and *Poète à Cuba*.

30. René Dépestre *Un arc-en-ciel pour l'occident chrétien* (Paris: Présence Africaine, 1967) p. 138.

7 A Prophetic Vision of the Past:[1] Jacques-Stéphen Alexis and 'Le Réalisme Merveilleux'

revolutionary literature is a filial impulse . . . Maturity is the assimilation of the features of every ancestor
Derek Walcott, *The Muse of History*

The role of Jacques-Stéphen Alexis as a student activist in 1946 was to all appearances an undistinguished one. One cannot help but feel that he stood, at that time, in the shadow of his vocal contemporary René Dépestre who was very much both the ideological and literary 'voice' of that generation. Alexis's writings in 1946 were restricted to the stridently anti-establishment column in *La Ruche* entitled 'Lettre aux hommes vieux' and signed 'Jacques La Colère. Indeed, even in the general outline of his career there is little to distinguish him from Dépestre or, for that matter, many of the student leaders of that generation. Like the rest, he was deeply influenced by Jacques Roumain when the latter returned from exile in 1941. After the fierce political *engagement* of the mid-forties he left, like so many, for Europe to further his studies – his particular field was medicine, specialising in neurology, which may explain his ability to evoke a range of mental states in his novels; from madness to catalepsy. He returned to Haiti in 1955 and along with his contemporaries of 1946 was actively involved in the politics of that period. His violent opposition to the Duvalier regime, which eventually led to his death, was also characteristic of the general Marxist opposition to Duvalier's politics of racial mystification.

However, his prose works published in the relatively short period between 1955 and 1960 have established his reputation as one of the most original and influential literary figures to emerge since the Occupation period. There is no evidence of any published creative writing by Alexis before 1955[2] and we witness in his later work the extent to which he had begun to shift away from the sentimental Marxism of the forties and assert a truly independent literary talent. For instance, the short story 'Le sous-lieutenant enchanté' which appears in his last published work *Romancero aux étoiles* (1960) is easily one of the most original pieces of fiction to be inspired by the American Occupation and gives us an insight into the strength of his creative imagination. This short story can in many ways be seen as the key to Alexis's major literary preoccupations. Many of the themes which recur in his entire works coalesce in this tale: the subversive power of the spiritual; the affirmation of a strong creolised culture in the Haitian heartland; the notion of intense bonds that are created between pursuer and pursued and invader and victim in history; the essential oneness of all men.

The plot concerns an American soldier, Earl Wheelbarrow, who penetrates into the Haitian interior in search of gold. This quest for material wealth by a white foreigner can be seen as an allegory of the larger New World experience of the Conquest and colonialism and Wheelbarrow represents the archetypal invader/coloniser figure. Traditionally such a story would be a vehicle for anti-colonial polemics. Alexis's intentions are quite different as most of the story is told from the Lieutenant's point of view. What Alexis elaborates are new possibilities which can emerge from such a clash of cultures. The Lieutenant faces an alien and hostile environment initially, yet one to which he is increasingly drawn. A strange woman who is the legendary 'Mistress of the Water', a creature of folk mythology, causes his eventual surrender to a world whose values are opposed to his own. In an ancient grotto, which early in the story is likened to a gothic cathedral, the Lieutenant succumbs to this primeval world. The tension between invader and invaded has released untapped spiritual resources in the former, indicating the novel reconstruction of New World history attempted by Alexis. Wheelbarrow is not simply a prisoner of race nor is he a lovelorn romantic figure wandering across unknown terrain like Chateaubriand's *René* but rather a conception of man as infinite potential beyond racial conditioning or historical explanation. At the end of his journey Wheelbarrow who came to possess, is possessed but tragic historical reality eventually intrudes. When the marines invade in 1915 the Lieutenant is accused of high treason and executed:

> Plusieurs vieux paysans . . . m'ont raconté avoir vu le lieutenant
> garrotté, lié à sa compagne, qu'il fut jugé et fusillé sur les lieux,
> accusé de haute trahison et d'intelligence avec l'ennemi.[3]

> [Several old peasants have told me that they have seen the
> lieutenant tied up together with his companion, and that they
> were judged and summarily executed, accused of high treason
> and consorting with the enemy.]

In the absurd cycle of New World history where the cynical
materialistic quest is interminably repeated, Wheelbarrow's experience is a challenge which is not tolerated. It is, however, a more
durable challenge since it represents for Alexis the real legacy of the
past and retains its immediacy in the legends of the folk.

Before his tragic death in 1961, Alexis had begun to elaborate a
vision of Caribbean history which for once did not depend on a
catalogue of greed and injustice. Instead, he saw the past as a
continuous process of synthesis which combined the accretions of
previous cultures and the residue of earlier confrontations to create
a distinct creole presence in the Caribbean. It was one of the more
daring and complex ideas to emerge from the intellectual effervescence of 1946. The origins of these theories can be found in some of
the earliest influences Alexis was exposed to. It is, perhaps, a
simplification to restrict these influences to the ideas of Jacques
Roumain and André Breton. However, these two figures provided a
range of ideas within which individual choices were made among
the generation of 1946. Alexis was to combine the ideas of these two
very distinct figures in order to create his own original view of New
World history and Haitian culture.

In perhaps one of the more sober observations made by Alexis in
his effusive homage to Roumain in 1957, Alexis says, 'Contact with
Jacques was an extraordinary thing. I am very moved when I recall,
our too brief encounters.[4] Alexis, in fact, was so moved by Roumain
that two of his novels describe in some detail the life of Jacques
Roumain. The novels *Compère Général Soleil* (1955) and *Les Arbres
Musiciens* (1957) do not deal exclusively with this subject but both
contain an important protagonist called Pierre Roumel whose life is
identical to that of Jacques Roumain. For instance, in *Compère
Général Soleil* the main character, Hilarion, meets Roumel in prison

and is exposed to the latter's Marxist theories. Later in the novel Roumel is forced by President Vincent to go into exile. In *Les Arbres Musiciens* Roumel is described as having returned from a long stay abroad and, as was the case with Roumain after he returned from exile, he takes an active part in the politics of the early forties, making a strong stand against the Catholic Church and its *campagne anti-superstitieuse*. Perhaps this admiration for Roumain's politics may even have been indirectly responsible for Alexis' own death. In commenting on Roumain's active role in the nationalist movement during the Occupation, Alexis is full of admiration for the fact that 'Jacques abandons literary activity which was too restricted for his liking and launches into the political fray, without looking back, with the impetuosity so characteristic of him'.[5] It is a similar impetuosity, a desire for 'le travail dans les conditions concrètes', that seems to have driven Alexis to attempt a clandestine invasion of Haiti in 1961, during which he was caught and later executed by the Duvalier regime.

In many ways Alexis's work reveals how great an impact Roumain's ideas had on the former. This not only applies to the sentimental Marxism of his early political articles in *La Ruche* but also to such questions as class division, race, the peasantry and cultural authenticity which are all important themes in Alexis's novels. For example, on the most obvious level, many of the political homilies that are delivered by Alexis's characters seem to echo Manuel's vision of peasant solidarity and the inevitable day of reckoning:

> Un jour le peuple reconnaîtra les siens, alors sa justice sera terrible. Tous ceux qui travaillent viendront un jour à nous, tous les véritables nègres d'Haiti. Ensemble nous chasserons de ce pays les Américains.[6]

> [One day the people will recognise its own, then its justice will be terrible. All the workers will one day come to us, all the true men of Haiti. Together we will chase the Americans from this land.]

Alexis's general perspective on Haitian society is clearly derived from Roumain's *L'Analyse Schématique*. The comments made by Roumain in this Marxist critique of Haitian society are illustrated in Alexis's presentation of the complicity between Church, State and foreign interests in his novels. This is particularly true of *Les*

Arbres Musiciens in which the harmony of interests shared by Lescot, the Catholic Church and American investors forms the political background to the story. In his analysis Alexis, like Roumain, is particularly critical of the Haitian elite. He revived in his novels, the tradition of social satire which originated with Marcelin and Lhérisson at the turn of the century and which reappears in Roumain's short stories. He, for instance, satirises the pretensions and opportunism of a bourgeois politician and his wife in the grotesque caricature of M. and Mme Jerome Paturault in *Compère Général Soleil* (pp. 182–92). Alexis may also, like Roumain, have been one of the few to be sensitive to the political presence of an ambitious black middle-class in Haiti. In *Les Arbres Musiciens* he shows how two members of this class Edgard and Diogène Osmin, in serving the cause of Lescot's government are ironically instruments of oppression like their white or mulatto predecessors. Alexis went so far as to state plainly that the theory of racial authenticity was being used in the forties to promote the interests of black politicians:

> de dangereuses et curieuses théories para-racistes se développaient dans la petite bourgeoisie et le 'colorisme' pseudo-révolutionnaire faisait de ravages.[7]

> [dangerous and strange pseudo-racist theories emerged from the petite bourgeoisie and pseudo-revolutionary 'negrism' created havoc.]

The various digressions concerning Haitian politics and social tensions during the regimes of Vincent and Lescot, which provide most of the atmosphere in *Compère Général Soleil* and *Les Arbres Musiciens* respectively, show the extent to which Alexis was indebted to Roumain for the latter's predictions about the evolution of post-Occupation Haitian society.

Alexis can also be seen as Roumain's disciple in his treatment of peasant culture. Roumain's polemic on this subject in *A propos de la campagne anti-superstitieuse* revealed both an awareness of the limitations of peasant religion since it was seen, in terms of the Marxist dialectic, as simply the product of peasant ignorance and insecurity, and a feeling that voodoo also was a legitimate feature of Haiti's national heritage. More than anything else Roumain felt there was little to be gained from the peasants' conversion to Catholicism. Alexis takes an identical stand in his fiction concerning peasant culture. For instance, in the 'Romance du Petit-Viseur' Alexis recounts a familiar folk tale that contains the warning that the organic relationship between man and the world around him must not be disturbed. The hunter in the story shoots 'The Bird of God' and is punished for breaking this taboo. The same theme is repeated in *Les Arbres Musiciens* in which a misguided Diogène Osmin pays no attention to his mother's warning and destroys the voodoo temples in his zeal to convert the peasants to Catholicism. Léonie Osmin's fear that 'Cette terre a des secrets que nul ne peut profaner sans en être châtié' (p. 102), [This land has secrets that none can desecrate without being punished] is not a matter of mere superstition since Diogène goes insane after committing his act of desecration. Alexis valued very highly the *Weltanschauung* of the folk and this would form the basis for his theories of 'Le Réalisme Merveilleux'.

However, Alexis did not romanticise peasant culture in the manner of the Griot movement. His first novel *Compère Général Soleil* refers to Africa as 'collée à la chair du nègre comme une carapace' (p. 8), [stuck to the black man's back like a shell] and a burden which 'pèse sur les pauvres nègres' (p. 125), [weighs on miserable black men]. It is in *Les Arbres Musiciens* in the context of the *campagne anti-superstitieuse* that Alexis elaborates on his reservations concerning the voodoo religion. One of the main characters, the *houngan* Bois-d'Orme, is shown as a sincere believer in the power of his gods:

Il leur (aux Loas) avait été fidèle comme un chien! Il était leur élu et son coeur palpitait d'allégresse . . . il maintenait pur de toute souillure une vieille tradition, le lien de fidelité qui attache un peuple à ses anciennes valeurs.

(p. 140)

[He had been as faithful to the Loas (gods) as a dog! He was their chosen one and his heart throbbed with joy . . . He maintained free from contamination an old tradition, the manifestation of loyalty that attaches a people to its ancestral values.]

Yet Bois-d'Orme can do nothing against the Catholic Church's campaign and the expropriation of peasant land. His impotence is criticised by Gonaibo in his observation that 'la surnature était l'ennemie de la vie libre. Elle paralysait les hommes, aliénait leur courage et leur esprit de décision' (p. 209), [the supernatural was the enemy of freedom. It paralysed men, eroded their courage and determination]. Consequently, when Bois-d'Orme symbolically hands down his powers to Gonaibo, the latter later takes off the chain which symbolises Bois-d'Orme's power, indicating his refusal to continue that tradition. The point is further emphasised in the characters of Carles and Carméleau Melon who perform the same function in the novel. The former can be seen as the author's *porte-parole* in that he simply affirms Alexis's position on voodoo:

> je respecte tout ce qui sort de la terre. Les Loas sortent de la terre comme des bananiers, comme le manioc, comme le mais . . . Les Loas ne mourront que le jour où l'électricité fera irruption dans la campagne . . . le jour où 'les habitants' sauront lire et écrire, le jour où la vie changera, pas avant   (p. 270)

> [I respect everything that comes out of the land. The Loas come out of the earth like banana trees, like manioc, like maize . . . The Loas will only die when electricity floods the countryside . . . when the people learn to read and write, when life changes, not before.]

This could easily be a summary of Roumain's position on voodoo and the need for what he termed a 'campagne anti-misère'. Carméleau Melon is Alexis's answer to Manuel in *Gouverneurs de la rosée*. The latter's condemnation of resignation induced by peasant religion and belief that one day the peasants will unite in a revolutionary 'coumbite' are all echoed by Alexis's character:

> Moi, je ne peux plus me résigner et répéter que le Bon Dieu est bon, que les Loas sont nos péres . . . En attendant le peuple souverain, Carméleau Melon gagne sa vie . . . partout il dit aux enfants de Dessalines de s'unir en silence, de préparer les lambis et les torches, pour qu'un jour éclate de nouveau le cri de 1804 devant un peuple debout et rassemblé.   (p. 344)

> [I can no longer resign myself and repeat that God is good, that the Loas are our fathers . . . While waiting on the people who are the final arbiters, Carméleau Melon earns his living . . . everywhere he says to Dessalines' children to unify in silence, to prepare the lambis and the torches so that one day the cry of 1804 should explode before an upright, organised people.]

The very vocabulary used recalls the ringing rhetoric of Roumain's political verse.

To this extent it can be seen that Alexis had simply assimilated many of Roumain's theories. Alexis's originality becomes apparent, however, in his elaboration of one of the *raisons d'être* of Haitian Indigenism–cultural nationalism. What we find in Alexis is a refusal to see Haitian culture as an adjunct to any larger cultural bloc. This is evident in his anti-Americanism and in his ridicule of Haiti's *assimilé* elite. Much of this sentiment can be traced back to the nationalism of post-Occupation Haiti. Alexis also applied his confidence in Haiti's cultural independence to the notion of a monolithic African presence which was strongly supported in the fifties by the Negritude movement. Alexis's participation in the First Congress of Negro Writers and Artists involved an affirmation of his disbelief in this global homogeneity of black culture which the conference sought to establish.[8] He refused to see Haitian culture as simply neo-African and insisted that 'this permanence of cultural features always becomes enfeebled in the long run in an individualised nation'. To Alexis a common history of oppression was not enough to create cultural uniformity. Indeed, such a theory of cultural homogeneity simply denied the Haitian national identity: '. . . we must also say that all these glosses and all this gloating over an alleged "Negroness" are dangerous in this sense, that they conceal the reality of the cultural autonomy of the Haitian people . . .'[9]

What Alexis had attacked in 1956 was one of the basic tenets of the Negritude movement – the belief that culture was organic and not a system of conditioned reflexes. To Alexis, culture was, rather, a system of learnt attitudes, a network of responses created through historical experience. Naturally, it was being asserted by implication that Haiti did have a creative history. Alexis refused to see the past in terms of despair and what he articulated in 1956 was a theory that explained that elation Roumain earlier expressed through Manuel in his contemplation of the Haitian landscape – an elation that informs Alexis's own evocation of the Haitian milieu. Haitian man was not a casualty of historical injustice, the product of a degraded ancestor, but one who endured and prevailed.

Tracing the influence André Breton and Surrealism exerted on Alexis is a more difficult undertaking. Alexis himself had far less to say about Bréton's presence in Haiti than his contemporary René Dépestre and he further complicates the issue by later using the word 'surrealist' to describe what was wrong with Western culture. In 1956 he referred to 'the intellectual constructions of a certain decadent West, its cold-blooded surrealist researches, its analytical games'.[10] However, it is difficult to see how any aspiring Haitian writer in 1946 could not have responded to Breton's presence. This was so not only because Breton was obviously sympathetic to the strong anti-Lescot feeling but also because he brought fresh currency to certain ideas that had been launched by the Indigenous movement. Alexis himself strongly favoured – in fact, it was part of the cultural position taken by *La Ruche* – the Indigenist repudiation of the notions of civilisation and culture promoted by Haiti's westernised elite and the former's interest in less respectable areas of Haitian life. The fascination with Haiti's 'unofficial' culture can be seen in the many literary efforts inspired by folk mythology, hallucination induced by voodoo rituals, the low life of Port-au-Prince and the mysterious Amerindian past. This tendency is not unconnected to the Surrealist interest in spontaneous and pre-logical cultural forms as Breton himself made clear in his speech in December 1945 (cf. p. 157). The first explicit suggestion that Alexis shared similar concerns is in the use of the term 'marvellous realism' in 1956, in which he offered a tentative description of Haitian folk art as an uninhibited, mysterious perception of reality: 'Haitian art, in effect, presents the real, with its accompaniment of the strange and the fantastic, of dreams and half-light, of the mysterious and the marvellous . . .' (p. 267)

To Alexis the strength of the folk imagination is that it is non-rational. The creative artist in Haiti should aspire to a similar imaginative freedom which would provide him with a superior way of seeing the world around him. What he advocated was not a total surrender to mysticism. He clearly rejected what he termed 'the fetishist obsession of a certain kind of nationalistic, annoying Africanism'. His *Romancero aux étoiles* contains the narration of a dream which is pertinent to this question of the importance of the artistic unconscious. In 'Le Roi des Songes' Alexis recounts the following vision:

> La grande cité, l'énorme cité mangeuse de rêve, la dévoreuse de songe, la croqueuse d' illusions la grande métropole matérialiste est au-dessous de nous . . . plus elle s'avance, plus elle perd peu à peu son caractère iréel pour devenir l'absurde, l'inhumaine, la terrible ennemie de l'imagination   (p. 249)

[The big city, the enormous city that absorbs dreams, that devours fantasy, that crushes illusions, the great materialistic metropolis is below us . . . The closer it gets, the more it loses its unreal look to become absurd, inhuman, the terrible enemy of the Imagination]

Such a critique of the limitations of materialism and rationalism is reflected in much of his creative writing. In Alexis's novels we have the most thorough-going attempt to register the primeval, the marvellous in Haitian literature. One of the recurring motifs in Alexis's fiction is the individual who attempts to possess or plunder for one reason or another, the Haitian heartland and is unsuccessful. 'Profane intrusions' which to Alexis summed up the history of the New World. For instance, in the case of Diogène Osmin it is attempted in the name of the Catholic Church or in the case of Lt. Wheelbarrow in the name of material wealth. In both cases their efforts are futile as they are profoundly disoriented by the Haitian heartland. They need to be stripped of their initial urges in order to perceive fully the world around them. To this extent Alexis's novels invariably are novels of initiation. Wheelbarrow is initiated by the 'Mistress of the Water' and in the case of Diogène it is madness that finally gives him access to the world he wished to destroy:

Dans sa vésanie, la forêt est pour Diogène le peuple qu'il a ignoré, le peuple dans ses forces naturelles, les forces desquelles sont nés tous les hommes et tous les dieux.   (p. 388)

[In his madness, the forest becomes for Diogène the people he has ignored, the people with its natural strengths, the force which creates both men and gods.]

Madness has dislocated reality and revealed its true meaning. The character who is the key to the perception of 'le merveilleux' is Gonaibo the innocent 'dieu terrestre'. He is described as a child who has had little contact with the world of men. Consequently, his imagination is the least inhibited and he senses the land in its full primal force. The teeming luxuriance of his world is evidence of Gonaibo's heightened sensitivity. One has the impression of a world untamed which defies being fixed into rigid patterns, which is animated by poetic fantasy:

Rocs et végétaux s'accumulent, abrupts, dorés, dans le cristal-
lisoir du ciel. Plaques, cônes, cubes, oves et saillies se cuirassent de
couleurs plates et crues, se poussent à qui mieux mieux,
dégringolent, chutent d'un jet dans la vallée. Confluent de deux
chaînes fougueuses, d'un lac, d'une forêt et d'une plaine, ce site
est un haut lieu de la nation haitienne.   (p. 37)

[Rocks and vegetation are piled up, suddenly, golden under the
crystal sky. Planes, cones, cubes, ellipses and projections are
covered with an armour of flat, harsh colours, jostle, collapse,
cascade into the valley. This confluence of two impetuous ridges,
of a lake, a forest and a plain is a site which is a watershed for the
Haitian people.]

This contingent world perceived by Gonaibo (unwittingly) fulfills
the Surrealist ideal that art should evoke a pre-conscious state
unimpeded by selective or critical processes. Gonaibo's open poetic
sensitivity allows him access to this quality of 'le merveilleux' or
perhaps, 'le surréel' in the Haitian landscape. As the title *Les Arbres
Musiciens* implies, it is the medium of music, the least 'rational' of the
art forms and the one that most directly affects the senses, that is
used to symbolise this sense of wonder possessed by the initiated.

As was the case with Jacques Roumain, Alexis's pronouncements on
literary theory and his own novels were often too vague to be really
useful. In his polemical, often confusing literary observations we
find that he is primarily conscious of belonging to a particular
tradition of prose fiction in Haiti – the 'peasant novel'. It is not that
Alexis wrote, strictly speaking, peasant novels. His characters are
drawn from a range of situations that have more to do with urban
poverty and the '*lumpen* proletariat' than with the rural peasant.
However, he belongs to this genre because of the ideological quality
and social consciousness that pervade his work. In assessing
Roumain's contribution to the genre of the peasant novel, Alexis
uses the term 'critical realism' to describe what he finds is absent
from Roumain's poetico-mythical world:

In Roumain's work we find a kind of symbolic realism. The novel
is a kind of popular poem with classical contours and symbolic
characters. Without underestimating the enormous artistic value

of Roumain's style, one must make the comment that he does not continue nor develop our critical realism.[11]

The same point is expanded in his description of what he attempted in *Compère Général Soleil*. Here he insists on the need for a specific historical context, for the writer to be 'the chronicler of his times'. The novel, then, should not celebrate the peasant 'in an abstract form, undetermined in space and time'.

Alexis's first two novels clearly substantiate this point. They can both be considered *romans de circonstance* in that they are based on specific political events in recent Haitian history. In *Compère Général Soleil* he treats the presidency of Sténio Vincent and the massacre of thousands of Haitian peasants by Trujillo in the Dominican Republic in 1937. In *Les Arbres Musiciens* he centres the plot on the period during 1941–42 when President Lescot simultaneously gave an American company the right to plant rubber trees on land expropriated from the peasantry and unleashed a crusade directed by the Catholic Church against the voodoo religion. The religious campaign was being used to serve the economic venture by destroying the centres of potential peasant resistance. The various political incidents are recorded through a number of digressions that sometimes abruptly suspend the narrative to present historical details. His third novel *L'Espace d'un cillement* is not as closely linked to particular political events. Yet, Alexis still adheres to the tradition of giving imaginative expression to political issues since the heroine of this novel who is a prostitute, is a symbol of Haitian history. She, like Haiti, is manipulated and exploited for profit.

Alexis's success, however, in dramatising these areas of Haitian politics does not depend simply on these episodes that are parenthetically included in the text but on the persuasive characterisation of those who figured in these events. He seems to follow very closely Georg Lukács' precription that in order to bring historical detail to life 'the outwardly insignificant events, the smaller relationships, are better suited than the great monumental dramas of world history'.[12] In *Compère Général Soleil* it is the life of the dispossessed Hilarion which is used to refract the historical drama taking place around him. In *Les Arbres Musiciens* Alexis principally uses the lives of the members of the Osmin family – two of whom, Edgard the soldier and Diogène the priest, are unwitting tools of the conspiracy between politics, commercial interests and the Church –

to portray the sequence of events that eventually caused the collapse of Lescot's regime.

One is also tempted to observe that in spite of the sprawling exuberance and picaresque details of his novels, Alexis's essential genius lies in exploring the fortunes of the outsider in his fiction. Alexis's main characters can be usefully compared with Roumain's Manuel. The latter is very much a prodigal son who is reintegrated into his community. Alexis's characters are either orphans or have no family ties and no community to return to. This impotence or collapse of traditional authority makes Roumain's solution an inadequate one. Through the figures of the dispossessed Hilarion, the mysterious orphan of the forest, Gonaibo and the prostitute, La Niña Estrellita, whose past is described as 'anéanti à tout jamais' [forever obliterated], Alexis explores the world of the outsider. The point is explicitly and repeatedly made in these novels that the traditions of the community can be inhibiting. This makes the outsider freer to fashion a new order of things and to act. Hilarion in *Compère Général Soleil* most graphically symbolises the status of the outsider and the plot traces his evolution towards lucidity and an assertion of his humanity. At the beginning he is swallowed by the absolute blackness of the night – an existential nothing that emphasises his status as an outcast. Hilarion almost embodies Fanon's theory of the 'en soi', state of object, in which the world imprisons the black man making him invisible, non-human:

> La nuit respirait fortement. Il n'y avait pas de monde dans la cour . . . le nègre était presque nu, presque tout nu. Un nègre bleu à force d'être ombre, à force d'être noir.   (p.7)

> [The night breathed heavily. There was no one in the yard . . . The negro was almost naked, almost completely naked. A negro blue because he was a shadow, because he was black.]

From this zone of non-being he moves towards the truth of the sun at the end. The light of dawn symbolises a new awakening for Hilarion: 'Le général Soleil . . . juste sur la frontière, aux portes de la terre natale.' [The sun . . . just at the border, at the gates of my native land.] It is the final transition he makes towards lucidity before he dies. This can be seen as a prototype of Alexis's other characters who, in their solitude, show a determination to survive. Gonaibo decides to leave his serene adolescent world and join the world of men. La Niña Estrellita changes her name and leaves the brothel in a determined act of courage. The end of all three novels simply represents the beginning of the journey for the main characters. Alexis does not present a Utopian vision (as did Roumain in *Gouverneurs de la rosée*) but rather the entry into a profane world in which a new order is still to be created. This quality is most explicit in Gonaibo's departure from his primeval world for the band of men who are cutting down the trees. Gonaibo's conflict has just begun: 'Les arbres musiciens s'écroulent de temps en temps mais la voix de la forêt est toujours puissante. La vie commence' (p. 392), [The musical trees collapse every so often but the voice of the forest is always powerful. Life begins].

In all of Alexis's fiction it is the bewildered, watchful consciousness of these characters that holds the episodic structure of the text together. Alexis's faith is most decidedly not in ancestral tradition but in the spiritual resources of these individuals who can emerge from their marginal worlds and assert a new faith in man.

It would also be misleading to take too literally Alexis's statements that his novels are simply chronicles of certain historical situations. In the following admission made in his unpublished manuscript *De la Création Artistique*[13] Alexis confesses that his novels are more than simply an inventory of the misfortunes of Haiti's poor. As he says, 'if that were my only objective I would have been satisfied with political action and would not have become involved with the arts'. Questions of literary form were also very important to Alexis. Indeed, they became increasingly so after each novel. His third novel, for instance, *L'Espace d'un Cillement*[14] is from the outset a poetic allegory using the heroine as a symbol of Haiti's misfortunes. The plot then follows a highly stylised sequence in which each day of Holy Week corresponds to a greater awakening of La Niña Estrellita's senses. Good Friday is the sixth day that corresponds to the sixth sense 'le don de la voyance'. The emotional and political rebirth of Alexis's prostitute is consequently given added resonance because of this juxtaposition of religious ritual and the freeing of La Niña Estrellita's repressed sensibilities. In his collection of folk tales he is also conscious of communicating the atmosphere and the dramatic dimensions of the tradition of story telling. In *Romancero aux étoiles* Alexis must invent a language which will convey the image and rhythm of an oral tradition as well as the para-linguistic resources (music, mime, gesture) that are at the story-teller's disposal. In Alexis's tales efforts are made to create the illusion of the story-teller's physical presence by using a direct conversational style. Repetition, digressions and exclamations are all used to suggest the actual voice and dramatic presence of the old story-teller.

Alexis felt compelled to insist on the quality of socialist realism that he saw as fundamental to his fiction. Yet his prose style is rarely ever that of a sober chronicle of socio-economic conditions. He almost instinctively moves away from a detached recording of events to a dense, poetic prose. In attempting to define his own style he once rejected the 'linear, sober Cartesian' form of the French novel and admitted that the form that attracted him was 'in its disorder like the beautiful trees of our forest, chaotic like the contemporary Haitian consciousness, contradictory, poetic, violent however without betraying the internal logic of history'.[15] The self-conscious addition of 'the internal logic of history' almost contradicts the violent disorder that best describes his technique. The frenzied accumulation of verbs and adjectives in Alexis's descriptive passages creates visually striking prose poems in his narratives. This style owes much to the freedom in the use of imagery which was advocated by the Surrealists. This radical juxtaposition of incongruous images is used to represent the convulsions of the sea in the following passage:

> Monstres de diamant aux insinuants sourires magnétiques; animaux de quartz en fusion dont les yeux de pierreries décochent des oeillades ensorcelantes; griffons de métal lancent leurs pattes aux ongles d'or.[16]

> [Monsters of diamond with suggestive magnetic smiles; animals of melted quartz whose jewelled eyes flash enchanting leers; metal griffons hurl their golden clawed paws.]

The flash of light as well as the monstrous threat of the storm are graphically evoked in 'monstres de diamant', 'animaux de quartz', 'griffons de métal'. This prose style which is characteristic of Alexis shows that his strength does not simply lie in 'critical realism'. He, like Roumain, belongs to a poetic tradition. In his case, however, the exuberant flourish of his technique is contrasted to the sober lyricism of Roumain's style.

Alexis's fiction also derives its force from the use of certain symbols which pervade the chronological sequence of the text. For instance, darkness and light bring a kind of formal unity to *Compère Général Soleil*. Similarly in *Les Arbres Musiciens* the point at which the river meets the sea is presented as a sexually charged figurative representation of the politics of the novel: the fusing of the individual destiny (the river) with the unknown – by extension the human adventure (sea) mirrors Gonaibo's own descent into the world of man at the end of the novel:

> Vorace au point de sembler vouloir avaler tout le large, cette embouchure béante, sensuelle, ravie, inassouvie, s'accouple avec la grande mer, étalant des muqueuses frissonnantes, presque charnelles sous la lune. (p. 9)

> [Voracious enough to appear to want to swallow the entire sea, this yawning mouth, sensual, ecstatic, unsated, is joined to the open sea, spreading ripples of mucous, almost erotically in the moonlight.]

This encounter which is central to the story, is presented in terms of birth and fecundity. Again it demonstrates the extent to which the politics of Alexis's novels are animated by poetic allegory.

In his contribution to the First Conference of Negro Artists and Writers Alexis entitled his paper 'On Marvellous Realism in Haiti' and in a lengthy article on the novel and national identity in the following year, 1957, he makes constant reference to 'le merveilleux' when describing the art of the Haitian people. This curious term had never before been used by a Haitian writer nor did it appear to have a metropolitan origin. Its origins were, if anything, Latin-American as it had been used by the Cuban novelist Alejo Carpentier to describe fantastic phenomena he had observed during a visit to Haiti in 1943. In his article on the novel, Alexis, however, makes no mention of Carpentier when he lists the various novelists who have influenced him. These include the Guatemalan Asturias, who shared many of Carpentier's theories of a New World sensibility but even he is not singled out for special mention.

In many ways Alexis's statements on 'le merveilleux' are remarkably close to those of Carpentier. The latter's novel based on the Haitian revolution *El reino de este mundo* was published in 1949 and anticipates some of the ideas that are found in Alexis's own fiction which appears almost a decade later. In his prologue to that novel Carpentier describes in some detail what he means by 'la real maravilloso'. His theories are based on his own involvement with the Surrealist movement in Paris in the inter-war period.

The point of departure of Carpentier's argument is his dissatisfaction with the contrived fantasies of the Surrealist movement. He agreed with the need to transcend the objective world and free man's imagination but he felt that the various Surrealist games had become stylised and repetitive. As he observed: 'through wanting to create the marvellous at any cost these miracle workers became bureaucrats'.[17] Surrealism was a desperate attempt by a fatigued society to capture the spontaneity of other cultures but one that was doomed to failure because these very experiments in the irrational were inhibited by inhibiting rationalism. In his later novel *The Lost Steps* the main character, who is a thinly disguised version of the author, comments on a collection of primitive artefacts on display:

> For more than twenty years a weary culture had been seeking rejuvenation and new powers in the cult of the irrational. But now I found ridiculous the attempt to use masks of Bandiagara, African ibeyes, fetishes studded with nails, without knowing their meaning, as battering-rams against the redoubts of the *Discourse of Method* . . . By labelling such things 'barbarous' the labellers were putting themselves in the thinking, Cartesian position, the very opposite of the aim they were pursuing.[18]

What Carpentier felt in Haiti – and this held true for the New World as a whole – was that the marvellous or Breton's 'l'insolite' existed naturally and was evidence of a civilising force in the region. The marvellous was facilitated by myth and Haiti was steeped in it. Carpentier speaks of 'finding himself' in daily contact with something that one could call 'marvellous realism'.[19] It was a world that did not differentiate between the mythological and the real. What he sensed was this strong presence of a creolised culture which made the Caribbean into the Mediterranean of the New World. It was an awesome elemental world which defied rational interpretation. A repository for the vestiges of various civilisations whose heterogenous traces made Surrealist experiments with the unconscious seem gratuitious and inadequate. In Christophe's 'Saint Souci' and his 'Citadelle' he saw fantasy come to life. This notion of the marvellous secreted in the landscape and cultures of the New World was also the focus of Alexis's literary attentions in the late fifties.

The point of departure of Alexis's definition of 'marvellous realism' was based in Marxist notions of spiritual alienation created in capitalist society. Alexis felt that capitalist development and materialism had had a debilitating effect on the European imagination. It is worthy of note that unlike the Negritude theorists this attitude to Europe and the West is not a racial one but one which depends on being conditioned by historical circumstance: 'Popular culture has lost its poetry in the West . . . One sees enormous armies of industrial workers, slaves to giant corporations, slaves who are exhausted by daily life and the pace of production in their ant-hills.[20] This is to a large extent a restatement of Carpentier's comments on the 'weary culture' of Europe. This exhausted world is contrasted to his own which is privileged because it has not been forced to lose contact with the spiritual:

The under-developed populations of the world who have had until quite recently had to live in contact with nature, have for centuries been compelled particularly to sharpen their eyes, their hearing, their sense of touch. The peoples among whom industrial life is most highly developed, have, for their part, used their senses to a lesser extent during the last few centuries . . . [21]

This motif constantly recurs in Alexis's novels as his characters can be divided into those who possess this heightened sensitivity and those whose senses are less acute. This is not done on racial lines since characters as diverse as Lieutenant Wheelbarrow, Diogène Osmin and Hilarion are initially unable to attain this perception of reality whereas Gonaibo is gifted in this way and each day of La Niña Estrellita's life in *L'Espace d'un cillement* means greater immersion into a world of the senses. (Each chapter deals with one of the five senses). This ideal state is embodied by the mythical 'Anne aux longs cils' in the *Romancero aux étoiles*:

Anne aux longs cils n'avait donc que trois sens pour percevoir le réel: le velours incarnat de sa bouche papilleuse, sa narine ovale, aigue, creuse, la chair de poule de sa peau aux grains frileux.

(p. 55)

[Anne of the long lashes had only three senses to perceive reality: the pink velvet of her sensitive mouth, her oval nostril, pointed and hollow, her goose-pimpled skin, sensitive to the cold.]

Alexis is suggesting that man's ideal relationship to reality is essentially a sensuous one and not as many of his deluded characters assume, a materialistic, rational one.

These conclusions on peasant culture contained obvious literary implications. Alexis saw in this unique perception of reality an opportunity to break away from the dead literary codes of Europe and create a new literary aesthetic from this sense of the marvellous. He, unlike Carpentier, does not single out Surrealism for criticism but simply categorises European art as characterised by order, logic and control. Traditional Realism – the most obvious product of reason and positivist thought – is unable to convey the primal force and the disorienting timelessness of the Haitian landscape. The demarcation between consciousness and the free association of dream and myth is an inhibition. In the fantasy of the legends and myths of the folk Alexis attempts to discover a suitable model for representing his world: 'The marvellous is the garment in which certain peoples clothe their wisdom and their knowledge of life.'[22] The populist thrust of Alexis's argument – which is absent in Carpentier – shows how he intended to fuse his politics with this Modernist literary position, which made no attempt to represent the world in an objective fashion. The unbridled luxuriance of the Haitian heartland – what Carpentier saw as the supreme Surrealist fantasy – which is described in Alexis's novels shows how this new 'baroque' sensitivity informs his creative imagination:

De toutes parts fulgurent, fleurissent, s'irisent, embaument, poudroient tant de pièces de féerie que le merveilleux fuse irrésistiblement de chaque parcelle de terre, du ciel et du vent, vraisemblable, vivant, péremptoire . . . Cette île a des accents de grandeur qui autorisent les plus folles equipées de rêve! (p. 10)

[From everywhere the flash, flower, iridescence, perfume, dust of so many manifestations of the unreal emerge, fusing irresistibly with particles of earth, sky and air, real, living, undeniable . . . This island strikes chords of grandeur which encourage the most insane adventures in fantasy!]

Alexis's exuberant, textured prose insists on a representation of reality in which the real and the fantastic overlap.

This exploration of the union between man and landscape in Haiti also provided Alexis with an insight into the history of Haiti and the Caribbean. He, like Carpentier, felt that there were areas of Caribbean history that had been ignored by European historians. Too Eurocentric a view of Caribbean history had been responsible for the stereotype of a fragmented, disadvantaged local society since it was the victim of the European quest for wealth and Empire. What such a perspective on the history of the New World does not elucidate is the process of creolisation that inevitably takes place in the native consciousness. In opposition to the stereotype of plurality and fragmentation Alexis, again like Carpentier, sees the Caribbean as a Mediterranean culture in which the process of *métissage* has created a cohesive cultural whole.

The landscape and the relics of the past bear witness to the cycle of grandeur and exploitation that recurs in the history of the region. The land becomes a repository for vestiges of past presences, historical encounters. In a surreal collage of disparate objects, Alexis shows how Haitian history is recorded: 'vestiges Ciboneys, de splendeurs de Chèmes . . . d'armes de conquistadors, de ouangas, de chaînes et de masques des premiers nègres marrons' (p.38), [Ciboney relics, grandeur of the Chemes . . . weapons of conquistadors, charms, chains and masks of the first maroons]. When Gonaibo encounters the men from S.H.A.D.A. he sees it as simply a repetition of the Conquest. The Americans are simply modern-day Conquistadors:

Une cavalerie d'hommes blancs, en kaki, galopait sur d'étranges chevaux de fer, à une vitesse folle, telle une ruée d'archanges destructeurs se ruant sur la lande tout humide encore de rosée . . . Voilà cinq siècles les guetteurs d'Anacaona La Grande ne pouvait avoir ressenti d'autre impression quand, dans un surgissement apocalyptique, survinrent à leurs yeux les cavaliers d'Ojeda.   (pp. 82–3)

[Cavalry of white men, in khaki, rode mounted on strange iron horses, at a crazy speed, like an unrush of destructive angels pouncing on the land still wet with dew . . . Five centuries ago the guards of the Great Anacaona could have felt no differently when, in an apocalyptic surge, the horsemen of Ojeda suddenly appeared before them.]

Here history responds to a 'primitive' notion of time – immutable and impervious to change. This profane intrusion is seen as a simultaneous perception of the present and the past. It is a vision of passionate fatalism for like the Conquest, S.H.A.D.A. eventually will fail, leaving like its predecessor the rusting vestiges of its presence.

What Alexis emphasises is that history does not produce a vision of despair – one that fed the self-contempt of the colonial mind. It is prophetic in that it presents the past as a continuum that restores meaning to the present and asserts the continued survival of the collective experience. The Artibonite river in *Compère Général Soleil* (pp. 165–7) which 'knows the history of the land' is a symbol of this free flow of memory. The symbol is given its full poetic force by Alexis when he describes it as 'un monstrueux boa liquide'. Both the restorative, maternal associations of the river and the deep subterranean connotations of the snake image are linked in this symbol. In *Les Arbres Musiciens* the character of Gonaibo is an embodiment of the cosmopolitan memory that is characteristic of the Caribbean *métis*. Gonaibo is a symbol of that indigenous consciousness which is rooted in the past. However, unlike the other characters he does not belong to any of the various cultural enclaves in Haitian society – neither elite nor *vaudouisant* – and can therefore grasp more easily the process of creolisation that has taken place from as far back as autochthonous pre-Columbian cultures:

Il était le dernier fils de la terre rouge du royaume de la Fleur d'Or, il était cette terre elle-même, croyait-il. Il avait ressucité la vie de la lande comme elle se déroulait naguère. Il avait les goûts, la couleur, le visage, les cheveux des hommes archaïques de Xaragua. Peut-être par un cheminement insoupçonné du sang, leurs gênes héréditaires avaient-ils été transmis jusqu'à lui?

(p. 85)

[He was the last of son the red earth of the kingdom of the Golden Flower, he has become this land itself, he thought. He had revived the life of the land as it unfolded, formerly. He had the tastes, the colour, the face, the hair of the ancient men of

Xaragua. Perhaps by some unsuspected transference of blood their genes had been transmitted to him?]

Alexis's conception of such a composite ancestral past stands in stark opposition to the racialist poetics of *Les Griots*. Like them he asserts the importance of an ancestral past – 'man cannot be no one's offspring, one cannot deny the past and history'. He, however, refuses to minimise any aspect of that ancestral heritage. He uniquely situates Caribbean man in the Caribbean – not exclusively in Africa or Europe. In describing his own situation, he confesses:

> If I have chosen without hesitation the human families which appear to be the closest to me, the negro family and the Latin-American family, I am equally determined not to deny any part of my heritage. I am close to the thought and sensibility of the French and France has given me so much that I am obliged to reciprocate with the little I have to offer.[23]

In this theory of 'marvellous realism' we have the culmination of one of the most positive tendencies within Haitian Indigenism. Alexis not only responds to the need to repossess the entire Haitian experience but also to assert the wealth of tradition that lay unexplored because of anti-colonial polemics.

There lies an enormous distance between the shrill prose of the young firebrand of *La Ruche* and the eloquence of Alexis's more mature poetic imagination. To understand Alexis's importance we must place him in the context of the tensions between metropolitan and indigenous culture that are evident throughout Haitian literature. 'Marvellous realism' as an imaginative response to Haitian culture not only surpasses the spectre of anarchy and barbarism that Haitians feared in their own culture in the nineteenth century[24] but also the excessive nationalism of the twentieth century which sought to reverse this prejudice in a self-conscious Africanist ideology. Alexis's generous resolution of this conflict is seen in his view of an authentic Haitian identity which is cross-fertilised by both victor and victim, metropolitan and indigenous. It is out of this that emerges his passionate vision of a civilising presence that is secreted in the culture of Haiti and the Caribbean.

NOTES

1. This phrase is taken from the Martinican novelist Edouard Glissant. He uses it in the preface to his play which treats the Haitian war of independence – *Monsieur Toussaint* (Paris: du Seuil, 1961). He speaks, like Alexis, of the need 'to unveil the past, deformed or obliterated by others, which allows us to better understand the present'.
2. In an article 'Où va le roman', *Présence Africaine*, no. 13, May 1957. He claims that he did not wish to publish anything before he was thirty (p. 95).
3. Jacques-Stéphen Alexis, *Romancero aux étoiles* (Paris: Gallimard, 1960) p. 212.
4. Reprinted as a preface to Jacques Roumain's *La Montagne ensorcelée* (Paris: Français Réunis, 1972) p. 29.
5. Ibid., p. 15.
6. Jacques-Stéphen Alexis, *Compère Général Soleil* (Paris: Gallimard, 1955) pp. 68–9.
7. Jacques-Stéphen Alexis, *Les Arbres Musiciens* (Paris: Gallimard, 1957) p. 157.
8. G. R. Coulthard in his *Race and Colour in Caribbean Literature*, (London: Oxford University Press, 1962) is unfair to Alexis by dismissing his paper as 'quite clearly a restatement of the fundamental tenets of negritude'. James Baldwin is far more sensitive to Alexis's position in his article 'Princes and Powers' in *Nobody Knows My Name*, (London: Michael Joseph 1964).
9. Jacques-Stéphen Alexis, 'Of the Marvellous Realism of the Haitians', *Présence Africaine*, nos. 8–10, June–Nov. 1956, p. 260. Page numbers are quoted from the English edition of this special issue.
10. Ibid., p. 268.
11. Preface to Roumain, *La Montagne ensorcelée*, p. 24.
12. Georg Lukács, *The Historical Novel* (Harmondsworth: Penguin, 1969) p. 44.
13. *De la Création Artistique*, unpublished manuscript, n.d.
14. Jacques-Stéphen Alexis, *L'Espace d'un cillement* (Paris: Gallimard, 1959).
15. Alexis, 'Où va le roman', *Présence Africane*, p. 100.
16. Alexis, 'Dieu Premier' (second chapter of an unfinished novel), *La Nouvelle Revue Française*, July 1972, pp. 65–6.
17. Prologue to Alejo Carpentiers *El reino de este mundo* (Havana: Union, 1964) p.x.
18. Alejo Carpentier, *The Lost Steps* (Harmondsworth: Penguin, 1968) p. 228.
19. Prologue to Carpentier, *El reino de este mundo*, p. xiii.
20. Alexis, 'Où va le roman?' *Présence Africaine*, pp. 85–6.
21. Alexis, 'Of the Marvellous Realism of the Haitians', *Présence Africaine*, p. 268.
22. Alexis, 'Où va le roman?' *Présence Africaine*, p. 98.
23. Jacques-Stéphen Alexis, 'La belle amour humaine 1957', *Europe*, Jan. 1971, p. 21.
24. The ambivalent attitudes of the nineteenth-century Haitian intellectual to African retentions and the voodoo religion in particular are treated on pp. 15–16.

Epilogue: a Case of
Two Literatures

ESTRAGON: We always find something, eh Didi, to give
us the impression we exist?
VLADIMIR: Yes, yes, we're magicians

The literary and political effervescence of 1946 is as close as Haiti would get to a literary renaissance in recent times. The successful overthrow of the arch-conservative Lescot, the strong Utopian impulse of Marxism and the taste for revolutionary politics encouraged by Bréton's presence as well as the optimism of the post-war period created a euphoria that approached the frenzied activity of the Indigenous movement in the 1920s. This is clearly reflected in the ideas and the creative imagination of two of the *enfants terribles* of 1946 – Jacques-Stéphen Alexis and René Dépestre. The former's theory of 'marvellous realism' with its passionate pan-Caribbean commitment and faith in the cultural survival of the Haitian people and Dépestre's continued belief in the political realisation of Surrealism's *révolution permanente* show the extent to which they were confident of the creative writer's ability to transform the world.

Even though the iconoclastic urges of the forties are muted in the late fifties, the tendency was to continue to see the writer as a visionary. The point of departure for most of the poetry of this generation tended to be lyrical celebrations of the brotherhood of man. The most important literary group to emerge at this time was *Haiti Littéraire*. It was more a loose alliance of artists who belonged to the generation that followed that of Dépestre and Alexis than a literary school. A selection of statements made by members of this group reveal the need to treat in a rather idealistic and philosophical way the human condition and modify the sometimes limiting and strident nationalism which they considered one of the negative features of the Indigenous school:

> Our writers have not understood that literature must not be made exclusively for local consumption. The literary work must be able to travel, to impose itself on and find a worthy place among others. Local colour is of little importance, what counts is the human colour of the work.
>
> (Anthony Phelps)

> We refuse to do like others, to imprison ourselves in a narrow poetic regionalism, to write according to imposed norms . . . Out with determinism. We want Haitian literature to take its place among other literatures.
>
> (René Philoctète)[1]

> Poetry . . . must be a collective human explosion which is filtered through the artistic heart. From this perspective, the externals of nature can only serve as a framework for this broadly humanist poetry.
>
> (Franck Etienne)[2]

The tendency to avoid a narrow, self-conscious local colour is evident in their various publications which invariably celebrate an ideal of human solidarity: René Philoctète's *Saison des hommes* (1960) and *Tambours du Soleil* (1962); Anthony Phelps's *Eté* (1960); Roland Morisseau's *Germination d'espoir* (1962). The position taken by this generation can be usefully compared to that of many writers of the late nineteenth century who also avoided the strident nationalism and local colour of such members of *L'Ecole Patriotique* as Oswald Durand and Massillon Coicou. However, the promised rebirth of *Haiti Littéraire* was short-lived for by the mid-sixties literary activity in Haiti became hazardous and even absurd as the regime of François Duvalier became increasingly oppressive.

1961 is a crucial date in this period as it was in April of that year that Alexis attempted to land clandestinely in Haiti, was captured and executed by Duvalier's forces. The Communist witch-hunts and the system of rigid censorship which followed were evidence of how paranoid and brutal the Duvalier regime had become. The number of aborted invasions and foiled assassination attempts, the reprisals of the dreaded Tontons Macoutes in the sixties and

Duvalier's 'acceptance' of the presidency for life in 1964 had created the atmosphere of gloom and fear that Graham Greene exploited so dramatically in *The Comedians* (1966). The terrors of this decade are primarily responsible for that dazed silence that characterised the literary scene at this time. The tragic sense of isolation and vulnerability felt by the Haitian writers has, perhaps, a precedent in the movement of *La Ronde* at the turn of the century. Because of the anarchy of that time literary activity resigned itself to hermeticism and the efforts of a small initiated coterie. By the mid-sixties the grand fraternal gesture of *Haiti Littéraire* could no longer be repeated. Indeed, René Philoctète's *Les îles qui marchent* (1969), which reads like a Haitian version of Césaire's *Cahier d'un retour au pays natal*, contains a desperate nostalgia and visionary passion that seems ill-suited to this spirit of defeat that was pervasive then.

The only really significant literary movement in recent Haitian writing is Spiralisme. It was founded by Franck Etienne and René Philoctète in the late sixties and represents the efforts of those, who, for one reason or another, did not leave Haiti, to maintain an interest in literary activity. The most obvious feature of this movement, particularly as it manifests itself in the sixties, was its apolitical nature. It was closely linked to the polemics of New Novel in France and Structuralist Criticism and restricted its attentions to questions of form in literary creation. To this extent it again brings to mind *La Ronde's* use of Symbolism to create a disinterested, hermetic verse that was a means of shutting out reality. Franck Etienne's difficult, allegorical prose work *Ultravocal* (1972) is the only obviously *spiraliste* work to have emerged from this movement. Its fragmanted narrative makes no attempt to deal openly with Haiti's political tragedy. However, a sense of futility seems to be concealed by what Etienne himself calls his 'délire verbal': Le possible pèse si peu dans le creux de nos mains que nous flottons sans cesse. Et la poussière du miroir use nos voix.[3] [What is possible is of such little weight in our cupped hands, that we float incessantly. And the dust on the mirror wears out our voices.] What is even more obvious is that the faith in the writer's ability to alter reality is now lost, as one recurring motif in *Ultravocal* is that of the lonely, impotent artist: 'Nous répétons mal nos tirades la solitude a rouillé nos voix.'[4] [We rehearse our tirades badly. Solitude has rusted our voices.] Even more recently this tendency to retreat from political reality was again apparent in the somewhat eccentric literary manifesto of *Pluréalisme*[5] whose ideas are built around the *désengagement* of the writer.

It would have been folly to attempt to deal explicitly with Haitian politics from within the country. *Le Ficus* which appeared in 1970 is a veiled tribute to Alexis and an indirect comment on the pervasive evil of the times:

> Je médite sur l'Etoile Absinthe . . . Un roman psychologique qu'un ami m'a raconté. Celui-ci a eu la tête tranchée pour n'avoir pas voulu lécher le cul aux salauds . . . Alors à un autre ou à moi de la compléter. Mais qui donc y arrivera? Personne.[6]

> [I meditate on l'Etoile Absinthe . . . A psychological novel which a friend related to me. He had his head cut off for not wanting to lick the backsides of scum . . . It is up to another or myself to complete the work. But who will do it? No one.]

The novel is an allegorical work in which 'le ficus' which is the symbol of evil is defeated by the unified trees of the forest. No Haitian novelist would dare to convey the full horror of Duvalier's dictatorship. However, this may have ironically been done by the Columbian novelist Garcia Marquez. When the recent French translation of his *Et Otoño del Patriarca* (1975) was read by Haitians they finally found their absurd and tragic world depicted in the bizarre Messianic figure of Garcia's patriarch.

The word 'diaspora' has acquired a new resonance for Haitian writers as it can now refer to all those who were forced into or chose exile. Among those who fled from Duvalier's nightmarish world were those like Jean Brierre who settled in Senegal and Dépestre who headed for Havana. The vast majority, however, ended up in French-speaking Canada. In this latter community a whole body of literature has been produced, generally published by Editions Nouvelle Optique. Two themes predominate in this writing – nostalgia for the Haiti they left behind and derision aimed at the Duvalier regime. The theme of exile and the need for *enracinement* are present in Dépestre's *Arc-en-ciel pour l'occident chrétien* (1967) and Brierre's *découvertes* (1966) in which both poets try to avoid anonymity as literary voices by re-immersing themselves in their native culture. Dépestre conceives of himself as a *poète-houngan* Brierre lyrically invokes memories of his hometown Jérémie, in an epic and largely autobiographical poem which poses the following question to all those who are in exile: 'Lequel de nous sera le premier mort, s'il n'est déjà un mort?'[7] [Which of us will die first if he is not dead already?]

Much of the work published by Editions Nouvelle Optique contains strident Marxist criticism of Duvalier's government. This is apparent not only in the many articles that appeared in the journal *Nouvelle Optique* (1971–4) but also in the fiction published by this group. The unchecked hysteria of Gérard Etienne's *Le nègre crucifié* (1974) and the disturbing fantasy of fear and sadism, *Mémoire en Colin-Maillard* (1976) by Anthony Phelps both of *Haiti Littéraire* are inspired by their outrage at Duvalier's politics. Only time will permit a proper evaluation of this *littérature du dehors* as it is seen by those in Haiti. Yet one senses an unbridgeable gap of mutual suspicion and distrust yawns between those who write in exile and those who are *du dedans*. The fierce political language of exile literature is necessarily different from the more muted and intro-verted vision of endurance seen in the few serious works published in Haiti.

Since Duvalier's death in 1971 there have been moves within Haiti to test the much vaunted liberalism of Jean-Claude Duvalier's new regime. In this respect the journal *Le Petit Samedi Soir* es-tablished in 1972 has played an outstanding role in reviving an interest in literary matters as well as commenting on risqué political topics. The writer who has made the most important contributions to this new, potentially militant phase in Haitian literature is Franck Etienne. His work is interesting from two points of view. Firstly, most of his recent work is in Creole and suggests a revival of serious interest in the literary potential of the vernacular. So far his success has been particularly evident in his two Creole plays. Also, his novels treat in an indirect way the dark years of Duvalierism. For instance, his Creole novel *Dezafi* (1975) – which later spawned a French version *Les affres d'un défi*[8] – uses the myth of the Haitian zombi to explain what happened in Haiti in the 1960s. There is precedent for this image of the mindless, submissive, reanimated corpse in Roumain's symbol of passivity and defeat – old Delira squatting in the dust in *Gouverneurs de la rosée* and Hilarion swallowed in an existential nothingness in *Compère Général Soleil*. Etienne's plot revolves around the voodoo priest Saintil who controls a colony of zombies. His daughter, Sultana, falls in love with Clodonis, one of the zombies, and in order to free him from further torture feeds him life-giving salt. Interestingly it is not ideology that liberates the 'living-deal'. The revolt against Saintil by the now freed zombies has resulted from Sultana's love for Clodonis.

Les affres d'un défi which follows in structure and plot the Creole original owes as much to Kafka as it does to Jacques-Stéphen Alexis. In the case of the former, the irrational and arbitrary intrusions of official violence into the normal world is conveyed in all its casual brutality in Etienne's morbid universe as it is in Kafka's dark fantasies. Radical shifts in points of view, fragmented narration and variations in style which are first effectively used in Alexis's *Les Arbres Musiciens*, provide Etienne with the proper medium for describing the macabre swirl of events – 'l'epidémie zombificatrice' – in Saintil's world.[9] These techniques also, as Alexis anticipated, work well in Creole since traditional story-telling in the vernacular is not limited in a formal way. Mime, song and dialogue are the resources of the traditional story-teller and likewise, Etienne shifts from standard prose narration to poetic prose which is simetimes broken by scenes which are presented in terms of a theatrical *mise en scène* and dialogue. *Les affres d'un défi* also continues Etienne's concern with the role of the writer and the value of literary activity that was first raised in *Ultravocal*. There are a number of authorial intrusions in the text which reflect on the act of literary creation:

> Qui nous écoute? Qui cherche à nous comprendre? Plutôt que de nous entendre, ils nous traitent de fous, puis ils s'empressent de nous museler.   (p. 2)

> [Who listens to us? Who tries to understand us? Rather than hearing us, they behave as if we are mad then they hasten to silence us.]

Etienne also cleverly likens the writer's problems of expression to those of the zombi. The latter's loss of humanity and freedom is evident in his limited grunts. Similarly, the writer is paralysed by limitations in literary expression: 'de mots tronqués et de cris inventés' (p. 161), [mutilated words and invented cries]. Etienne is implying that language is only freed when political oppression is removed. The end of the novel witnesses the successful revolt of the zombies against Saintil and the vision of all humanity freed by the life-giving salt. It is only then that 'les mots clés pour exprimer la vérité' (p. 226), [key words to express the truth] are found.

Perhaps Etienne's sensitivity to the exhaustion that now exists among Haitian writers as well as the desperate hope that a renaissance is still possible provides us with the best insight into current literary activity in Haiti. Too many have seen Haiti become the political swamp that is Saintil's world and have seen their contemporaries tortured as Clodonis is. The collective narrative voice that is used in *Les affres d'un défi* speaks constantly of a journey whose many obstacles and detours have made endurance difficult. But for the first time in his more recent work an optimistic note is sensed in his belief in the possibility of a new beginning.[10] Perhaps this image can best sum up the mood of weary expectancy that now exists among Haiti's writers:

Nous venons tout juste de naître. Pourtant, nous sommes en route depuis longtemps. Un bruit de clé tournant dans une serrure nous tire de nos songeries. (p. 157)

[We have just been born. However, we have been on this road for a long time. The noise of a key turning in the lock wakes us from our dreams.]

NOTES

1. *Rond Point*, no. 12, Dec. 1963, pp. 26–7.
2. Franck Etienne, *Au fil du Temps* (Port-au-Prince: Antilles, 1964) p. 8.
3. Franck Etienne, *Ultravocal* (Port-au-Prince: Serge Gaston, 1972) p. 387.
4. Ibid., p. 408.
5. An interview with the founder of this movement, Gerard Dougé, and the manifesto of 'Plurealisme' can be found in Christophe Charles, *Dix nouveaux poètes et écrivains haitiens* (Port-au-Prince: Coll. UNHTI, 1974).
6. Rassoul Labuchin and Michaelle Lafontant-Medard, *Le Ficus* (Port-au-Prince; Theodore, 1971) pp. 12–13. *L'Etoile Absinthe* is the title of Jacques-Stéphen Alexis's unfinished novel.
7. Jean Brierre, *découvertes* (Paris: Présence Africaine, 1966) p. 31.
8. Franck Etienne, *Les affres d'un défi* (Port-au-Prince: Henri Deschamps, 1979).
9. Etienne admits this technical debt to Alexis in an interview with Christophe Charles in *Dix nouveaux poètes et écrivains haitiens*, p. 51.
10. Dépestre's recent 'roman à clef', *Le mât de cocagne* (Paris: Gallimard, 1976) also affirms the capacity of the individual to prevail against the submissiveness of a 'pays anesthésié.

Index